Piece of Work

A MEMOIR

Danielle Tantone

Copyright © 2022 Danielle Tantone.

All Rights Reserved. This book contains material protected under International and Federal Copyright Laws and Treaties. Any unauthorized reprint or use of this material is prohibited. No part of this book may be reproduced or transmitted in any form or by any means, electronic or mechanical, including photocopying, recording, or by any information storage and retrieval system without express written permission from the author/publisher.

ISBNs:
Hardcover: 979-8-9869308-0-0
Paperback: 979-8-9869308-1-7
Ebook: 979-8-9869308-2-4

Contents

Author's Note v
Introduction vii

Part One: Faith and Doubt

Chapter 1   Looking for Love 3
Chapter 2   A Refreshing Adventure .13
Chapter 3   Come to Jesus. 24
Chapter 4   Be Transformed 34
Chapter 5   Believe 43
Chapter 6   Baptized with the Spirit .52
Chapter 7   The Woman at the Well .58
Chapter 8   Cracks 70
Chapter 9   The Fall 76
Chapter 10 The Winter 84
Chapter 11 The Scarlet Letter 96
Chapter 12 Searching for a Fix 104
Chapter 13 The Ring 115
Chapter 14 Roller Coaster 119
Chapter 15 Turn Around 130

Part Two: Growth and Resilience

Chapter 16 Chasing Butterflies 145
Chapter 17 Where do I Belong? 154
Chapter 18 God Blessed the Broken Road 164
Chapter 19 Give us Grace 172
Chapter 20 Generational Trauma 181
Chapter 21 Reconciliation 190
Chapter 22 Fight Song 196
Chapter 23 Surrender 207
Chapter 24 Silver Linings 214
Chapter 25 Paradoxes 220
Chapter 26 Final Breaths and Other Small Things 230

Author's Note

Almost all names have been changed, and some details altered or omitted to protect the privacy of people who didn't sign up to be characters in my book.

Changing the names of the people I love was a hard choice, as names are meaningful to me, and they're part of the story. But I had some fun coming up with pseudonyms that had a similar vibe or meaning as the real names. In the end, I changed even my daughters' names, adapting the tales of how we came up with them to capture pieces of the truth.

This memoir *is* my truth, as accurate as possible. It's not my whole life story, but a story *from* my life, one that has been burning to come out for years. It includes some of my darkest chapters, but even in the darkness, God's light has always shown through.

Introduction

A friend on social media asked me earnestly what compelled me to want to write a memoir, and I never really answered her. The desire to write this book has pervaded my life, been at the back of my mind through everything else, for almost two decades now. It can feel narcissistic to share such a personal story, but I feel called to do it, even while slogging through nursing school in my 40s, raising kids, trying to make a living and a life. I believe that individual life stories can teach us about humanity. The specific informs the universal.

My book was always going to be called *Believe*. At first it was the story of a spicy Jewish girl who became a sweet Christian wife, but then some "poor life choices" made me a less than perfect poster child for Christianity, and I didn't know what to do with that. Who would want to read a story about a villain? And how could I ever become a hero when I had messed things up so royally?

For years I struggled with love addiction, depression, anxiety. And it became a story about infidelity and divorce, seeking love and never quite finding it. My faith shifted and evolved as I learned more about myself and the world. And then it became a story of my own growth and transformation, becoming whole, becoming new, starting over. Ultimately, it was a story about forgiveness, love, and empathy. And the person who most needed *my* forgiveness, love and empathy was myself.

By the time COVID came to play in 2020, I had somewhat peacefully straddled two opposing worldviews - the multicultural Jewish open-mindedness of my youth, and the Bible-focused Christian conservatism of my adult life - for more than 15 years. I had never been a political person, not even when I worked for the Associated Press after college. Ever since the first time I registered to vote at 18 years old in 1992, I'd found I couldn't completely identify with either party, just as I didn't quite fit into either religion. I was a mixture, a middle ground, which at times made me feel like a wishy-washy shade of gray.

Recovering from breast cancer treatment just as the pandemic hit the world, while working "on the frontlines" at the hospital, made me feel still more in the middle - physically, politically, and personally. I was holding the hands of dying patients while friends on social media rumbled their disbelief and my own extended family visited only on driveways. The rift between left and right grew wider and harsher than ever before. With friends and family on both sides, I tried to wave my white flag from the middle, but often felt trampled on the battlefield.

As I reflected on my own story, slowly and quietly, the colors of my life started peeking through. I realized that I wasn't a shade of gray, but a rich colorful tapestry full of all my history, ancestry, failures, and triumphs. And being in the messy middle wasn't an accident. Being able to see both sides of any situation with almost equal clarity and understanding, knowing what it feels like to be broken and bereft, and knowing how to build people up when they're feeling small, was a gift - something I needed to share with the world. I eventually learned that *We are all a Piece of Work, a Work in Progress, and a Work of Art - all at the same time.*

And that is the heart of this book. It's not a political book, a religious book, or even really a spiritual one, though my story contains so many miracles. It's not a self-help book, though I hope you may learn from my mistakes - and a few things I've gotten right.

Saying goodbye after a catch-up lunch with a friend recently, she thanked me for listening to all her drama, encouraging and inspiring her without being "preachy."

"You're just easy to talk to," she said. "I feel like I can tell you anything and there's no judgment."

I smiled and my heart swelled.

"Well, I may look sweet and innocent. I may walk around like I have it all together, but if you only knew my story," I said. "We are all a piece of work…"

"Piece of work," she said. "That's what you should call your book."

And so, it is. This book is a *piece of my work*, a piece of my life, a story about a girl who's a real *piece of work*. But aren't we all if we're honest? *And though I may be a piece of work, I'm also a work in progress, a work of art, a masterpiece - a piece of The Master, The Great I Am. And you are, too.*

PART ONE

Faith and Doubt

CHAPTER 1

Looking for Love

SATURDAY, NOVEMBER 8, 2003

I take a bite of the best peanut butter and jelly sandwich I've ever tasted, soft bread bursting with sticky grape jelly and smooth salty peanut butter. *Mmm.* It's possible anything would taste good right now, but I close my eyes to savor *this* delicious bite.

After almost eight hours on the tiny hard seat of my road bike, I'm sitting alone at a picnic table outside the cafeteria of the only high school in Gila Bend, Arizona. I can almost feel my blood sugar perking up, my muscles refueling on carbs, fat, and protein. Always watching my weight, I mentally calculate my calories in versus calories out. I've burned maybe 2000 calories, and only eaten a few energy bars, some banana halves, a turkey sandwich at lunch, and a packet of chocolate Gu. Surely, I must have lost a few pounds in all these hours. I've always been short and curvy, never quite as skinny as I wanted to be.

It's Saturday - no kids on campus today. Just a bunch of crazy adults participating in the 2003 MS150, a two-day, 150-mile cycling event that benefits Multiple Sclerosis.

A glob of jelly plops down on my thigh and I look down in an exhausted haze at my aching, tingling legs. They don't look any leaner.

Maybe a little tanner, though? Or perhaps that's just a layer of sweat and grime. Regardless, I scoop the jelly up with my finger and lick it unabashedly. *God made dirt and dirt don't hurt.*

My right calf has some chain grease on it, a *rookie mark*, my cycling buddies in college would call it. I should be out of the rookie phase by now. But I think the guys I worked with at Outdoor Adventures would be glad to see how far I've come on the little purple Cannondale road bike they helped me pick out 10 years ago. It's like it was waiting there for me at the bike shop: on sale, mounted up on a pedestal, extra small just for me. I rode it around the parking lot, and I've been working hard to become a real cyclist ever since.

I'm 29 now, still not fast on the bike, and hardly the ideal image of a cyclist, but I'll give myself credit for being one persistent little Energizer Bunny. My head is pounding, and I don't think I could get up if I tried, the hard wooden picnic bench cradling my tired butt. But somehow, I feel strangely great, powerful, like I could accomplish anything.

It's been a warm day, but now a cool breeze blows through my hair and whisks the sweat from my skin. It's hard to believe it's November when it feels like a typical summer day in New York or Chicago. November can go either way in Arizona. There may be a week of chilly temps, rain, and wind, then another where it starts to feel like someone's summer again.

I look around the school yard: sunburned grass, a few good-sized trees, pretty dismal. I take a long, hard swig of cool water and then another bite of my sandwich. Gila Bend has, until today, been nothing more than a stopping point on the way to California or Mexico. When I was a kid, we'd stop and eat at the Space Age Diner, an iconic place right on the main road through town, outside a dingy motel that tries to look like some sort of futuristic space station. I'm glad this road trip won't take off again until tomorrow morning, especially since getting back on the road means another eight hours on a hard bike seat pedaling.

"Hey, do you know where Liz is?" I hear a male voice say. I look up. Three young guys in Bank of America jerseys that match my own stare down at me and my sandwich. The tall guy on the right gives me a shy grin. I must be quite a sight, my hair a frizzy mess, dried sweat on my face, jersey unzipped, lavender sports bra and probably an ample amount of cleavage exposed. I peek down and discreetly zip my jersey up a tad. *Well, at least they can tell I'm a girl.* The shapeless jersey doesn't do much to show off my curves, and these Lycra cycling shorts show too many curves, making my short legs look even chunkier than they are.

"I'm Steve," says the guy on the left. "This is Luke and James," he gestures toward his friends.

"Hi, I'm Danielle," I say, swallowing hard on a glob of peanut butter, then taking a quick swig of water to wash it off my tongue and flash them a smile. "I'm sorry, I was really hungry. I just finished a few minutes ago and that was the most I have ridden in a long time!" *Is it ridden or rode? Is ridden even a word?*

I think about the "Century" I rode in college, 100 miles to Picacho Peak from Tucson on a Super Bowl Sunday. A full day of hard exercise and a free pass to enjoy all the chips and dip at my boyfriend's Super Bowl party that afternoon.

"Ah, we understand. Good job," Steve says, evidently the designated speaker. "Did you happen to be riding with Liz? She crashed after the first rest stop and we haven't seen her since."

"Oh my gosh, no. I didn't even know she crashed," I say. "We were supposed to ride together today, but right before we started, she realized she forgot her helmet and went back to her car to get it. She told me just to start and she would catch up, but she never did. And I didn't stop and wait because I was afraid I'd never get going again if I did. I didn't want to end up last!"

I feel a pang of guilt for not insisting Liz and I start and finish together, and I hope my friend's OK.

"Oh, you were far from last. There are still people coming in, probably will be for a few hours yet. You didn't do so bad," Steve reassures me. "Eighty miles is no joke. They call it the MS150, but it's actually 80 miles each way, 160 miles."

"Well, no wonder I'm so tired," I quip. "Who decided to add on an extra five miles each way!?"

All three boys laugh lightly, and Steve says, "Well, we're gonna go get our camp set up. Maybe we'll see you later."

"And I'm going to sit right here and eat this amazing peanut butter and jelly sandwich. I'll tell Liz you were looking for her," I say, smiling.

Liz is my best cycling buddy. We met at the Saturday morning ride our local bike shop puts on each week. They call it the "ABC Ride." As are super-fast, think Tour de France. Bs are just a little less quick. And Cs are speedy compared to an old lady on a beach cruiser, but too slow to keep up with most serious cyclists. Liz and I fit squarely into the C category, which is fine with us. The way we figure, we're still doing way more before 8 am than most people do all day. We usually ride around 30 miles each Saturday.

The MS150 is our first stab at a big ride. Just like runners train for marathons, a few months ago, we decided we should train for something more than just getting around the mountain and home in one piece on Saturday mornings. Liz organized a corporate team through Bank of America, where she works. She got the bank to sponsor us and match all our donations. But other than a few introductions at the start with some of the team members, and the brief conversation just now, I really don't feel much a part of a team. I rode solo most of the day, meeting people along the way, even catching a couple of fast cyclists from my real estate firm and drafting off them for a few minutes before falling back into my own slower cadence.

Eventually I find Liz, unscathed by her crash, aside from a small scratch on her leg and a bruised ego. We collect our bags from the neatly staged rows where they've unloaded them from the trucks. Then we lug our stuff over to the big circus tent where we'll sleep tonight, pump up the queen-sized air mattress my sister Courtney let us borrow, and set out our sleeping bags. We gather our shower supplies and head off to the girls' locker rooms by the gym, passing a few tents along the way. Our group of a few thousand cyclists has completely invaded the small campus, some under the community tent, and others in their own tents scattered among the school buildings.

In the locker room, there are girls in various stages of undress, not at all bashful to be taking a public shower in a high school gym.

Apparently, most of them haven't heard of using a razor "down there," I notice, without wanting to have that much information. Though I like to think I'm comfortable with my body, and I'm in decent shape from all the riding and yoga I've been doing lately, I have a hard time baring it all in front of a bunch of women, or in front of anybody for that matter. I sheepishly undress, wrapping myself in my teal green towel as quickly as I can, and only removing it a moment before I slip under the stream of warm water. The water stings my chafed skin, but it feels good to be clean.

I pull on a pair of comfy Abercrombie jeans and a light blue tank top, then zip on a gray hoodie. I grab my makeup bag and walk over to the mirror. *Not bad*, I think, checking out my reflection. Rosy cheeks, deep brown eyes, pretty face and a curvy, but fit body. Even if I'll never be drop-dead gorgeous, I look casual, yet feminine. It would be nice to meet a cute cyclist tonight at dinner, I muse, already tasting the spaghetti and meatballs. I think I'll even have a nice cold craft beer with dinner. Beer is not usually my drink of choice but sounds amazing right now, after all that hard exercise.

I've only recently resolved to spend less time obsessing over guys and more time focusing on what I love to do, like cycling, yoga, singing and writing; and of course, real estate, which is how I make a living. But my secret hope is that by not focusing on it so much, a great guy will magically show up. And as far as I'm concerned, tonight would be as good a time as any.

I brush on a little pressed powder to even out my sunburned complexion, and just a tiny bit of mascara and lip gloss. I don't want to look too made-up. It's dinner in a tent on a high school football field, and I think cyclists tend to like the natural look anyway. I rub some gel through my naturally curly hair and twirl it with my fingers so it will dry smooth and wavy. Content with the result, I slip on my flip flops and head back to camp.

After dinner, Liz heads off to make a phone call and I hang around to mingle in the makeshift bar area. I notice several cute guys, but each time I start to consider one, a girl walks up and grabs his arm. It's pathetic really. Are all the good guys taken? I've certainly dated my fair share in the year and a half since my divorce, but now I'm at a crossroads. Sick of all the men who only want one thing. Weary of giving it to them and then getting hurt. But not sure how to find a nice one who's also good looking, fun and likes me back. I glance at my watch. It's only 8:00, but I'm beat. I head back to the tent, thinking I'll see Liz there.

She isn't there, but I pull off my jeans and slide into my sleeping bag. I lie wide awake for about five minutes before I realize I still have my contacts in. I consider taking them out right there in the dark but decide that could be a disaster. Besides, as exhausted as I am, I just don't feel sleepy. And I wonder again where Liz is. She showed me where the BofA guys had set up their tent, so I slide my jeans back on and head over. When I walk up, they're chatting along a low wall under a large tree just outside their tent.

"Hey guys, hope I'm not interrupting anything," I say brightly.

"Hi Danielle. Not at all. I just got here myself. Glad you found us," Liz says.

"I tried going to bed, but it was just too early, so I thought I'd come look for you."

"Good to see you," says Luke with a smile. He's boyishly cute, tall, and very lean. Some people might say he's too skinny, but I've always preferred long and lanky muscles over short and bulky ones like my own. He re-introduces himself and the others - James, who, it turns out, is his brother, and an older guy, Ken, who I didn't meet earlier. Steve has gone home to be with his wife and new baby.

"Why don't you girls have a seat and stay awhile," says Luke, offering his fold-up camping chair to Liz. James stands up wordlessly, looks at me, and gestures toward his own chair. I smile up at him. Wow, I didn't notice how tall he was earlier.

"How sweet you boys are, giving your chairs up to the girls. Your mom must have raised you right," I say, flirting. I glance furtively at Luke and notice his bright blue eyes and chiseled jaw, but then my eyes fall to his bright gold wedding band. *Yep, all the good ones are taken.* Then I turn to James. No wedding band there. He's sitting behind me in the shadows, so I can't check him out without being obvious. He seems kind of shy, a little scruffy in a way that could possibly be sexy, and very tall. I've always liked tall guys. Six feet, maybe 6'2" feels just about right to me, even though I'm barely 5'1". But I'm pretty sure James is closer to six and a half.

We talk and joke for a few hours. The conversation moves to careers, and I tell them I'm a realtor.

"Cool. Maybe you can help Jimmy find a house when he gets on with the fire department," Luke says brightly.

I smile at the childish nickname. James wants to be a firefighter? How cool. Most of the potential clients who stop by the real estate kiosk at the Scottsdale mall where I've recently started working are single guys. Although I'm sure some of them are looking for a date more than a home, I think I'm just approachable and relate well on a professional level to guys.

We start talking about tandem bicycles, where two people ride together on one bike.

"It'd be so cool to find someone to ride a tandem with," I say. I notice a quick, almost imperceptible glance between Luke and James.

Finally, yawning, Liz and I get up to go get some sleep for the big ride back to Phoenix tomorrow. James hasn't said much to me, but he seems interested in an innocently shy sort of way, and I feel butterflies in my stomach at the anticipation of something new. I did ask God for someone different from the typical guys I usually fall for. Maybe shy and innocent is a good thing. I'm pretty sure he's not Jewish, but it never seems to work out with the Jewish guys anyway, even if I do manage to find one I'm attracted to. Hardly any of my past boyfriends, or even my ex-husband, were Jewish, though my faith is a big part of who I am.

I wonder if he's Mormon, I think, just before drifting off to sleep.

I'm woken up several times during the night, once by someone's coughing spell on the other end of the tent, once because I have to pee (slide on the jeans, go outside and around the corner to the

J-Johns and then hightail it back to the tent, still a little scared of the dark, even at 29 years old.) Finally, in the wee hours of the morning when it's still pitch dark out, I lie awake as some truck-mounted machines loudly and slowly suck all the waste from the J-Johns. It feels like I've just fallen back asleep when the alarm on my watch starts beeping me awake. I feel around for the button that makes it stop, hoping I hit snooze instead of off.

I peel my eyes open when the beep wakes me up again eight minutes later. *Ouch!* My body screams in pain as I carefully pull on a clean pair of cycling shorts and the light pink, form-fitting jersey my sister got me for my birthday a few months ago. The BofA one is still damp and smelly from yesterday and this one is way cuter anyway. I grab my toiletry bag and head once again to the girls' locker room to brush my teeth, wash my face and pull my hair back.

I'm so sore I can barely walk over to the cafeteria for the pancake breakfast. How on earth am I supposed to ride another 80 miles today? I don't even think I could sit on the seat. I'm feeling grumpy as I nibble a few pancakes and gulp a cup of sweet coffee. After breakfast, I rest on the air mattress for a few minutes and then take some Excedrin, hoping it will dull the pain and give me a caffeine rush of energy. Then I pack up my sleeping bag and clothes and lug them back over to the trucks that will carry them back to Phoenix. I long to curl up in the truck with my bags. *Nope. Not an option. You are tough. You can do this!*

Reluctantly, Liz and I mount our bikes and start pedaling, wincing with every stroke. Even my wrists and ankles ache. The wind is blowing hard, which makes the whole thing feel like a futile plight. But we keep pedaling and soon we make it to the first rest stop, 10 miles in. I'm not hungry, but I grab a few orange wedges and some Gatorade, fighting for a burst of energy. I still haven't quite woken up.

We're just getting back on our bikes when the BofA guys – James, Luke, and Ken - pull up next to us. They started later than everyone but have quickly caught up to the main group.

"Look at you all *bright-eyed and bushy-tailed*," I say with a smile, making air quotes with my fingers and shaking my head in mock disgust. "*Like this is just a walk in the park.*"

Mercifully, it's decided the guys will pull Liz and I for a while, blocking the wind so we can draft and ride easier. This will force them to slow their pace, but I get the feeling that behind all their bravado, they're tired too and don't mind taking it easy today. And I sense James' friends playing wingmen, trying to nudge him toward me.

The 80 miles pass in a blur. I spend most of them within a few feet of James, but I still haven't gotten a good look at him, our conversations brief and breathless as we pedaled our bikes. I've learned that he's the head mechanic and manager at a local bike shop, he's interviewing to become a firefighter, and he loves to mountain bike and go four-wheeling with his friends in a rock buggy he and Ken built together.

James is more blue-collar than most of the guys I've dated, a *guy's guy*, and I like that. I can tell he's religious, or at least traditional, and his wholesome innocence is intriguing. I feel attracted to his essence, his soul. I've never felt anything like it - although I've always been dramatic with my feelings. Once I decide I like someone, I'm thinking about marriage before most guys think about a second date, which often leads to getting intimate too quickly and then getting attached just when he's ready to run.

I remember when I first realized that kissing a boy didn't necessarily mean as much to him as it did to me. I was in high school, and he was a friend of a friend, kind of a bad boy. I was surprised and flattered that he even liked me, although looking back, I don't think he bothered to take me out on a date. He did kiss me, though. And I thought that kiss sealed the deal, making us boyfriend and girlfriend. I probably asked him, "Does this mean we're dating?" or "Am I your girlfriend now?" I was such a dork. And of course, that scared him away. I never heard from him again. Don't even remember his name. I can't tell you how many more times a similar scenario would play out in my life. It hurt me every time, deeper than I realized. I've gotten numb to it, and I've learned not to expect much; to be a playful, fun sort of girl rather than a needy, emotional one. I've never understood why some girls have boyfriends that last forever - the guy they dated freshman year of high school is the one they marry - but everyone I like either ignores me or likes me for a day and then moves on. And on the rare occasion that a guy does want to stick around, then I'm the one who runs.

I want something different from that now. But I feel like these initial experiences with love and lust, crushes and obsessions, have scarred me, and I'm not sure I'm even capable of forever love.

But I'm overthinking it, I decide as James and I finally pedal into the parking lot of the Phoenix High School where the ride started yesterday. We join the rest of the group and enjoy barbecue sandwiches and free massages. I meet Luke's wife, Amanda. Long legs clad in stretchy pants under a stylish sweater. Freshly highlighted shoulder-length blond hair framing a lightly-made-up, heart-shaped face with sparkly blue eyes. She hardly looks like a woman who just had a baby three weeks ago. All three of them - James, Luke, and Amanda - are like caricatures of this wholesome all-American family that feels just out of my reach, and I instantly find myself longing to be part of it. I hand James my glossy realtor business card, complete with the requisite headshot in the upper right-hand corner, not so much because I hope he'll call me to buy a house, but because I want to get to know him, and it's a convenient way to give him my number – and a picture to remember me by.

He's different, refreshing, and I sense a possibility of... something with him.

CHAPTER 2

A Refreshing Adventure

November 10, 2003

Monday morning, back at home, every muscle in my body is stiff, and I can barely get off the couch to get a glass of water. But it's a "good hurt," I tell myself. My little body did something amazing this weekend.

As I lie on the couch, aching but happy, thoroughly enjoying my self-imposed recovery day, I watch TV, read a book, eat, sleep - and wait for James to email or call. I feel a giddy anticipation thinking about him, but he was so shy and reserved that I'm not sure he'll call. I'm thinking he probably is Mormon. The Mormon kids in high school choir were always the nice, wholesome, polite ones. My sister, Courtney once had a Mormon boyfriend. But when it comes to marriage...well, Jewish moms want their daughters to marry nice Jewish boys, and I imagine a Mormon mom would want her son to marry a Mormon girl. And I don't want to waste any more time. I'm ready to start a family and begin a real adult life.

I hear the garage open, and Courtney's car pull in. She's a law student at ASU and we've recently bought this cute little house together. It's been fun having my little sister as a roommate, and the house I found for us is perfect - in a small infill community of newer homes right in the middle of South Scottsdale, where most of the homes were built in the 50s and 60s. It has vaulted ceilings, a kitchen island, and a nice open great room. We got it re-tiled before we moved in last month. It's a three-bedroom, so we decided it was fair that I get the master bedroom and Courtney get both tiny secondary bedrooms. We share the open den office, but I work from home, so I use it more than she does. Courtney is eternally at the law library, studying with friends.

"How are you feeling?" she asks as she sets her keys and books on the counter.

"Everything hurts, but I feel good," I say, whining just a little. I tell her about the cute, shy guy I met on the ride. When I finally see his name in my inbox, my heart leaps.

> Hey Danielle,
> James here from the MS150. Sorry I didn't get the chance to say goodbye yesterday. I hope you recovered well. I think I have a cold coming on, but other than that I feel OK.
> The sale I was telling you about at the shop is this Friday. We are located on the northeast corner of Alma School and Southern. 480-649-3394 is the number, Adventure Bicycle Company is the name.
> I haven't been able to get a hold of the girl I know who has a mountain bike your size. She night rides with us on Wednesday, so I'll ask her then.
> Later
> -James
> Adventure Bicycle Company

"It doesn't really sound like he's all that interested in you," Courtney says matter-of-factly when I let her read it. "It's not at all flirty or anything."

"Yeah, I guess not, but he's kind of shy. Maybe he's just not the flirty type," I say defensively. I sense that he does like me and that sending this email was a big deal for him. I read between the lines of his actual words to the meaning beneath. He wants to see me again.

As I walk into the bike shop Friday afternoon, the hanging bells on the glass storefront door jingle to announce my arrival, and James looks up from the bike he's working on at the back of the shop. The floors are made of weathered hardwood boards and my heels click as I walk toward him, past rows of bikes. I admire the shiny metal and pretty colors, the familiar smell of rubber and grease. James meets me at the glass counter that separates the sales floor from the service area. I look down at the various bike parts displayed in the case.

"You look nice," he says, and I feel the sparks despite his reserve.

"Thanks. I came from work, so not exactly dressed for a bike shop today," I say, smiling up at him, *way* up. "I had a realtor home tour this morning, so I had to be professional and all that."

The truth is I took careful pains to appear classy and professional, but cute and a little sexy at the same time, without trying too hard. I settled on a pair of navy capris and a fitted, slightly sheer white button-down, and I decided to blow my longish, curly hair straight, which I rarely do. I wanted him to see that I clean up nicely.

James doesn't own the shop, but he explained to me during the ride that he works alongside the owner, Greg, managing it and practically running things. He's known as a great bike mechanic, and cyclists come from all over town to have him fix their bikes. Greg trusts him implicitly and, despite his shyness, I can tell James is also a great bike salesman because he has an honest and gentle way about him, knows his product, and listens well. People always think that being good at sales is all about the talking, but I've found that people who know how to listen rather than talk all the time can connect with their customers and have far more success in sales. James does this naturally. It's something I'm still working on. I tend to talk more than I listen.

He's invited me to a special sale they're having today for their regular customers, and I've stopped by for some bike shorts and socks, but mostly to see James and talk more about the mountain bike ride he suggested for this Sunday. He's an expert mountain biker, just one step down from professional. I've never tried riding off-road, and I'm excited for my first time to be with him. He shows me the cycling gear, and I pick out a pair of women's shorts from among the two or three choices. It's obvious this shop caters more to men than women.

"Can you show me some of the mountain bikes?" I ask. "I don't know anything about mountain biking, but I've always wanted to learn, just never had someone to teach me."

I briefly wish I had bought a mountain bike back in college instead of a road bike. But then I guess I wouldn't have met James on the MS150 road ride. *Everything happens for a reason.*

"I'll teach you," James offers shyly.

"That would be awesome. Hope you're not just saying that. It would require lots of time together, I would think," I flirt.

"I can handle that," he says with a half-smile.

This whole exchange feels old-fashioned and simple, G-rated and sweet compared to my recent interactions with guys. James is a different breed. I feel like I'm being taken back into another time, and I absolutely love it.

Later that evening, after attending a *Shabbat* dinner for local Jewish singles, I decide to call James at the shop, under the pretext that I need another pair of shorts, which isn't untrue. Old-fashioned or not, I can tell that if I want anything to happen here, I'm going to have to push things along just a bit. Greg answers and calls James to the phone.

"Your *girlfriend's* on the phone, Jimmy."

I grin into the phone, thrilled at this tiny confirmation that he does like me, and thinking again what a departure this is from my previous experience of dating, which usually involved hooking up after some drinks and hoping it would turn into something more.

I ask James to charge a second pair of shorts to my credit card and tell him I'll get them from him the next time I see him, thus ensuring there will be a next time soon.

"By the way, what are you guys doing after the sale tonight?" I ask, thinking maybe they're going out for drinks as a group.

"Nothing that I know of," he says.

"Oh. Well...do you want to go grab a drink or something then? I was out with some friends earlier, but I'm not tired," I say, not specifically mentioning that it was a Jewish thing. It's not that I'm ashamed of my Judaism. I'm just not ready to explain it yet.

"Sure, that would be great," he says. He calls me back when he gets off work about 20 minutes later and we decide he should just come over to my place.

That night we talk a lot, flirt a little, drink one beer each, and get to know each other. I learn that he's not Mormon, but Christian. And I don't mean Christian, as in celebrates Christmas and Easter, and goes to church occasionally. He's one of those people who read and study the Bible, applying it to every aspect of life. I realize he probably thinks I'm going to hell because I don't believe in Jesus. He doesn't specifically say so, but I knew some *born-again Christians* in high school, and that's what they told me. They seemed unaware that the fear of hell was a poor sales pitch since I didn't believe in a literal hell any more than I believed in Jesus.

I've always believed in God, talked to him in my head, bounced things off Him. I guess you'd call it praying, though Jewish prayer is generally more formal. In synagogue, we recite specific phrases in Hebrew - excerpts from the Psalms or verses from the *Torah* - during a formal service, led by a rabbi, followed by a poetic translation into English *en masse*.

I love the haunting Hebrew melodies that pepper our prayer services, the beauty and symbolism of God's sacred *Torah* scroll and the *Ark* that holds it. But along with the formal prayers, we're encouraged to pray silently, too. I speak freely to God about anything and everything. I ask him about stuff. Thank him for things. I feel like God is part of me. I know He hears my thoughts, knows my intentions - and loves me, just the way I am. God is everywhere and everything. I am made in his image.

I believe people are basically good. We don't need a savior or an intercessor. There's one God, and I already know him. Judaism teaches that we are God's chosen people. I believe this, even though I can't quite wrap my brain around why God needs to choose favorites. But I'm content with knowing that there are some things I won't fully understand until I see God face to face. And I can't help but wonder if perhaps all the world's religions are more similar than different. Maybe we're even worshipping the same God and don't even know it.

In my earliest memory of grappling with the concept of God in an intellectual way, I'm looking up at the arched stained-glass window above the slump block western wall of the main sanctuary of Temple Solel in second grade religious school.

Al shlosha d'varim, ha'olam omed, we sing —the world stands on three things: *Torah, Avodah, and Gemilut Hasadim*: learning, ritual practices, and acts of lovingkindness.

Reform Judaism is the most modern of the three branches of Judaism, emphasizing the evolving nature of the faith, focusing on progressive values, ethics, human reason, and intellect, with less stress on ritual observance and traditional Jewish law. I was raised in a community of inclusiveness and acceptance, taught to participate in *Tikkun Olam* - repairing the world, making it a better place, healing, helping, caring for the marginalized.

But the main tenet of Judaism, whether you are Reform, Conservative, or Orthodox, is that *there is one God.* Period. End of story. We chant it in the most sacred and simple Jewish prayer: *Sh'ma Yisrael Adonai Eloheynu Adonai Echad*, "Hear, Oh Israel, the Lord is our God, the Lord is One." And the *V'ahavta*: "And you shall love the Lord your God with all your heart, with all your soul, with all your might."

But I've always been curious about Jesus. Who was he really and why do so many people think he was God's son? What's the deal with the Trinity - three-in-one? In high school choir, I loved singing those beautiful Christmas carols, even the ones that mentioned Jesus.

I longed to be part of all that was Christmas instead of feeling like an awkward outsider. But believing in Jesus, or even thinking about him, is simply unacceptable for Jews, and he is inaccessible to us. To believe in Jesus would be blasphemous. Jews for Jesus is like a conflict of interest, a type of cult we learned about in high school religious studies. You can't *be* a Jew and be for Jesus. If you're *for Jesus*, you're a Christian, not a Jew.

And at the same time, what I believe isn't really what makes me Jewish. Judaism is funny that way. It's both a religion and a heritage. I'm Jewish because my mother is. Jewish lineage follows the mother's line. It's a birthright, not something someone can take away from me. Once a Jew, always a Jew. Even if I were to convert to Christianity, I'd still be a Jew by lineage. And if the Nazis were in power today, I'd be marched into that concentration camp right alongside my parents, my sister, and all my second and third cousins, regardless of what I told them I believed. I have Jewish blood coursing through my veins because both my parents are Jewish. My dad is not the least bit religious, but he's still Jewish. His family is French and spent generations in Alexandria, Egypt, so they followed the Sephardic traditions of Judaism, a whole different flavor from my mom's Ashkenazi Jewishness most common in the US.

My first husband, Ian, didn't believe in God, but we still celebrated Christmas. I even cut down my first live tree with him in upstate New York and then decorated it in our Manhattan apartment. According to him, I was too religious. But the truth is I've always been more spiritual than religious - seeking truth, trying to understand God and people, never simply following the rules and reciting prayers and rituals by rote. In my mind, *religious* is doing things the way they're supposed to be done, without asking why. It's a lot of shoulds and shouldn'ts. There are religious Jews, Christians, Catholics, Mormons, Muslims - even atheists. That's not me.

But I've always been interested in religion, faith, humanity - and understanding the divine power that to me is undeniable on this earth and in each of us. I guess that's one reason my first marriage didn't last long. How could I be with someone who doesn't even believe there's a God, when I see the evidence of His amazing handiwork everywhere I look - in a baby's smile, a patch of grass, a bird's song, the kindness of people, the tiny miracles of everyday life?

As soon as James and I start talking about past relationships, I'm struck with the absolute certainty that this handsome 26-year-old, 6'4" man is a virgin.

I make sure he understands that I've been married and divorced already, and that even if I hadn't, I never even considered saving sex for marriage. I tell him a little bit about Ian, and he reveals that he's recently broken up with a girl named Janie, the first girlfriend he'd had since high school, when he decided to swear off dating in favor of mountain biking.

"Did you have sex with Janie?" I ask, already knowing the answer.
"No."
"Have you ever had sex?"
"No."
"Are you waiting for marriage?" I ask, knowing he is.
"Yes," James says, breathing a sigh of relief and looking at me with a bewildered expression, his eyes asking, "How on earth could you have guessed that?"

I know because this conversation is like a déjà vu of another conversation 10 years ago with Lewis, a Christian guy I dated briefly in college. It's because of Lewis that I even know this is still a thing people do: saving themselves for marriage in the name of Jesus.

I met Lewis on an Outdoor Adventures rock climbing trip I was co-leading. He was an engineering student. I was a Journalism Major with a French minor, who had, up until recently, believed engineers were the drivers of trains. Of course, I knew there must be more to it, since there was a large prominent stone building on campus with the name "Engineering" carved into the top, but I didn't quite understand what engineers did.

After hours of subtle flirting while we practiced rock climbing on Mount Lemmon, I had convinced Lewis that I owed him an ice cream. Sitting on the curb outside the brand-new Cold Stone Creamery, where they hand-mixed your ice cream creation on a marble slab, Lewis stretched out his sleek shaved legs. He was a cyclist on our college team, and I was thinking he must be quite the ladies' man with those bedroom eyes and that rock-hard cyclist body. I imagined he had slept with many girls. Not that *I* was promiscuous or anything. I had only had sex a few times, but I usually assumed I was less experienced than most people around me, not more.

"Do you have a girlfriend?" I asked.

"Nah, haven't really met anyone I like," Lewis answered, smiling at me.

"Well, there must be lots of girls you mess around with though."

"You mean like sex? I don't do that," he said softly.

"You don't?" I asked, incredulous. "What do you mean?"

"I'm waiting until I get married."

"What? You can't be serious. But you're gorgeous. You could get any girl you want! Why would you want to wait 'til you get married? For all we know, we may be like 30 before we get married."

"Well, I'm a Christian and I believe in the Bible, and I try to live my life as Jesus did," Lewis said, absolutely serious.

"And did Jesus actually *say* not to have sex until you're married?!"

"Yeah, you know that commandment, 'Thou shalt not commit adultery?'" he said with a smile, giving my arm a gentle punch. He had a slight Southern drawl that was very sexy. How ironic that the sexiest guy I had ever gone out with wasn't even looking for sex.

"Adultery is having sex with someone other than who you're married to, or someone who's married to someone else," I retorted. "If neither of you is even married in the first place, you can't really commit adultery! And anyway, didn't Jesus live thousands of years after the ten commandments were delivered to the *Jewish* people?"

"Well, whatever," he said, a little flustered, "then it's fornication. All I know is I'm saving myself for my future wife, just as she will do for me." So, there we had it. I knew where that relationship was going. Nowhere.

I wonder if it will be like that with James. If he too will push me away because I'm not Christian.

Despite our religious differences, Lewis and I dated for several months. I was pretty sure, even then, that if Jesus didn't want him having sex with someone who wasn't his wife, then he also wouldn't want him *not* having sex but being with her the way we were. I still blush when I think of all the things he taught me about the male body. But they weren't my rules to follow, and we had a great time together. He came home with me for Thanksgiving and met my parents and everything, but even though I imagined a future with him, he made it clear he didn't see one with me. He never tried to convert me or even really wanted to talk much about what he believed. He kept it to himself. I guess he thought I was a hopeless case. There was no way I was becoming a Christian, so he might as well have a little fun with me. I wasn't marriage material. Lewis was out of my reach.

We broke up when I headed to Paris to study abroad the spring of my junior year, and I don't think the French had ever considered reserving sex for marriage. Half the time they didn't even bother with marriage, but simply lived together and had kids without that religious and legal permission slip.

But now I realize that Lewis did plant some seeds all those years ago. He introduced me to the crazy notion that even in this modern age, one could, and maybe should, save sex for marriage. I started asking questions about Jesus and his relationship to Judaism, bought a few books on the subject, and fell in love with the Christian pop music he listened to. I still have the cassette tape of Michael W. Smith songs he recorded for me. And sitting here with James now, I can't help but wonder if there isn't some reason I had that experience with Lewis back then. Was it preparing me for something? Is God trying to tell me something? I've always believed that everything happens for a reason…

"I think we should go out to dinner tomorrow night," I announce as James is getting ready to leave.

"I agree," he says with a shy smile.

"Do you like Mexican? My sister, Courtney told me about a great little place just up the street."

"Sounds perfect. I'll pick you up at 7:00?"

Despite our vastly different backgrounds, I wonder if James and I have a future together, or if he will be just out of reach like Lewis was.

CHAPTER 3

Come to Jesus

November 22, 2003

The following weekend, James takes me out on my first mountain bike ride at Usery Park in East Mesa. He's a calm and patient coach, and I'm smitten - with James, the mountain biking, and his refreshingly conservative life.

His brother, Luke and sister-in-law, Amanda meet us out there after our ride with a picnic breakfast of homemade cinnamon rolls, a dark green tin thermos of coffee, and fresh berries. They bring their adorable three-year-old, William and their new baby, Hannah.

I sit at the concrete picnic table in the gorgeous desert park, cradling one month-old Hannah and getting to know them all, and I yearn to be a part of this Norman Rockwell family, all blue-eyed and wholesome. It's funny that I'm so attracted to this version of family when I once yearned just as strongly to become part of Ian's exotic and multicultural one. I'm a chameleon, with so many different skins I can wear, all of them real, but none of them capturing the entirety of who I am.

The first time I saw Ian, he was standing at the top of the rickety wooden staircase of his mom's rented brownstone in Harlem. He smiled down at his cousin Eloise and me as we awkwardly fumbled our way up, laden with black trash bags and an assortment of suitcases containing all our clothes and personal items from Eloise's minuscule Greenwich Village apartment.

"*Salut, Cocotte*," he called down to Eloise in perfect native French, barely glancing at me as he gestured toward a bedroom at the end of the hall where we should put our stuff, without offering to help carry anything. We lumbered past a tiny cupboard of a kitchen packed with giggling French-speaking girls who looked like they were still in high school. Everyone went about their business as if it were a perfectly natural and supremely uninteresting thing for two young women to arrive like vagabonds on a stifling hot Friday night in July, carrying garbage bags full of stuff. Sweat dripped down my back and I wiped perspiration from my brow after finally setting the bags down on the worn hardwood floor of the large bedroom that would be ours for the next week.

You might think a New York City heat wave would have nothing on a girl who grew up in the hot Arizona desert, but this was an entirely different heat. In Arizona, sweat doesn't drip down your back. The arid air that feels like a blow dryer on high instantly dries any perspiration the minute it forms on your skin, which does serve to cool you off just a little. And in Arizona, we have air conditioning. Everywhere. Whereas here, in these pre-war buildings, central air was a rare luxury. People opened their windows to the hot, muggy outside air, and electric fans moved things around to provide some relief.

Ian wasn't really my type: dark hair and eyes, medium height, olive-toned skin, and the kind of nose I've always thought of as a "Jewish nose," even though he wasn't Jewish. But he had nice eyes and a warm smile. He was cool and aloof, which of course sparked my interest, almost as much as the way he spoke French and English with equal fluidity and a native tongue. I'd always wished my dad had spoken his native French to me as a child so that I could be fully bilingual. Instead, I had to study French for years in school and only finally achieved fluency after living in Paris and spending time with all my dad's cousins and their families there.

"*Salut, je suis Danielle,*" I introduced myself, even though he hadn't bothered to ask.

"*Ian, le cousin d'Elo,*" he responded.

I had only been in NY for a few weeks, there on a summer internship at Bates Worldwide, an international advertising firm.

I'd met Eloise during my semester in Paris a few years earlier. She and her friend Caroline were the token *françaises* who lived in the American house at the *Cité Universitaire*, a campus of dorm housing at the edge of the city just before the *banlieue*, that served all the nearby colleges and universities in Paris. Eloise was sweet and fun, and had that unique ability, just like Ian, to speak both French and English with equal ease. Now she was a lawyer in New York City and had invited me to stay in her tiny apartment on Bleecker Street in the Village for the summer. I was only supposed to be there for a 12-week internship I had arranged through the international business graduate school program I was attending, but I never returned to grad school after the summer.

Her apartment was barely 400 square feet, with a tiny ancient kitchen, and just one window air conditioning unit in the cramped living room where I slept on a navy-blue IKEA sofa bed. With all that noise, there wasn't much sleep happening those first few nights, but I was thrilled to be living in New York City and I didn't care. I would open the window and sit out on the fire escape like they do in the movies, taking in the sights and smells from the bars, restaurants and falafel stands below.

It was a fifth-floor walk-up tenement building above a pawn shop for which she paid an exorbitant rent. In fact, that's why we had made the trek up to her Aunt Brigitte's house in Harlem. Eloise and her aunt had discovered the fine art of home sharing long before it was common. Being French expats, they advertised in a magazine called FUSAC, France USA Contacts. Brigitte's Harlem brownstone felt like an international hostel full of young French travelers.

Since Eloise had planned to be out of town that week, she had decided to rent out her apartment to a French couple visiting New York. Her trip got canceled, but thankfully Brigitte had an open bedroom, so we had spent the evening packing up our clothes and personal items and headed up to Harlem for the week. I could hardly complain since I was a glorified houseguest myself. Plus, I was secretly thrilled by the idea of staying in Harlem. A small white girl in the notoriously black neighborhood, the streets of Harlem made me feel strong and kind of hip, even though I was anything but. Staying there was an adventure and I loved it. Just the name Harlem had a tough, rough ring to it. I grew up in a middle class, white suburban area - maybe three or four black people in my entire graduating class of 600 or so - but my mom was raised *on the streets of New York* in a diverse Brooklyn neighborhood, and I liked to think that I inherited just a bit of her street smarts. My dad was born in Egypt and half his family now lived in France. I was fascinated by diversity. I loved immersing myself in other cultures and finding the ways we were all more similar than different.

I wasn't Ian's type either, as he liked to point out often. He usually dated Black and Hispanic girls and listened to rap and hip-hop, with some Latin music mixed in. From his perspective, I was too straight-laced, conventional, vanilla. Too white and too "religious." He and his mom had always lived a Bohemian lifestyle that looked like an adventure to me. I think that's what attracted me most to Ian and his family, that combination of freedom and Frenchness. Ian didn't even have a checking account when I met him. He'd just cash his paychecks at one of those check cashing places and pay for everything from lunch to utilities with $20 bills. We came from two very different worlds. My family may have been French also, but my grandpa, *Papi*, was a banker, first in Alexandria, Egypt, then in Paris, then in New York. My dad was a realtor, and my mom was a dental hygienist who taught me how to write a check around the same time she taught me how to put in a tampon. We were much more conventional.

A few weeks after our Harlem stay, my internship over, I had decided to stay in New York. I was getting ready to move into an apartment with a new roommate, a friend of a friend moving to New York from the Midwest. Eloise was out of town for the weekend and Ian showed up at the Bleecker place one night, a backpack slung over his shoulder and a bottle of wine in one arm, needing a place to stay. His mom's lease on the brownstone had ended and she was staying with other friends until she found a new place, so he was on his own.

Wine and conversation led to kisses and cuddling, and soon we were dating. Several weeks later, I got a urinary tract infection that turned into a serious kidney infection and landed me in the hospital for five days. Ian really stepped up during that time, visiting me, communicating with my parents, and moving all my stuff into my new apartment so it was ready when I got out. My roommate and I decided he may as well just move in with us. Splitting the rent three ways instead of two helped us all out.

By the time he proposed a year later, our lives were so enmeshed that I never had the space to explore whether he really was the perfect partner for me, so I ignored my doubts and pushed forward. Until I couldn't anymore. Our marriage lasted less than a year.

How interesting that Ian thought I was so religious, but compared to James, I feel irreverent and secular. I think about some of my recent sexual experiences particularly, and I feel aware of my *sin* in a way I never really have before. Jews don't generally think about sin like Christians do. The only time you even hear the word sin is on *Yom Kippur*, the Day of Atonement, the most sacred and solemn of all the Jewish Holy Days when we name our sins against God in alphabetical order, like a chanted poem: adultery, blasphemy...

I was too vanilla for Ian, but I fear I may be a bit too spicy for James.

James recently moved out of his parents' house only to squeeze all his belongings into a bedroom in his brother's house two blocks away. He's naïve and inexperienced. Maybe I'm just too much for him. We talk about being "just friends," because it's crazy to consider a future together when we come from such different worlds. But at the same time, we both feel an undeniable connection. I'm ready to be in a real relationship that could lead to marriage and kids, and James has almost completely avoided dating since high school. Not being close to girls made it easier to stick with his resolve to not have sex until he got married. Of course, not dating also made it unlikely to ever get to the point of marriage, I think, but that works out for me since now he's a 26-year-old man ripe for a real relationship, and that's just what I want. I have enough experience for both of us, I think wryly, and I'm glad he's all mine. But I worry that someday he'll regret not saving himself for someone who had saved herself for him, and he'll leave me for another girl.

On Thanksgiving night, after we each finish dinner with our families, James comes over and we head to the old dusty Scottsdale Six drive-in movie theater to see *Elf*, a cute new Christmas movie. We dress warmly, and James has filled the bed of his forest green Dodge pickup with a foam mattress covered with blankets and pillows. It's the best drive-in movie experience I've ever had - a far cry from when my dad used to make Courtney and me duck down in the back seat as we passed through the entrance, so he only had to pay for two people instead of four. I hated when he did that.

James and I still haven't kissed or had much physical contact, but the cold weather gives us an excuse to cuddle up close. After the movie, we continue cuddling in the back of the truck, parked in the curve of our cul-de-sac. Finally, James nervously proclaims, "I really want to kiss you."

"Just do it," I say, breathless. And he does. It's electrifying, like nothing I've experienced before. It just feels right, like I'm home. *Oh no, there's no way we're just friends.* I feel my insides heat up.

The day after Thanksgiving, I'm invited over for dinner at James' parents' house in Mesa. I wonder what a born-again Christian mom will be like. Different from Ian's mom, I'm sure. I half-expect a frumpy woman with her hair in a bun singing hymns. I dress carefully in sky blue corduroy Banana Republic pants and a modestly cut scoop-neck black sweater. My style and personality have always been eclectic, so I just reach into my more modest side, the part of me that craves tradition and an old-fashioned life. It's always been there. I used to love baking cookies and singing Christmas carols at my best friend Anne's house with her conventional Christian family. And I often wished my own family was more traditional.

As it turns out, James' parents seem normal. His mom is pretty and slim, with shorter frosted hair, jeans, and a colorful fitted top. His dad is a big, tall man in a nice flannel shirt and jeans, with a graying beard and sparkling blue eyes that smile along with his mouth. The food is delicious and it's a nice, easy evening spent talking and eating around their large wooden farmhouse table. James' Uncle Leo and Aunt Renée are also there.

"*Renée*. That means reborn, or born again in French," I note aloud. *Interesting.* I've always been intrigued by language and the roots of words. *Reborn. A born-again Christian. What does that really mean? Why do they call it that?*

A few weeks later, I invite James, Luke, Amanda, and the kids over for dinner on a Sunday night, but James says they can't make it.

"We're going to the 6 PM service at church this Sunday," he says.

"Oh, what kind of church do you actually go to?" I ask, wondering why he hasn't invited me to go with them.

"A Christian one!"

"I know that, but like what denomination?"

"Just a biblical Christian church," he says.

"Oh, well maybe some time I could come with you and check it out," I say. "I've always loved going to church with friends...if that would be OK."

"Sure. That would be great," he says. I don't know it, but he's screaming with joy inside at the prospect that I am perhaps open to knowing Jesus.

I finally make it to church two weeks later, after a full day selling new homes from a trailer on the west side of Phoenix. I'm glad they go to the evening service so I can join them now that I'm working weekends.

James and I arrive late and the place is packed so we're forced to sit in the lobby where they've set rows of folding chairs and the sermon is piped in through speakers in the ceiling. It's a nice lobby, but I'm distracted by the setup. The pastor speaks casually and has a dry sense of humor. He sounds like a regular guy, not a holier-than-thou preacher. I peek in the small window of the door to the sanctuary to catch a glimpse of him. He has longish gray hair and a short beard, and he's wearing jeans and a golf shirt. This is so different from temple where the rabbi wears a formal robe over dress clothes. I fall in love with the music, which is modern and upbeat, a band playing along with harmonizing singers.

Music has always been at the heart of my own spirituality. A singer myself, once upon a time I dreamed of becoming a professional one. I even briefly considered becoming a cantor, the worship leader in Jewish services. My first year of college, I majored in musical theater. But at the end of the year when I bombed an important audition - mostly because I was too busy hooking up with a hot guy the night before - I took the advice of one of my professors who had said, "If there is something else, anything else, that you can see yourself doing, that you are good at, then go, do that. Because show business is hard. It must be your one thing, the only thing you can see yourself doing."

For me there were always lots of other things. But sometimes I want to go back and punch that professor for saying that to 18-year-old me. Because I've since wandered from one thing to another, always looking for the path to fulfillment. I think if I would have just stuck with one of the things, any of them, I'd be much further along professionally by now. But oh well. Everything I have done has brought me to where I am now. And this. This is interesting.

I start wondering anew what Jesus really said, did, and believed in his lifetime, and who he really was. I review everything I learned about Jesus growing up. I remember the shock and horror I felt the day my childhood neighbor Sonnet told me that the Jews killed Jesus.

I was about eight years old and across the street at her house. We sat at the table in her sunny kitchen. She slurped the last of her vanilla milk loudly through her straw. I sipped mine slowly, tentatively. Sonnet's house was the only place I had ever tasted vanilla milk, not a sweetened Nesquik version, but simply a tall glass of whole milk with a teaspoon of vanilla extract added for flavor. The whole milk her mom bought was so much creamier than the 2% I was used to. It was almost hard to swallow. Sonnet's mom - tall and dark-haired, with a straight back and a stern face - did not allow junk food. It was nothing but whole wheat bread, whole milk, meat, potatoes, and vegetables. Sonnet would gorge herself on cookies and Twinkies whenever she came to my house, which made me think that maybe her mom had missed the boat. Not being able to have the thing made her want it way more than I ever did. I actually liked fresh fruit and vegetables and really didn't eat that much junk food. My friends with the strictest moms were always the most rebellious ones.

"You know the Jews killed Jesus," Sonnet blurted out, smirking an almost evil grin my way, her long bare thighs making a farting sound on the yellow vinyl kitchen seat as she repositioned herself. Even though it was late November, in Arizona, it was a warm day and we'd been running around outside.

"Did not," I said, not knowing what else to say but never one to calmly avoid an argument. *How could we have killed Jesus?* I wondered to myself. *We don't even believe in Jesus.* I slumped back home across the street. *The Jews are God's chosen people. Why would we have killed Jesus?*

My mom was in the kitchen preparing stuffing and getting the turkey ready for Thanksgiving dinner the next day. Cooking wasn't her favorite thing, but she always managed to feed us well, and she especially rallied during the holidays.

"Mom, Sonnet said the Jews killed Jesus. I'm confused. Does that mean he's real? I thought we don't believe in Jesus, just like we don't believe in Santa Claus."

"Oh, Danielle, Sonnet is just trying to be mean and get you riled up. Of course the Jews didn't kill Jesus," she said calmly, seething under the surface at Sonnet's audacity.

"But was he real? Did he live and die like a real person?"

"Yes, Jesus lived a long time ago. He was a good Jewish man, a rabbi. He was a pacifist in a time of war. He brought a message of peace, and ultimately, he was killed for it. He never tried to start a new religion. Paul did that after Jesus died. Jesus was a Jew. It's complicated, but it was Roman soldiers who killed him, not Jews."

"Oh."

My mom was very wise. I figured if she said it, then it must be true.

CHAPTER 4

Be Transformed

December 17, 2003

But now I want to find out for myself who Jesus said he was. Back when Lewis and I were dating, I bought a few books about him, but they were more about coming to terms with who he was from a Jewish angle, or a historical perspective. I really want to understand what the Christians believe Jesus said and did while he lived on this earth, who he said he was and what he expected his followers to do. And why in the world these two Christian cyclists who rolled onto my path a decade apart both felt so compelled to preserve sex for marriage in his name.

Not knowing where else to begin my research, I walk into the Scottsdale Public library, the same branch where Nana, my dad's mom, has been a beloved volunteer for years. it's right down the street from Nana and Papi's townhouse, and Nana is a fixture here. Employees and patrons alike love her French Egyptian accent and her cultured elegance. Thankfully she's not here today, because I feel like I'm on a secret mission.

I head to the non-fiction section and follow the signs to the books about religion. There are shelves and shelves of books, and I wonder how exactly to go about doing research on Jesus Christ.

Which sources can I trust to be true and unbiased? Is there even such a thing where religion is concerned? I hear James' voice in my head from a conversation we had the other night. He's saying, *The Bible is the inspired word of God. It doesn't contradict itself. All the answers can be found in the Bible...*

And I think maybe I should just start there. *Can you check out a Bible from the library?* It seems logical to see what the Bible says about Jesus first, then later I can compare to other sources. I reach for a paperback bound with the title, *The New Testament*. Perfect, I think, this is the Christian part of the Bible, the part I've never read, would never have even thought of reading. There's a foreword by Billy Graham and it's written in clear modern language, not that hard-to-understand Old English like the Bibles in the hotel room nightstand drawers that I've peeked into over the years. I'm excited to finally know what the Christian Bible claims Jesus said about himself.

I've never believed that God meant the Bible to be taken literally. I've always thought of it as a collection of stories from which we could learn lessons. Surely those people didn't really live hundreds of years and Jonah wasn't literally swallowed by a whale. Could God have actually parted the Red Sea so the Israelites could cross? I suppose so, but it's hard to imagine today. I do believe in God the Creator, and I have a constant dialogue with Him in my head. And despite Reform Judaism's attempts to neutralize God's gender, I still picture God as more male than female, but really, I feel Him like an ever-present spirit more than a true bodily male. I have a sense that everything happens for a reason and that God is omniscient (knows everything), omnipresent (everywhere all the time), and omnipotent (capable of whatever he wants to accomplish). I just don't necessarily believe he chooses to act on those things in our everyday lives. I believe He has a greater purpose for each of us, but I don't have any idea what my purpose might be. I assume He does though.

I remember writing an essay on *The Problem of Evil* for a college philosophy of religion class, defending how a good and decent God could allow such evil in our world. It's an issue philosophers have debated for ages, but my humble conclusion after examining the arguments was that evil is necessary to contrast with the good, that even though God could just control everything and make it all good and perfect, He gives us free will, and that makes life interesting. I'll have to track it down from the boxes of special papers my mom keeps for me in her garage. I'd love to read the philosophies of my 19-year-old self.

I slither over to the check-out desk with my New Testament in hand, half-afraid that someone I know will see me or that Nana will find out I checked out a Christian Bible and I'm reading about Jesus Christ. It's one thing to go to church with a friend. That could be perceived as more of a social thing, not as a seeking for truth. Reading a book about *their* God, especially *their* Bible, is more serious. Though in truth, I've never thought of their God as separate from my God. I want to believe, in fact, that all religions are essentially reaching for the *same* God, grasping at understanding that which is not completely fathomable in this lifetime.

But some religious groups seem far away from truth and enlightenment, I think, as my mind conjures up the still-vivid images of two planes crashing into the two towers of the World Trade Center two years ago, and all the other tragedies of that day and the days that followed. I watched it all unfold live with Ian in my mom's cozy office TV room just a few months after we moved home to Arizona from New York.

September 11, 2001 - Ian and I were engaged and planning an October 13th wedding. We were staying at my mom's place in Scottsdale, in the process of buying our first house.

The final signing at the title company was scheduled for 9 am and my alarm was set for 6:30, but around 6:00, Courtney knocked on my bedroom door.

"Wake up. Something's happening," she said.

We all stood wordless, wiping the sleep from our eyes as the events unfolded on the TV. Watching incredulously as they played fresh footage of that first plane hitting one of the towers of the World Trade Center, I said, "That didn't look like an accident. It's like they slammed that plane right into the building on purpose." *Why would someone do such a crazy thing?* The newscasters at that early hour were eerily silent. They didn't have anything to say yet, so they just played the live feed.

"It looks like another plane just hit!" I said. And we watched as one of the buildings started to ripple, then collapse. I didn't know a building could do that.

Just a few months earlier, the night before we left New York to move to Arizona, we had visited Top of the World, a fancy cocktail lounge on the top floor of the World Trade Center where you could see views of the entire city. The elevator ride up took forever.

I thought of all the people trapped inside their offices, even the shopping center and huge subway station underneath the buildings, and I wondered how many had been able to get out.

Eventually, we had to peel our eyes away from the TV to shower and dress for our appointment. *Can you still do something as mundane and monumental as buy a house on the day of such a historic tragedy?*

At the title company, our escrow officer had a mini-TV perched on her desk. We watched continuing coverage of all the day's events as we signed the hundreds of pages of documents that made that cute three-bedroom, two-bath house in Surprise, AZ our own.

Those people on those planes performed those atrocious acts in the name of their God, I think now. They really thought they were doing something good and right. Since the dawn of time, people have killed people different from them in the name of religion. It's heartbreaking, when I truly believe we *all* are God's children, we *all* have inherent value.

Still, when I've visited churches with friends over the years, attended weddings and funerals, held my hands in prayer position and said *Namaste* at the end of a great yoga class - I've been struck by the commonalities among religions more than the differences. It's crazy people who mess things up, not the actual religious teachings.

Back in my master bedroom in the house I share with my sister, I've made sure Courtney is safely in bed and unlikely to barge in and catch me reading my borrowed copy of the New Testament Bible. I don't know if she would have questions or think I'm silly - or worse - for wanting to read a book that goes against everything our religion stands for.

Tucked into my four-poster bed, my dog Myka curls up against me. She's a German Shepherd mix that people have said looks more like a dingo. Ian and I rescued her from the pound right after we were married. Her official name is Mykonos, like the Greek Island where we spent part of our woeful honeymoon a month after the September 11 atrocities.

We had settled on October 13th for our wedding date despite the well-known superstitions about the number 13. It may have even been a Friday. I don't remember now. And maybe the fact that I glued my eye shut with nail glue that I mistook for a bottle of contact lens rewetting drops on the night of our wedding rehearsal should have been a sign that the marriage was doomed.

Ian worked for Starwood, an international resort chain, so we got discounts at all the hotels. We planned a honeymoon in Greece without knowing the world would change a month before our big day. October was already the very end of the tourist season on the Greek islands, and we were warned that it may be a little quiet during that time, with some businesses starting to close for winter. But after 9/11, almost no one was traveling, so the beautiful Greek Isles felt deserted and depressing. I felt tired, jet-lagged, in a fog the whole week, which is too bad, because it really was beautiful. But my memories of Greece will always be shrouded in the sadness of 9/11 and a marriage that probably never should have been.

Back in Athens the last few days before heading home, we stayed in a posh French hotel with an ornate lobby and furniture that felt royal. We went out to dinner that night, but then got in a fight about what we wanted to do after. *Are you supposed to fight on your honeymoon?* Finally over the jet lag, I wanted to go out dancing, but he had no interest.

Immediately after the wedding, I had felt relieved, like a weight was taken off my shoulders because I no longer had to agonize over whether I was making the right decision in marrying Ian. It was done now. I chose not to think of forever. But now that the honeymoon was over, I wondered again whether I had made a mistake. He was a decent guy, we had fun together sometimes, but did we have a love to build a life on? Maybe not.

It was only eight months later that we started the divorce process.

I crack open the Bible. It starts with the book of Matthew. I skim through a detailed genealogy of Jesus Christ, recognizing some of the names from the *Torah*: Abraham, Isaac, Jacob, Judah, Ruth, King David... Then I read about the virgin birth, a story I've heard many times at Christmas, in movies and books, and when I've visited churches with friends. But I try to really pay attention as I read it now, looking for clues, willing God to speak to me if this is OK, good, right.

An angel tells Joseph, "Do not fear to take Mary as your wife, for that which is conceived in her is from the Holy Spirit. She will bear a son, and you shall call his name Jesus, for he will save his people from their sins."

It says that all this took place to fulfill a prophecy from Isaiah: *Behold the virgin shall conceive and bear a son, and they shall call his name Immanuel* (which means God with us).

I skim quickly through the rest of the story about Jesus' birth and early life, wanting to get to the part about who he said he was and what he told Christians to believe and do. I can't find anything about waiting until you're married to have sex, even though Jesus' words are printed in red and stand out from the rest of the prose.

"Man shall not live by bread alone, but by every word that comes from the mouth of God," he said. "You shall worship the Lord your God and him only shall you serve."

Sounds like Judaism to me.

Then the famous sermon on the mount:

"Blessed are the poor in spirit, for theirs is the kingdom of heaven. Blessed are those who mourn, for they shall be comforted. Blessed are the meek, for they shall inherit the earth…"

"Do not think that I have come to abolish the Law or the Prophets; I did not come to abolish them but to fulfill them…" he said. "Unless your righteousness surpasses that of the scribes and Pharisees, you will never enter the kingdom of heaven."

So, he didn't come to abolish Judaism, but to fulfill its prophecies? *Which prophecies?* I'm confused by the part about righteousness. I've always believed I was a good person with a good heart. I've always cared about people. But I certainly wouldn't call myself righteous. I read on.

"You have heard that it was said, 'You shall not commit adultery,' but I say to you that everyone who looks at a woman with lust for her has already committed adultery with her in his heart."

Wow. And what, then, if you really have committed adultery, I wonder, because technically I was still married to Ian when I started dating - and sleeping with - other men. The divorce process takes months.

"It was said, 'Whoever divorces his wife, let them give her a certificate of divorce.' But I say to you that everyone who divorces his wife, except on the grounds of sexual immorality, makes her commit adultery; and whoever marries a divorced woman commits adultery."

This is a little too much for me, I decide, closing the book. I'm a divorced woman. It might be harder than I thought to figure out whether Jesus said he was God's son and came to start a new religion. Furthermore, it's beginning to look hopeless for me if this is what James' "God" thinks about divorce and remarriage. And besides the fact that I was born Jewish instead of Christian, I have thoroughly failed to live a righteous life. According to this Bible, I'm nothing but a divorced adulterer.

It's ridiculous to think that a Jew could become a Christian anyway. If James and I do get married, I suppose I could just celebrate the Christian holidays, which I love anyway, and even go to church with him occasionally. But I was born Jewish, and I'll always be Jewish. I don't even know how I would go about converting if I wanted to. I've known people who converted to Judaism from Christianity, but not the other way around.

The next day James comes over with a DVD copy of *Lord of the Rings*, his favorite movie. I haven't seen it yet. I lay my head in his lap as we watch Frodo battle the forces of evil. After the movie, I casually mention that I checked out a Bible at the library, which he finds hilarious.

"Any Christian in the world would have gladly given you your own Bible to keep! All you had to do was ask," he says.

"Oh, well I didn't really plan on checking out a Bible. I was looking to do some research and I just figured I might as well start at the source," I giggle. Then I ask if he thinks his mom would be OK if I just celebrated the Christian holidays but wasn't technically a Christian myself. I tell him that after reading Matthew, I've realized there's no way I could measure up since I haven't lived this perfect Christian life, kept myself pure, and all that. He kind of laughs at me as he explains that this has nothing to do with what holidays I celebrate or what his mom thinks. He says you don't need to come to Jesus a perfect Christian.

"When you become a believer in Jesus Christ, He takes your previous life and all its sin away. It's forgiven and forgotten, as if it never happened. Jesus died for *our* transgressions. That's the gospel, and that's all you really need to understand."

Wow, I think, *that sounds pretty good - so simple and yet so unlikely, impossible really. Because how on earth could this man who lived thousands of years ago forgive all my transgressions? Why would he even do that? If God wanted to forgive me, why wouldn't He just do it? Why would Jesus have to die for me to be forgiven? And yet... I've done a few things I'd like to erase. Starting fresh sounds wonderful. Where do I sign up?*

CHAPTER 5

Believe

December 22, 2003

It's the Monday before Christmas and James and I have been dating about six weeks. I'm cruising along the I-10 freeway, heading East toward Scottsdale from the western outskirts of town where I just started working as a sales agent in a new home community.

My office is a single-wide trailer on the side of a dusty road, a far cry from the upscale kiosk at Scottsdale Fashion Square Mall. It's a brand-new project, and they've just started breaking ground on the model homes that buyers will eventually peruse.

It's been a quiet, cloudy, wintery day, rare in Arizona, even in December. I spent most of it - between the occasional phone call or pop in by a prospective buyer - reading the Bible and trying to wrap my brain around it all. The Christian Bible is confusing, intriguing, and captivating, all at the same time. I feel a beckoning, a calling... to something. I'm still making my way through the book of Matthew, trying to understand this Jesus guy.

"Ask, and it will be given to you; seek, and you will find...For I came not to call the righteous, but sinners...Come to me, all who labor and are heavy laden, and I will give you rest..."

"You shall love the Lord your God with all your heart and with all your soul and with all your mind. This is the greatest and first commandment."

My heart leaps in recognition of the English translation of the *V'ahavta* prayer I diligently memorized for my Bat Mitzvah at 13 years old, the folksy Debbie Friedman version of this important Jewish prayer springing to my lips.

"And a second is like it," Jesus continues. "You shall love your neighbor as yourself. On these two commandments depend all the Law and the Prophets."

This sounds perfectly reasonable, familiar, of God. The same God I have always known. But reading it makes me feel squirmy, guilty. I'm in forbidden, heretical territory. And at the same time, I'm wondering if I could possibly believe this stuff? *Should* I believe it? Does God want me to see it as true? Is it just a coincidence that James is the second born-again Christian who has captured my heart, even though he was saving himself for marriage, presumably to a virgin Christian girl as devout as himself?

And if I go forward on this strange new path, what then? How does this fit into my liberal Jewish upbringing, my dad's French Egyptian heritage, my mom's streetwise Brooklyn feminism? I feel like I'm on the precipice of something important.

I turn off the radio so I can just think. I contemplate the words that Pastor Rick spoke last night at church. This time we got there early enough to get a spot in the main chapel. He talked about the day he became a Christian and how he was "saved." He hadn't grown up Christian like James had. He was a regular guy who did bad stuff, but he told the story of God reaching down and changing his life. *How did he know it was God?*

As the congregation prepared to take communion, gilded metal trays were passed from row to row, and you could hear peoples' rings clinking against the metal as they grasped the plate from the person next to them. On each tray were tiny plastic thimbles of grape juice and little crackers that reminded me of thin bits of *Passover matzo*.

Rick said, "If you have not taken Jesus into your heart, then it's OK to simply pass the plate along. It's not for you. But think about that. Think about what you're saying. You're saying, 'No thank you God. I'm good. I don't need your provision. I will go my own way.'"

I swallowed hard and passed the tray.

Speeding down the freeway now, I'm thinking about how I've always been taught that Jesus was not for the Jews. Jesus himself didn't even want to start a religion. That was Paul. Why am I now feeling like maybe this is for me? What do you have for me, God? What should I do in this strange situation? Can a little Jewish girl from Scottsdale believe in Jesus? Is this curiosity coming from you, or am I a heretic? How will I ever know whether this is right or true? Could Jesus really erase my bad choices and make me clean? How would I know if I were saved? Would I feel any different? And how...on Earth...would I ever even begin to tell my mother? *What should I do?*

I'm in a sort of daze as I drive down the freeway, wondering and praying about these things, but suddenly I look up from my reverie and my gaze lands on the back of the car in front of me. There in big bold letters on the Arizona custom license plate, like a sign proclaiming God's answer to my questions, it says: BLEEVE!

A shiver runs down my spine. Believe. Just believe. I think God's telling me it's OK to believe in Jesus. I guess this is about the closest thing I'll ever get to a burning bush, and my silent response is, "OK. I will. I do..."

Over the next few days, I feel elated as I replay the dramatic scene in my mind. James and his family are thrilled by my story, tell me they have been praying for me. *Praying for me?* What a strange concept. I pray, officially, that God will forgive me for my sins, and I feel light and free, excited to be alive. I guess this is what it feels like to be *saved*.

At church Sunday, butterflies flutter in my belly as we approach communion time. Taking communion is such an unJewish thing to do, almost like wearing a cross around my neck. But Rick reminds us again that to pass on the elements is to say, "No, this is not for me. I can do this on my own," and I decide that I don't want to pass them on, that Jesus is for me, that I need to live my life God's way, that my way *has not* worked.

Telling my mom the news is worse than I could have imagined.

James sits quietly next to me at the heavy sage green wrought iron dinette set, surrounded by flowering plants in the spacious front courtyard of my mom's Scottsdale patio home. I've told her I have something important to share. I don't know what she's expecting, and the whole thing feels awkward and formal. Birds chirp, cars whir by on the nearby freeway, a dog barks in the distance. A heat rash breaks out on my chest, the way it does whenever I'm nervous, excited, or worked up in any way. Finally, I take a breath and tell her about going to church with James, the borrowed Bible, the license plate.

I think it would be easier if the *news* was that I'd become a lesbian, a porn star, a drug addict, or a criminal. She would understand and support me if I told her I was moving to Africa, quitting my job to tour with a band, or heading to New York to try to make it on Broadway. Or even that I was marrying a Christian instead of finding a nice Jewish husband. After all, I didn't marry a Jew the first time around either. But as I spit out the story about how I have *become* a Christian, it's like I've driven a dagger into her heart. Her voice breaks and tears spring to her eyes. She shakes her head slowly.

"I can't respond now," she says, rising from the table. "I love you, but I can't feel anything but betrayal and sadness right now, and I need some time to process this."

My mom is passionate and outspoken, loving, encouraging. She has always been my biggest champion. But she doesn't understand this at all, and I've never seen such sadness, anger, and disappointment on her face. My heart aches and I ask God silently how this could be right if it hurts my mom so much.

Jesus said, "Do not think that I have come to bring peace to the earth. I have not come to bring peace, but a sword. For I have come to set...a daughter against her mother...Whoever finds his life will lose it and whoever loses his life for my sake will find it."

My mom and I talk on the phone a few days later and her voice is hard as she tells me that my choice to become a Christian is the ultimate betrayal.

"How could you turn your back on your faith, your heritage, your family? You've always had such a strong Jewish identity."

"I didn't turn my back on my faith," I try to explain to her. "This is a continuation of that faith, a strengthening, a deepening. And I still have that Jewish identity," I plead. *Don't I? Can't I? Am I still Jewish?*

The answer I hear silently screaming from both my mom and my soon-to-be Christian family over the next few weeks, months, years, is a resounding no. I feel as if I've been locked out of the temple without a key. No longer welcome there. So, I push forward on this new path I've chosen. Or that has chosen me. I don't really know which. And I hope I have gone the right way. Jesus said, "I am the way and the truth and the life. No one comes to the father except through me."

The synagogue we attended as I grew up was called Temple Solel, which means Pathfinder. This was the place that guided my path, taught me about God and His *Torah*. My path has always been a wandering, complicated one, even before this. I've tried to discern God's voice in the noise of my life. Now Jesus says *he is the only way*. And I believe him. But absolutes are hard for me. And if he is the only way to God, what does that mean for my family and friends who don't believe in Jesus, who think I'm ridiculous for believing? I don't have these answers and don't know if I ever will.

James proposes in February, and we get married in a small, simple ceremony in an adorable sunken flower garden on the grounds of the Scottsdale Civic Center on April 25, 2004, less than six months after we met. My mom is there, along with the rest of my family, despite my betrayal. She loves me unconditionally, no matter what.

I've always known that, as surely as I know my name. Although, ironically, I will have to change my name. Again.

I wear a simple, flowy cream silk dress rather than a formal gown like the first time. James' nephew William is the cutest ring bearer, carrying his beloved stuffed hippo as the ring pillow. The whole event feels whimsical, provincial. It's simple and beautiful, and I feel so much love.

"For whenever two or more of you are gathered in His name, there is love," Amanda sings sweetly.

And I just know this time will be forever. With Jesus as our foundation, there is no way we could fail.

Rather than head off on a honeymoon, we decide to stay in town. April in Arizona is beautiful, so we get a room in nearby Fountain Hills and spend the next two days encased in its plushness, making up for lost time with the physical stuff. We have sex 10 times in our first 24 hours as husband and wife.

We move into our new house in East Mesa, just around the corner from both Luke and Amanda's and James' parents' homes. My second house and my second marriage in as many years. The house is in rough shape and fixing it up keeps us laughing. Like the day James is checking out some electric lines in the attic crawl space above the kitchen and falls through the ceiling. I hear a crash and run into the kitchen to see only his long bare legs dangling from the ceiling. I don't know whether to laugh, scream, grab a ladder or a camera. I run up and grab hold of his legs, as if I could catch him and bring him safely to the ground. We can't stop laughing about it.

That summer we set out on a road trip to Durango, stopping in Flagstaff on the way. We've brought our mountain bikes, of course, so we ride a scenic trail through a forest of aspen trees and up over a steep ridge. It's so different from the desert riding I'm used to, even though we're only a few hours from home. In Arizona, you only need to increase your elevation a little bit to find yourself in a whole new world.

We cross a gorgeous open meadow full of fresh green grass sprinkled with wildflowers. There in the middle of the field stands a big black bull, the most evil-looking creature I've ever seen in real life, in stark contrast to the pretty grass, trees and flowers surrounding it. The bull is a powerful presence and I feel a chill as we pass him. But the thought crosses my mind that in real life, true evil rarely looks like a big, black bull, but more like a beautiful rose. You don't even sense its danger until you've already been pricked by its thorn.

The following February, James and I are out on an early morning mountain bike ride back home. I'm getting pretty good, a lot more confident on the technical Hawes trails near our house. I've even won a few races. Granted I compete in the Beginner category, for the 30-35 age group, so maybe the competition isn't so steep. But I've never been fast at anything in my life so getting that first-place medal was a thrill.

I love mountain biking with James. Though he's so much faster and more skilled than me, he never makes me feel like I'm slowing him down. He gently encourages and praises me. But today I'm feeling tired. I wish I had opted to stay in bed instead of forcing myself out on the trail. I feel flat and heavy and just want to turn around and go home.

James gently encourages me to keep going, thinking that's all I need. We're riding a hard section of the trail called *Twisted Sister*. I've only tried it once before. I know I need to gain some speed to be able to power over the rocky part coming up, but as I pedal hard, I fumble going over a rock and tip over to my left, falling into a ravine and landing with all my weight on my left wrist. I know immediately that this is more than just a scrapes-and-bruises kind of crash. I look down at my wrist, bent at an odd angle and already starting to swell. I snatch off my glove and wedding ring.

"I'm pretty sure it's broken," I say to James, standing on the trail above me. He scrambles down and lifts me out of the ravine and onto the trail, checking me over for other injuries and instructing me to drink some water. We both have inadvertently and uncharacteristically left our phones in the truck, which is several rocky miles away.

After a few minutes' rest, we get up and begin making our way down the trail on foot, James walking both bikes. But fives steps in, I feel woozy and light-headed, and I'm forced to sit down. I feel like I should be able to walk since it's only my wrist that's hurt, but I think I might pass out if I try.

James is a trained EMT, and he's hesitant to leave me alone, but I know I won't make it down this rocky terrain on my own two feet clad in cycling cleats, and the idea of being slung over his shoulder as he tries to carry me down on his own cleats sounds even worse.

"I think you should go get help, Baby. You could be down there in 15 minutes on your bike and call your friends at the fire department. You can tell them exactly where I am, even show them the way, and I'll be fine," I say. "I didn't hit my head; I have plenty of water and snacks. I'll just sit here on this rock and wait."

He looks worried, but reluctantly agrees that's the best course of action. He takes off racing down the mountain on his bike, and I sit on that rock, looking up at the birds soaring across the cloudless blue sky and feeling very close to God. My wrist is throbbing in pain, but I feel completely peaceful.

Since no one is around to hear me, I begin to sing. First the Jewish songs that have always made me feel close to God. The *Shehekianu* prayer, the *Sh'ma*, the *Va'a hafta-* you shall love the Lord your God with all your heart. And I do. Oh, how I do. I feel such love, sitting here on this mountain in terrible pain. It reminds me of Shwayder Camp in Colorado, where I spent all my teenage summers and could hear God whistling in the surrounding pines, bubbling in the nearby creek. In addition to being the place where I solidified the Jewish identity my mom was so proud of, Shwayder was where I first learned to love the outdoors, hiking, and backpacking. In the beginning, it was a love-hate relationship, but soon it became a major part of my life.

I move on to the contemporary Christian music from church and the radio: "Blessed be the name of the Lord," "Amazing Grace" and my favorite, "Untitled Hymn" by Chris Rice.

Forty-five minutes later, I spot a helicopter circling the area and realize they're looking for me but can't see me. I manage to walk up to a higher spot and wave to them, and they find a clearing where they can land nearby.

Two men walk over, and we determine that, with help, I'm able to scramble to the helicopter. They settle me in, and I wonder aloud how much all this is going to cost me. But they explain that this isn't a medical transport, but a police chopper, intended to locate me only. Since they were able to land and had a paramedic on board, I got the privilege of enjoying a free ride over the rocky desert that has never looked so gorgeous to me. I watch in awe as we soar above God's beautiful creation, and I'm so thankful to be alive.

I decide that I'm ready to get baptized. Baptism isn't a requirement in our church, but an outward sign of an inward spiritual commitment. Believing in Jesus made me a Christian. The baptism just announces the news to the world.

CHAPTER 6

Baptized with the Spirit

July 17, 2005

I heave the heavy white polyester gown up to my knees and sink into one of the blue plastic school chairs set up along the wall in the backstage area of the church sanctuary. The gown reminds me of the choir robes we wore at Temple Solel, but it's at least five sizes too big.

Alone in the bright fluorescent-lit room, the air conditioning steadily humming as I wait for my cue to go out onstage and be baptized, I can hear Rick's preaching - or rather *teaching* as they like to call it - piped in through the speakers. I hug my arms across my chest and shiver despite the 118-degree mid-July desert heat outside. They always cool the church down to arctic levels, but I know this trembling is more from nervous excitement than cold. I've performed onstage a hundred times in musicals, speech competitions, singing engagements, but tonight is not supposed to be a performance. I'm getting baptized, making a public proclamation, in front of my family and the church, of my internal heart change and faith in Jesus. At our church, baptism isn't something you do to babies, but a conscious choice that someone makes when they're mature enough to understand the gospel and follow Jesus personally. It's not the thing that makes you *saved*, but rather an obedient step of faith. Lots of times we see kids around eight or nine getting baptized, sometimes teenagers, and many times adults who were raised in the church but then strayed and came back like the prodigal son.

Usually they do baptisms in batches, about once a month. Each person reads a little snippet of their testimony and then they get dunked in the tank while joyous worship music plays in the background. But tonight, I'm the only one. Whether it's because it's the evening service, the middle of summer and everyone has left town, or that I'm special, I don't really know. But they've told me I could make a longer speech. It's unique to come to Christianity from Judaism, and people at church are always amazed when they hear the dramatic story of how God got my attention with James' choice to remain a virgin until marriage, and then sealed the deal with a license plate.

As I review my notes, my mind wanders back through all the scenes of my life, the divergent paths I walked that somehow brought me to this most unexpected destination.

I think about all the years at temple, staring up at that colorful stained-glass window and the ornately carved ark on the pulpit that housed the *Torah*, God's word. I remember how we used to do the high holiday services at the nearby Presbyterian church, because our own sanctuary was too small to hold the droves of Jews that came only on those few days of the year. They'd cover up the crosses to make it feel less Christian, but I was always curious what it would be like to attend church there on a Sunday.

A memory of visiting my friend Carly's church in fourth grade after a Saturday night sleepover pops into my highlights reel - a low table in a Sunday school classroom, a story about Jesus and these felt cutouts of the manger scene that had felt foreign and forbidden to me.

Christmas carols at Anne's house on Christmas Eve in high school, feeling the joy of the words and melodies, even though they weren't part of my personal belief system then. "Fall on your knees, oh hear the angel voices! O night Divine! O night when Christ was born." That one was always my favorite.

And then Lewis, my first Christian cyclist. I wonder what he would think if he learned that I've become a Christian.

I think of all the very unchristian things I have done in my life and feel so thankful I'm forgiven, that those choices are *as far as the East is from the West*. And I think of that crazy license plate that just happened to be in front of me as I drove down the freeway and wondered what I should do. Believe. Just believe. So easy, and so hard.

As I prepare to take this next step in my faith journey, I picture my sweet, handsome husband, who takes care of me and expertly captains the bright yellow tandem road bike we had custom made to fit our vastly different heights.

I believe he's proud of me, though pride isn't really a sentiment Christian people express. We're supposed to give all the glory to God. It's a whole new vernacular I've had to learn. Instead of feeling lucky, I'm *blessed*. Instead of taking credit for accomplishments, or being proud of our own hard work, we *praise the Lord*. For me, it's a new way of thinking about life. I don't dislike or disagree with it; I just have to remind myself to change the way I verbalize things. Kind of like when Anne's mom taught me in high school that when I say, "Oh my God," I'm *using the Lord's name in vain* and therefore cursing him. Even though I meant nothing by it, I learned to change my words around her, and eventually I just stopped saying the phrase altogether. I still think about her every time I almost say "Oh my God" when I'm not directly praising Him.

Anne and I first met in Mr. Moore's fifth grade class, and we've been friends ever since. Growing up, I spent many afternoons ensconced in her family's conservative Christian life, baking cookies or banana bread in her mom's country kitchen. Her family planted seeds of Christianity in me without even knowing it. I'm not sure if Anne even believes in Jesus anymore. We really don't talk about it. But she's here at church today to support me regardless. Our friendship has ebbed and flowed over the years. There was a time during those middle and high school years when I wanted so desperately to fit in with the popular crowd and I thought Anne wasn't quite cool enough for me. I watched her make other friends, friends who ended up being much cooler than the ones I so badly wanted to like me. But we've stayed close through it all, 20 years now.

Luke and Amanda are here with William, who's five now. Hannah's in the church daycare. My mom and Courtney are also here to show their support and love, despite everything, along with Nana, who considers my mom her daughter even though she's my dad's mom, and my parents have been divorced for years. That's just how my family is, especially the women. We stick together. We love no matter what. My mom is a living, breathing example of the unconditional love she taught me about, and I couldn't love her more. She's perhaps the most Jesus-like example in my life, ironically. Our relationship is strained right now, but I know it will heal.

My dad is not here. He tries to stay away from anything religious, emotional, controversial - or important. These things make him feel uncomfortable. But his absence today doesn't bother me as much as it has in the past. In this moment, I'm more hurt by the fact that James' parents - my Christian family - didn't come to celebrate with me, when my Jewish family, for whom this is *no* celebration, are here, even though they don't understand or agree with my choice to become a Christian.

My father-in-law, Glenn, has carefully explained that although he still believes in Jesus and studies the Bible faithfully, he no longer believes in the ordinances of the church, such as communion and baptism. He believes the "Church Age" is over and God is no longer using the church to reach his people. He believes that the true Christians are being called out of the church. And Sheri believes what Glenn believes. Or if she disagrees, she doesn't let on.

So, they cannot or will not attend church, even for an important ceremony in a loved one's life. I can't help but think that if William or Hannah were getting baptized, they'd overlook their principles and just be here for them. Their not being here for my big day makes me feel like maybe I'm not a loved one after all, even though they show me love in all kinds of other ways.

James and I had an angry fight with them about it a few weeks ago when our air conditioner broke, and we had to stay at their house over the fourth of July weekend until a technician could get out to fix it. Our relationship with James' parents is generally light and easy. We live around the corner and see them almost every day.

Arguing is unusual in James' family, but totally normal in mine. My whole life, I've been called *argumentative* even though I'm also a peacemaker at heart. But I just can't help myself from speaking up and standing up for what I believe is right. James is a stoic man who does not enjoy confrontation and rarely shows a lot of emotion. And I'm trying to be a good Christian wife for him - less outgoing, less impatient, less interrupting, less talkative, less dramatic...less me. Even though he's more than a foot taller than me, I feel like I have to make myself just a little smaller to fit into his world.

Glenn had been muttering about the "abomination of desolation" that was in the church for a while, but James had never asked him to expound. I'm unquestionably the more inquisitive of the two of us. We knew Glenn spent hours each day studying the Bible. But it was only when I walked into his study one night after a family dinner at their house and asked about the strange website open on his computer, that he started talking to me about it in detail. He said they were supporters of Harold Camping and Family Radio. I had never heard of either.

When I investigated it later, I learned that Camping had already twice predicted the end of the world, and then quickly changed his pronouncements when his dates came and went without event. Now he was proclaiming "the end of the church age" and calling on people to donate to his radio mission instead of their local churches. James and I both tried to reason with them, get them to see that this guy looked like a false prophet, remind them that the Bible says no one can know the hour of the Lord's coming. I pointed out that it sure looked to me as if God was still using the church - He used it to reach me.

I really love Glenn and Sheri. We work on DIY projects, cook and bake, shop, celebrate holidays and birthdays together. They're willing to help anytime we need anything. But arguing with Glenn is like trying to reason with a brick wall. After a few failed attempts to get our point across, James and I realized it wasn't worth it. If we continued the discussion, we would destroy our relationship with his parents completely. Despite our disagreements, we want them to be as involved in our future children's lives as they are with Luke's kids. So, now we avoid talking about this sore subject. I love them where they are. And I swallow my sadness.

I hear my cue and head out to the baptismal bath built into the stage at the front of the sanctuary. I chose Isaac to baptize me. He's one of the other pastors on staff and he's also a Jew who became a Christian, so I feel a special kinship with him. We carefully step into the warm water and the heavy robe floats up around me. Isaac stands in the water next to me as I boldly read the story about how this little Jewish girl became a Christian.

As he lowers my upper body and head backwards into the water, I'm thinking about water getting up my nose, my mascara smearing, losing my balance. I forget to listen to the exact words he proclaims. But when I emerge from the water, triumphant, I think, *Well, it's official. Even though I didn't need the baptism to make it so, Danielle Malka is a born again Christian. Life certainly has its twists and turns.*

CHAPTER 7

The Woman at the Well

August 18, 2005

A month later, I see those precious two lines on the pregnancy test that tell me I'm finally going to become a mother.

I've seen a lot of positive pregnancy tests lately, but none of them my own. The idea that these two lines represent my own baby growing in my belly makes me want to leap with joy. Which feels inappropriate while I'm standing with a couple of other girls in the back room at Crisis Pregnancy Center where I've started volunteering once a week on my day off from new home sales.

CPC is a Christian organization that offers free pregnancy tests and other resources to young women facing unexpected and usually unwanted pregnancies. My role is a sort of client advocate/counselor who comes alongside a woman and helps her to understand her choices regarding her pregnancy. No one hides the fact that the goal is to dissuade these women from seeking an abortion, and to share with them the good news of the gospel. The organization is decidedly pro-life, but we never bad-mouth or castigate a woman who is "abortion-minded." Rather, we lovingly show her some other options and pray that God opens her eyes and heart. We also offer support and love to women who have already had an abortion. Many of the volunteers and staff members have had abortions themselves.

I remember when I first started learning about and contemplating the big issues like abortion as a teenager. Although I was generally surrounded by people who believed in a woman's right to choose, *no one* I knew was actually "pro-abortion." I hated the terms "pro-life" versus "pro-choice," as if the two options were mutually exclusive, when I had never believed they were. My mom told me stories about girls she knew who had died following desperate back-alley abortions, and I knew even then that making something illegal was not the way to change people's minds and hearts about it. But if I had to pick a side, I would have called myself pro-choice before.

Now, a Christian, I find myself morphing, little by little, into a more conservative version of myself. I could always see both sides of an argument. I've always been someone who walked the line in every way. But I feel myself silently creeping over to the opposite side of the court from where my home team plays. I check myself frequently to be sure this is right and true. And so far, I have always decided that yes, it is. *That's a baby in there.* Still, I'm glad abortions are no longer illegal and that women who do choose them, whatever their reasons, can get them safely. I'm glad they have the freedom to make that choice. I don't see abortion in the same light as murder, as many evangelical Christians do. I believe a fetus is a living human being that God is knitting together in its mother's womb, but until it's born, that baby is wholly inseparable from its mom. They are two and one, at the same time. Although the baby is a separate life, it's part of its mom's body and cannot survive apart from her. These thoughts swirl around my head even as I'm enmeshed in a culture that doesn't see it quite the same as I do. I'm straddling two worldviews and can see them both so clearly. I wish everyone could. I'm aware that I'm weaving together a new narrative between my own background and belief system, and this new Christian understanding that I've inserted myself into, and this feels OK, beautiful even.

In any case, I've seen firsthand that teaching, loving, and serving these women with unwanted pregnancies is a much more effective way to reach them and prevent abortions than ostracizing and criminalizing them, regardless of our own beliefs. During our training, we learned techniques for talking to the troubled, possibly pregnant girls about Jesus and abstinence. It seemed a little late for abstinence, I thought. But the idea was that it's never too late to recommit to purity.

We teach them - using a paper heart as a visual - that God intended sex to be enjoyed within a marriage. Each time we have sex with a different partner and then break up, it's like ripping our heart apart, we say, as we dramatically tear the paper heart in half. It can never be put back together exactly as it was. Even if you try to tape or staple it together, there will always be an ugly scar where it was torn apart. Another visual we use is Scotch tape stuck to a piece of construction paper. You can peel the tape off the paper, but little bits - remnants of the union - remain stuck to the tape, and it will never quite stick to anything else again.

In the deep recesses of my heart, I wonder if all the relationships in my past will taint my beautiful marriage with James. Will I have trouble sticking to him?

When I met James, I was in a place where I had made choices that crossed the line from good girl to bad girl, and the possibility to be born again, forgiven, a new creature in Christ, was like a refreshing drink of water after a long drought. I had always walked the line, dabbled in the darker side. I had a spicy free-spirited streak that wanted to indulge in all of life's pleasures, but deep down I also had a very conservative side that prevented me from ever truly letting go and tumbling toward a path of destruction. So, when I was faced with the possibility of starting fresh and enjoying a happily ever after, I was ripe for it. It was as if everything in my life had led me to this. I felt cleansed and new, like that old sin could never touch me again.

During our CPC training, they shared a modern retelling of the story of Jesus meeting the Samaritan woman at the well, an excerpt from Max Lucado's book, *Six Hours one Friday*. It struck a chord within me. She was a woman who had been married five times, a Samaritan who was hated by the Jews, an outcast among outcasts, but Jesus asked her for a drink of water, spoke to her, listened to her, revealed himself to her, and accepted her as she was. She ran into town and proclaimed that she had met a man who knew everything she ever did and loved her anyway. *I* was that woman at the well.

I love sharing my testimony with the girls who come into the center. I feel like I have a unique ability to touch their lives and show them that God can love them just as they are, and that Jesus is for everyone. I use my own story to build rapport with them. I particularly love telling them that it was the very fact that James was abstaining from sex, waiting until he got married, that set him apart from the other guys I had known. The idea that their life, too, could be a testimony that could lead others to God seems to resonate. I tell them that God really can save anyone and following Him is a better way.

The irony of the situation has not escaped me. Here I am counseling young women who are pregnant and wish they weren't, when I want to have a baby more than anything. James finally agreed we could stop *preventing* a baby, but he still won't call it *trying* to get pregnant. But after more than six months of not preventing, I'm getting nervous. You spend your whole life avoiding pregnancy and then you decide you're ready and it's harder than you'd think to get pregnant when you want to.

In the back room at CPC, we're role-playing the part of our job where we run the pregnancy test. The client pees in a cup and we use a little pipette to place three drops of urine into the appropriate opening on the test kit. We've been trained to wait a full five minutes before determining the result, but usually you either see two lines immediately - which means positive, pregnancy - or you see only one line, the control line, which means it's negative, no pregnancy.

I'm playing the part of the counselor, but my partner who's playing the client didn't have to pee, so I peed in the cup for the test. As we wait the mandatory five minutes, we chat about nothing important, and I try not to stare at the test stick. Maybe it's like boiling water. "A watched pot never boils," my mom used to say.

"I've never seen one show up positive after the first two minutes or so, have you guys?" I finally ask.

"No, usually it either shows up right away or not at all," one of the girls answers flippantly.

My period is due in a few days, so I figure it's too early for there to be enough of the HCG hormone in my urine to make the test positive, even if I am pregnant. But I'm secretly hopeful.

It's been almost four minutes. I glance back at the test and imagine I see a faint second line next to the test line. I look away and then look back again. The line is not quite pink like the other one. It's so faint you almost can't see it. But I do, in fact, see something there.

"Um, can you guys come look at this, please? It's probably wishful thinking but…does that look like a second line to you?"

They peer over my shoulder, squinting their eyes.

"Hmm, I definitely see something," one of them says.

"And when it's negative, there's no line at all there, not even a faint trace, right? All the negative tests I have seen had no trace of a line," I say, getting increasingly excited.

Someone goes to get the manager, who confirms that indeed this is a positive result. I'm pregnant! *Should I call James?* No, I should tell him in person, I decide. But I want to scream from the rooftops that I'm finally pregnant! I'm going to have a baby!

Eight months later, my baby girl wakes me up in the wee hours of the morning with a contraction followed by a trickle of liquid on my inner thigh as I lie on my side in bed next to James.

We celebrated our second anniversary yesterday. Dinner, then Dairy Queen with Luke and Amanda and the kids, followed by a walk around the Riparian Preserve in Gilbert. James' family calls the preserve "Dinosaur Park" because, near the large lake with ducks, birds, and other wildlife, is a sand pit where kids can dig up plaster dinosaur bones like real archeologists. We'd already had a more romantic celebration last weekend, a sort of babymoon staycation at the hotel that overlooks the garden where we got married.

Sitting in a corner booth at Dairy Queen last night, six-year-old William placed his little hand on my belly to feel the baby's hiccups we could all see as my tight tummy bounced with each tiny spasm. We've all been anxious for Baby Girl to arrive. Even though her official due date is three weeks away, I've been told I will probably deliver early because of my special double uterus. I think it was last night's anniversary sex that has finally coerced her to make her entrance, though. Sex at eight months pregnant is hardly sexy, my tummy swollen and heavy. Of course, James doesn't mind. But for me, at this point it's more of a loving gesture, a marital duty of sorts, than something I truly enjoy. I hope that desire will come back eventually.

Another cramp constricts my belly and I feel another trickle. I get up and go to the bathroom, place a menstrual pad inside my underwear as I've read I should.

I gently nudge James awake.

"Baby, I think it's time. I think my water broke."

"Are you sure?"

"Well, no. But I think so..."

"What time is it?"

"Just after 3 AM."

He jumps out of bed and almost trips as he springs into action, gathering the pre-packed hospital suitcase, brushing his teeth, making sure I'm ready. I'm getting increasingly excited as I realize that if indeed my water has broken, they won't send me home. I'm going to have this baby today! I shower and dress in comfortable clothes: leggings and a soft long-sleeved maternity shirt.

When we get to the hospital, just a few minutes from our house, they decide to let me labor for a while before calling the doctor. Even though I have a C-section scheduled a few weeks from now, they tell me they want to see if the contractions progress and the baby can be delivered vaginally. But I suspect they just want to give the doctor a little more time to sleep. I'm only one centimeter dilated. My second cervix, the one most people don't have, is also dilated to one centimeter, even though there's no baby on that side of the uterus.

I'll never forget how cold, alone and scared I felt during my first well-woman exam, where I learned that I had a somewhat rare abnormality of my reproductive system, when before that I had thought I was a perfectly normal 19-year-old.

I walked into the campus health center, undressed as instructed, draped myself with the paper robe and sheet provided, and lay down on the exam table, only my toes reaching the cold metal stirrups. The nurse practitioner walked brusquely into the room and instructed me to scoot my butt all the way to the edge of the table and open my legs wide. She picked up a speculum from a tray and tried to stick the cold metal inside me, but after poking and prodding for a few minutes, she sighed deeply, set it back on the table, looked at me with a confused expression on her face and said, "You have…," then promptly left the room without finishing her sentence.

I lay there all alone in the cold too-bright room, wearing nothing but a paper gown.

I have what? I wondered. *Do I have a disease?* A few minutes later, she came back in with someone else in medical garb, presumably a doctor. He inserted the speculum and wriggled it around once again.

"You have a septum dividing your vaginal cavity into two halves," he explained. And within a few minutes, the two practitioners had identified two cervixes, one on each side.

That first visit prompted other medical visits and tests. It was eventually determined that I had a *bicornuate* or a *didelphys* uterus. I heard both terms thrown around, and different doctors had different opinions about which one I had. Reading the descriptions of each abnormality, it seemed mine was somewhere between the two. Essentially there's a complete division of my uterus into two separate halves, with two separate cervixes and a septum that divides the vaginal cavity into two halves. They told me the phenomenon is caused by an incomplete fusion of the uterus during fetal development. They were concerned about the kidneys, which are formed around the same time as the uterus. But an ultrasound revealed that my kidneys were fine.

I was told that I *should* be able to have a baby someday, but any pregnancies would be somewhat higher risk and I'd probably deliver early, most likely by C-section. So, I've felt anxious this entire pregnancy, worried that something bad would happen to my baby.

Around 7:30 AM two doctors come in and announce the C-section will be at 9:30. I call James, who has just left to grab breakfast with his dad. They hurry back, and Glenn awkwardly hands me a strikingly beautiful Mexican-style floral vase of roses he picked up at Albertson's across the street. My heart constricts as I set them down on the bedside table. My own dad is in San Diego. He won't be here to see his first grandchild born. He could have made arrangements to come, but he says he'll wait until we come out to visit instead. He doesn't like hospitals.

My mom is still working as a dental hygienist, but she's on her way. James' mom is also working. She's a schoolteacher at a Christian school nearby. We had instructed everyone to go about their day as usual, thinking we'd be here most of the day before we had a baby to show them. But now things are moving quickly and the whole family begins arriving, cramming into our large hospital room. It's like a little party. No one is accustomed to a scheduled birth that doesn't require hours of pushing.

Around 9:00, they wheel me out of the room to the OR, James scrubs in and they give me the spinal block. Other than being completely numb and immobile from the chest down, I'm fully awake and aware as they deftly work to produce the baby from my belly. I can feel a vague pushing sensation on my abdomen and then a strange scent that reminds me of Corn Nuts.

"What is that smell?" I ask James, fighting a wave of nausea. I glance over at the anesthesiologist, who quickly adds a bit more of the anti-nausea drug to my IV. James, who's tall enough to peek over the tent that separates my lower half from my upper half, stands up to look.

"I'll tell you later. You don't want to know."

But I insist, and he tells me I'm smelling my own flaming flesh as they cauterize the incision where that will remove my baby from the womb. After a few more minutes, I hear the beautiful newborn wail and the standard, "It's a girl!" They wrap the 6-pound dark-haired beauty in a blanket and James holds her next to my face so I can see her.

He walks back into our hospital room a few minutes later and presents our beautiful baby to our waiting family just forty-five minutes after they wheeled me out. The doctors quickly stitch me up and soon I join them back in the room.

"I waited my whole life for you," I say to my baby girl as I hold her up and gaze into her newborn-gray eyes later that afternoon. And it's true. I've always loved babies. As a kid, I would race home from school to babysit, preferring playing with babies to hanging with my friends at the mall. I loved to change their diapers and dress them, rock them and feed them. And now this one is my very own and will one day call me *Mommy*. God knit her together in my belly. Perfect and beautiful. She still doesn't have a name. We were calling her Rachel May before she was born, but as we marveled at her, still in the operating room after they lifted her from my belly, it was the classic, "she just doesn't look like a Rachel May!"

This baby naming feels like serious business. It's weighty to think that this human being will be saddled with the name we choose for her entire life.

We've started to scrawl a list of possible names on a paper towel from the hospital room sink. Each time a nurse or doctor stops in to check on me and the baby, they peek at the list, and we ask their opinion. We mark the names with check marks, asterisks. Finally, on the second day, James concedes to naming her Cadence. I love the multiple meanings of this beautiful name - the steady rhythm of feet on pedals pushing a bike up a tough climb, the iambic pentameter of a poetic verse, a sequence of notes or chords comprising the close of a musical phrase, a modulation or inflection of the voice. I'm glad James didn't let Luke's initial mocking of the name prevent him from giving it to our daughter.

I have many years of babysitting experience, but I've never cared for a newborn.

"Is that normal?" I'll ask as she burps loudly, or sleeps so soundly nothing could wake her, or the time poop shoots across the room as I'm changing her diaper. Yes, she's perfectly normal, I determine, and I love her immediately.

My breasts seem to think they should produce enough milk for a small army rather than a six-pound baby girl who falls asleep almost instantly a few minutes after beginning to nurse. These are fun, happy days. I loosely follow the nursing and feeding schedule outlined in the popular book, *Babywise*, but I try to be laid back and intuitive to the needs of my baby.

James got his real estate license and quit his job at the bike shop, and I decide to leave my new home sales job after my maternity leave to be home with the baby and help James with the real estate business. Cadence is an easy-going baby, and we tote her along to all of it. She falls asleep on the go and transfers well.

She starts talking even before walking, speaking in eloquent full sentences just like my mom tells me I did as a toddler. Despite her happy, easy nature, she's also strong-willed, which I think will be a good thing as she grows up and takes her place in the world.

The next two years pass in a blur of real estate, church, family dinners, breastfeeding, play dates, home renovations, even world travel. First, we head to Ixtapa, Mexico for Courtney's destination wedding, an almost two-year-old Cadence in tow and Baby Number Two kicking in my tummy. Then two weeks after that trip, I show

James and Cadence around the City of Love. Visiting Paris is a special adventure with a two-year-old and a big pregnant belly. James lugs Cadence's stroller up and down the steep stairs of the *Metro*. We enjoy baguettes, cheese, salami, and wine by a playground between museums.

Since Cadence is under two - for a few more weeks, anyway - she can travel on our laps for free. Seven months along, I don't have much of a lap available as my belly has taken over and my legs weren't long to begin with. But luckily, there are extra seats to spread out in. I'm so happy to return to my beloved Paris with James and Cadence, that I simply don't allow the heavy belly, constant trips to the bathroom and aching hips to ruin our fun. I love getting to use my French again. It's a bonus that French people, widely assumed to be rude and unfriendly to tourists, apparently have a sort of reverence for a pregnant woman. I'm treated like royalty, even whisked to the front of lines at museums and the Eiffel Tower. And we stay with family, my dad's cousin Yves and his wife Claudine. The trip is inexpensive and amazing. We return home on our fourth anniversary, and Cadence turns two the next day. Life is good. We're happy and healthy.

Two years and two months after Cadence's birth, my water breaks again in the middle of the night; the same tiny trickle, no big gush. James looks over at the tiny newborn as they clean her up after pulling her from the incision in my belly, then back down at me lying on the operating table and says with a smile and a twinkle in his blue eyes, "Well, looks like she got the short end of the stick. She looks like me!"

Though his joking comment implies that looking like him makes her less beautiful than looking like me, Alexandria - named after the city in Egypt where my dad was born - is a gorgeous baby. We had considered naming her Victoria - a strong and beautiful name, the female version of Victor, my Papi, my dad's dad. He's 94 now and such a character. Still going strong. Still as feisty as ever. But in Jewish tradition, you don't usually name a baby after a living relative, so we name her after that glamorous, cosmopolitan city that I've heard stories about all my life. We'll call her Alex for short.

Alex's coloring is lighter than Cadence's was at birth, and her eyes look like they actually will turn out blue, I think in wonder as I recall the Punnett squares we studied in AP Biology. I know my brown eyes are dominant, just like my personality, and James' blue eyes carry the recessive, less forceful version of the gene for eye color. But if Alex's eyes turn out blue, then that means that I have a recessive blue eye gene deep inside me too. I feel like this is a metaphor for something.

My mom brings two-year-old Cadence to the hospital, and she smiles wide as she presents her new baby sister with a brightly colored stuffed parrot she picked out at the dollar store. Alex's arms are snugly bound inside her swaddle, so Cadence holds onto the toy for safe keeping. She crawls up into bed with us and I nuzzle her hair. So dark at birth that she almost looked Mexican, it's now completely blond. But her eyes are brown, like mine. I hug my two perfect babies against me in the hospital bed and feel so full of love for these two creatures I created - or God created, I correct myself, using James and me as nothing more than vessels.

CHAPTER 8

Cracks

SPRING 2009

Cadence is three and Alex is almost one. And I've been able, miraculously, to get them both down for a nap this afternoon. James and I are each at our computers in our shared office den with the arched entryway and window to match.

I squint through the plantation shutters and see two bright green and blue lovebirds sitting on the low courtyard wall we built last year. It's not the first time I've seen them. They're like a little surprise that shows up every now and then, their striking colors against the brown desert making my heart sing. I don't know much about birds, but a friend told me our local lovebirds are a small African parrot species, escapees from the pet trade first spotted in the 1980s that have flourished here. They're beautiful and exotic. How amazing that they've survived so far from home and in such harsh conditions. That's some resilience.

Two kids is exponentially harder than one, especially when the oldest is three and both are strong-willed and sassy, like their mom. James and I are trying to work together in real estate. I show homes with him sometimes, help with listing presentations, marketing, and communications. But we have different styles and ways of doing things. There's also an awkward dynamic since I'm the more experienced one, but James is the man, and I don't want him to feel like I'm telling him what to do.

In Christianity, marital roles are much more traditional than I'm used to. I know James grew up that way. And I want to make him happy. So, I try to step into the background and quietly - or not so quietly, as the case may be - help however I can. I have a million projects of my own I'd like to start, too. I'm learning about blogging and internet marketing. And the days fly by between making and cleaning up meals, keeping the kids busy, laundry, church stuff, cleaning up messes. I'm hardly bored, but I'm not quite content either. Supporting our family 100% from a Real Estate market that is quickly falling apart is stressful for us both. Our life feels chaotic, and I wonder if I'm really cut out to be a stay-at-home mom, even though I know that's what James wants his wife to be. There's always so much to do, home and work blended into a 24/7 treadmill of activities. There's no daycare that takes kids at-will and ad-hoc, so we juggle our schedule. You can't pay for daycare when your job only pays you after the fact and once in a while, and our savings account is draining quickly. Gingerly, I bring up the idea of me getting a job, one with a regular paycheck.

"Yes, we'd have to put the girls in daycare, but people do that all the time. I could make good money that could really help us instead of feeling like an inadequate housewife all the time," I plead. "I have a college degree. I'm capable of more than this."

As soon as the words are out of my mouth, I realize they weren't quite what I meant. Being a mom is the best, most important job I've ever had.

"Are you saying that *just* being a wife and mom isn't enough for you," James asks sadly, an angry glint in his eye. It's the closest thing to a fight we've ever had.

"Of course that's not what I'm saying," I say earnestly.

"OK, let's see what kind of job you can get," he finally relents. I quickly land a few interviews, but I let the opportunities fizzle out as I feel his quiet disapproval.

Trying to come up with a way to make money without putting the kids in daycare, I dream up a plan to open my own home daycare business. I've always loved kids and have experience as a babysitter, a camp counselor, even a substitute teacher. I talk to a few friends and recruit a small group of children for a trial run of *La Maternelle*. I'm proud of this creative name I've come up with, the French word for nursery school, which also means maternal, or motherly. I'm just one mother helping other mother friends who go to work. The idea is ambitious and creative, and even James likes it. But I only last two weeks. Being stuck at home all day taking care of other people's children is harder than I thought it would be, even though I love my friends' kids and they play well with mine. I'm just someone who needs to be able to get up and go.

As it turns out, the following week, I have to get up and go to the hospital. Papi was up on a ladder pruning his prized fig tree, lost his balance and fell. He hit his head and he's in the ICU. There's a surgery they could do, but at his age, the prognosis isn't good. My dad calls a family meeting, including Nana, Courtney, Mom, and me. My parents have been divorced for years now, but they're still close friends. More than friends even. Married or not, they're family, and always will be.

Papi has never been a fan of doctors, drugs, or hospitals, but he tells my dad to do what he thinks is best. Even the surgeon is hesitant because of his age. He warns us that he may not be strong enough to survive the surgery, but without it, he will rapidly decline. We go forward with the operation, but he doesn't wake up after. They move him to an inpatient hospice facility, where we can all visit as much as we want. He holds on for a few days, strong and stubborn still. He never regains consciousness, but I talk to him as I sit beside his bed late the next day. He's lived a long and fruitful life. Ninety-five years old and still had all his wits about him, right up until he took this blow to the head. It's sad to see him lying here, dying.

I can't stop thinking of Kendyll, Courtney's friend who died a few months ago of a rare form of cervical cancer at 29 years old. I spent some time with her during our trip to Ixtapa, Mexico last year for Courtney's destination wedding, when I was seven months pregnant with Alex. Kendyll and I had the same time slot for pedicures the morning of the ceremony. She told me she and her husband were just starting to plan for kids. She was a teacher, a wonderful, joyful girl. I remember her complaining about her stomach hurting, a persistent gassiness and bloating that she'd had for a while. But still she danced and laughed with us all week long.

On her way back home to Chicago, she started bleeding, and her diagnosis came soon after that. She started a blog to share her thoughts and her story with her friends. Kendyll's sense of humor and sweet spirit came through in every post. Her friends here in Arizona rallied around her, hosting a car wash to help raise money to pay the mounting medical bills.

Courtney, a lawyer, and one of the smartest people I know, and Jack, her husband who owns a turquoise business along with his brother and best friend, created turquoise necklaces they called *Believe Beads*. People who didn't even know them or Kendyll bought the necklaces in support of this sweet girl.

James quietly rolled his eyes at the name *Believe Beads*. As if he found it vexing that we thought all we had to do was just believe and Kendyll would win this battle against cancer. I've started to notice a dry cynicism about him, and I sometimes think he's more concerned with what's *biblical* than what he truly believes. Meanwhile, the word *Believe* has become my personal mantra since *the license plate*. I do still believe that God put that license plate in my path to speak to me, to tell me that it was OK to believe in Jesus. I do believe in Jesus. And I also believe in miracles. And love. And family. And even myself. It bothers me that James, his family, and the church, subtly tamp down these deep beliefs that I was taught since childhood. *Only Jesus.*

"You can do anything you set your mind to do," my mom always said.

And I can hear a small voice in my heart start to speak up and say, "Yes, you can! It's not wrong to believe in yourself." Jesus himself said, "love your neighbor as yourself," implying that we are first to love ourselves.

Kendyll lost her fight against cancer less than a year after her diagnosis, despite all our believing. And that's sad. She had so much life ahead of her. Courtney told me that once, as she lay dying, Kendyll asked her husband, "Where will I go when I die?"

"You'll be right here," he said, gesturing to his head, "and here," holding his heart.

I swallowed a lump in my throat as I heard the story, feeling like I was an awful Christian for not sharing the gospel with her as she was facing death. While it was true that beautiful Kendyll would indeed live on in all our hearts and heads, it made me sad that that was their *only* answer, and it really hit home that if I truly believed what Christianity said, then where she was headed didn't look good. I was forced to acknowledge my beliefs as more than just theoretical. This was a kind and gracious young lady. But she did not know Jesus, as far as I knew. Would God send her to Hell? I pushed the thoughts away, unable to deal with them in that moment.

And now, sitting here at Papi's death bed, I begin to sing in Hebrew. I pray generically that God will keep him safe, free from pain. But I can't bring myself to quote scripture or beg him to accept Jesus Christ as his personal savior before it's too late. Does that make me a bad Christian?

"What do you see, Papi? *Qu'est-ce que tu vois,*" I ask him instead. "Can you see God? Is there a guy named Jesus there? Do you see all your loved ones who have died before you?"

Maybe Papi can even offer *me* some assurance. But there's no response. I don't know what he sees, hears, feels - or believes. And anyway, faith is believing without seeing. And mine is wavering.

After Papi dies, I try not to think too much about where he's gone. I choose to trust that my God will have mercy on all the people I love. I believe He has the power to either give them faith, showing them the truth at the very last moment, or whatever it is that He needs to do to take them to the good place. I can't believe He would shun His own people. I just can't.

I learn a few days later that Glenn and Sheri also went to visit Papi. Courtney's in-laws were there when they stopped by, and they told her they were appalled by the way Glenn and Sheri had brashly urged Papi to repent and believe "before it's too late." No one tells me exactly what they said or how it went down. But regardless of their intent, which I heartily believe was an intense Godly desire and burden to boldly share the gospel with a dying man they cared about, the way it was done only drives a rift between my in-laws and my family. And I feel more and more in the middle. Like a small boat rocking in the sea with nowhere to moor.

All these tiny cracks in my belief, in the strong foundation of our marriage even, but I ignore them, along with the rising sadness in my heart. I haven't learned yet that negative emotions and doubt are healthy and necessary, and that it's the very cracks that let the light in. So, I try to fill them instead. And though the cracks in our house seem rather small on a sunny day, we see their significance when the storm comes.

CHAPTER 9

The Fall

May 2009

After Papi's death, my focus returns to our finances. My friend Stephanie emails me about a new network marketing gig she's involved with - The Trump Network. The company has developed a way to test your personal biome to create a customized vitamin pack formulated just for you. Donald Trump has very little to do with it, but he's purchased the company and stamped his name onto it like he does his buildings and everything else he's a part of. He's convinced that network marketing is the financial vehicle for the masses, and that healthcare is the best sector to play in.

I love Stephanie. She was my partner at one of the new home communities I worked in, and I think it will be fun to work with her again, so I jump in and try it. There's a lot of rah-rah enthusiasm over how much money we're going to make and how many people we are going to help with this company. But despite the allure of residual income, I hate multi-level marketing.

After a few months of business overviews, product demonstrations, cold calls, and networking, I start looking at job postings on Craigslist. In late August, I see an ad for a job selling vacation ownership, which I know is just a fancy way to say timeshare, but I realize I know the guy who posted it and decide to apply. Sean and I worked together selling new homes in Surprise back when Ian and I were married. In fact, Sean and his wife were there the day Ian dramatically left both me and his wedding ring in Rocky Point, Mexico in the middle of a Memorial Day weekend trip a group of us took together in 2002. I can see the scene so clearly.

The group of us had been lounging on the beach in front of our rented condo, but Ian was sulky all morning after a fight we'd had the night before. We were all starting to talk about going into town for lunch soon, so he went inside to shower. He couldn't stand the sand and salt on his skin after being at the beach. Later, stomachs growling, the rest of us headed up to the condo to get changed and drive to the marina for lunch. As we meandered up the walk through the grassy pool area, I started as I heard Ian shout from our balcony.

"Danielle, I broke my fucking nose!"

"What?" I asked, straining to hear him above the sounds of people enjoying their vacation, but noting the alarm in his voice.

"I walked into the sliding glass door, and I broke my fucking nose!" he yelled.

Behind me, my coworkers Connor and Sean broke into cackling laughter. I suppose it was comically ironic that the one guy among us who didn't drink should walk into the door. And he had been acting so pissy. But I didn't find it funny. I dropped the chairs, towels, and bags I was lugging and raced up the stairs, on alert at an emergency and genuinely concerned about my husband. When I got inside, he told me what happened in an accusatory tone, as if his walking into a sliding glass door was my fault.

"Let me look at it," I said, reaching toward his nose.

He removed the blood-stained tissue, and I tried not to gag.

"Ouch. I'm sure that hurts," I said. "Well let's get you to the hospital. I know there's not much they can do for a broken nose, but at least they can assess and bandage you up."

"There is No. Fucking. Way. I am going to a Mexican hospital," he hissed.

"Why not? I lived in Mexico for three months. I had to go to the hospital once. They have perfectly capable doctors here. And it's not like you need open-heart surgery. It's a broken nose. They can bandage you up, give you some pain meds, and you can enjoy the rest of the trip."

"Are you crazy? You think I'm just going to *stay* down here with a broken nose?"

"What do you mean? What else would you do? Things happen," I said, thinking of the time I stepped on a stingray on the first day of a spring break trip to Mazatlán in college. That stinger slicing through my foot and the searing poison shooting up my leg was the worst pain I'd ever felt. I screamed and writhed on the beach like a woman giving birth. But my friend got some fresh aloe from a nearby plant, someone else fetched the hotel doctor, and I ended up having a great vacation with my friends.

I resisted the urge to add, "Suck it up, you big baby!"

"I want to go back to the United States immediately," he said.

"Honey, we can't. We didn't even drive ourselves down here. We're with our friends. We're going home tomorrow. Can't you just have a few shots of tequila, enjoy the extra attention, and make the most of it?"

"I'll take a bus home!"

"Now who's crazy? You won't let a Mexican doctor bandage you up, but you'll ride a Mexican bus from Rocky Point to Phoenix! If you really want to do that, then I'll go with you, but come on, you're being silly. Maybe you'll feel better after a little lunch."

"You know what, just leave me alone. You go to lunch. I'll stay here alone and rest."

"OK, if that's what you want. Do you want me to bring you back some lunch?"

"I'm not hungry!"

"Well, you probably will be later. I'll bring you something for later," I said, kissing his forehead then heading toward the door.

When we got back, the curtains in our room were drawn, the sheets thrown back, the bed empty. I walked over to the nightstand to turn on the lamp. There on the stand was a half sheet of notebook paper, stained at the top with a few drops of red blood. I picked it up and heard a small clang of metal hitting the tiled floor. I bent down to find Ian's titanium wedding band, the very one I had helped him pick out just eight months earlier.

"You can hold on to this. I won't be needing it," the note said. "I'm taking the bus home. You can try calling me when you get back in town. I'm not sure where I'll be staying."

Are you kidding me? Who does this?

His words stung me. I told him I'd go with him. We had been bickering all weekend, but I couldn't believe he wanted to end our marriage over that. He wouldn't be needing his wedding ring anymore? Tears streaming down my face, I brought the note out to show the others. Sean's wife grabbed it and gasped as she read it, her hand flying up to her mouth.

"Wow. The drama. A blood-stained note?"

"Maybe it will blow over," someone said.

But for me it was already over. You just didn't do something like that, take off your wedding ring and leave your wife in Mexico. Even if she *was* a flirtatious drunk. Even if you *did* feel hurt and left out. Even if you did walk into a sliding glass door and break your nose. You talk to her, listen to her. You tell her that you love her. That's what I wished he had done.

Everything we did after that day was just going through the motions for me. Even when he lay in our bed at home a few weeks later, drugged out on Percocet after his nose surgery, pleading, "Don't leave me. Don't divorce me," I had already moved on in my mind. *You left me when you took off your wedding ring,* I thought, shaking my head.

During and after the divorce process, I dated like crazy, to keep myself busy and to keep from feeling lonely and mistakenly getting back with Ian for comfort. I had a fling with my coworker Connor, who was also going through a divorce. I thought I was in love with him, and when he rejected me, I frantically latched on to someone else, then another, then another. I was lonely and empty, even though from the outside it looked like I was having the time of my life, and at times I was. But dating and sex was like a drug that never quite satisfied.

That's where I was, who I was, when James came along. Addicted to a high I could only get from guys. *I'm so glad to be past that now.* I naively believe that I'm not only *saved* but also *safe* from the demons of my past.

In any case, Sean knows I can sell. There was always a friendly sales competition back in the new home sales days, and sometimes I even beat him. He hires me for the timeshare job, and I start the next week, right after my 35th birthday.

James seems OK with me working. The job has these crazy hours that will allow us to get by without daycare. I'll work three evenings a week, plus all day Saturday and a half day Sunday. I'll be with the girls every morning while James works from his home office, then a few days a week I'll head off to work after I put them down for their afternoon nap. James can work some more while they sleep, then feed them the dinner I've prepared, or maybe have dinner with his parents as we often do, hang out with the girls for the evening, then put them to bed. Our parents are willing to help when he has evening and weekend appointments. I think it should work brilliantly. A perfect solution.

On the first day of work, our group of new sales agents sits in the small auditorium where they show the guests fancy footage of the timeshare resorts and all the places they can go. They're making us watch this cheesy corporate sexual harassment video. It makes me chuckle. I'm a 35-year-old Christian housewife with two little kids. Sexual harassment, workplace dating, these concepts are the furthest thing from my mind.

After a week of sales training, I start taking my own tours: 90-minute meetings where I sit at a small table building rapport with an adult couple, talking about travel and family and fun. Perusing the pictures I've compiled of me and my family on vacation, we laugh and joke, talk about the vacations *they* have enjoyed. I get to make them dream. I'm good at this. People trust me because I'm real and honest. I find things we have in common and connect with them. And they buy from me. This feels good. I'm having fun.

Though I think most people see timeshare salespeople as one step above - or even below - used car salesmen, I'm not that kind of salesperson. I learned long ago that you don't need to be a wheeler dealer to be good at sales. You just need to connect with people. And I love doing that more than anything. I'm enjoying this job more than any of the dozens of jobs I've held in my 35 years. And I'm good at it. With two small kids at home, Cadence three and Alex just a little more than a year old, it's the first time in years that I have extended amounts of me time.

Working in timeshare reminds me of the summer I spent as an OPC in Cabo with my college roommate Sophia. OPCs are the people who fill timeshare presentations with potential buyers by offering them a free breakfast and all kinds of other gifts for attending. I was good at it because I connected with the tourists rather than using the sneaky tactics most of the OPCs used. At our first weekly sales meeting, they dubbed me *La Revelación de la Semana* - the revelation of the week. Whether in Spanish or English, I loved getting those accolades.

And now, 13 years later, I still love being appreciated. Feeling successful gives me a thrill, an emotional high. I feel myself exuding energy and life. It's exhilarating to be using my mind and talents for more than reading stories, entertaining toddlers, and cleaning the house. At work I feel free, like me again, not just a wife and mother. And I think I'm a better mom because I have this time away to just be me. I enjoy the kids even more when I'm with them. I've even been able to finally shed the last ten pounds that I'd like to blame on pregnancy but that have been hanging around for most of my adult life.

But I can feel James' resentment growing. His real estate business is finally picking up and he grumbles about having to put the girls to bed without me several nights a week and then sit home alone until I get home after work. What I wouldn't do for a few evenings alone at home – to read, write, get stuff done. I don't understand why he can't make the most of that precious time instead of begrudging me for it.

My mom calls one day while I'm at work, tells me they had seen "something unusual" on her mammogram last week and did a biopsy a few days later. Today she got the results of the biopsy. It's not benign. She has breast cancer.

Courtney, newly pregnant with her first baby, and I meet Mom at Zipp's for an iced tea the next afternoon before work. We review the diagnosis and treatment options. While Courtney busies herself with the practical details of which doctors to call and in what order, I encourage Mom to dream about a trip to Italy once she's cancer-free. It's my way of dealing with it. It's the best thing I can bring to the table: get her looking forward to silver linings.

They schedule her surgery within a month. Since they caught Mom's cancer so early, she needs neither chemo nor radiation, just surgery, so we all feel like this is far from a tragedy. But still, it is cancer, and it is scary. I think maybe I should get a mammogram sometime soon. I wonder if I'll be considered higher risk because my mom got it. Our pastor's wife has been bravely battling the disease for a while and I know how bad it can be.

James feels distant, detached from the whole situation. Which I find strange since his brother survived cancer a few years before we met. Maybe he's just playing off my lightheartedness, but he doesn't seem to see it as any big deal. He doesn't ask me how I feel about it or hold me close. It makes me feel like he has little interest in my life and what matters most to me. But I swallow these feelings. It's a busy time and I pour myself into my work. I praise God for sparing my mom from what could have been. If you're going to get cancer, this version seems like the best possible scenario.

James' real estate business is booming, and he callously announces one day, "You can quit your job now."

"But I love my job!" I plead. "I don't want to quit. Plus, you know real estate is cyclical and unpredictable. My income will give us a consistent base to carry us through the lean months, which you know will come again."

"You're not making very much money anyway," he says. "And I hate being home alone at night while you're at work."

I don't want to make him unhappy. I want to be a good wife, but a bitter seed is sprouting within each of us, causing tiny cracks in our perfect marriage. He's feeling resentful and jealous of my love for a silly job, and I'm upset and hurt that he can't see how important this is to me, how I'm thriving. I feel far away from him, sad. He reluctantly agrees to give it another month and see how things are going then.

CHAPTER 10

The Winter

OCTOBER 2009

The first time I notice Brock at work, he's standing at the back of the large room where we meet at small round tables with our guests. They often have those of us who don't have a tour stay in the room to keep the energy and enthusiasm high. It helps with sales.

Brock has just returned to work after a few weeks off because his wife had a baby. He's training to be a manager. I can tell he's younger than me, and he emits a cool, aloof vibe that reminds me of the popular kids at school. He smiles at me from across the room and I feel a flash of a singular high I've felt before. I pray a quick prayer of thanksgiving that God has forgiven me and that I'm free from that sinful addiction. But in the next breath I decide to go talk to Brock, learn more about him. *Harmless.* He goes out to smoke, and when he returns a few minutes later, I casually walk over.

"You're way too good-looking to be a smoker," I say quietly, almost under my breath. It's probably not a very appropriate thing for a married Christian mom to say to a man whose wife has just had a baby, I think. But it feels nice when he reacts.

"Well, we all have our vices," he says with a white-toothed grin and a wink. I look him in the eye, smile and shake my head slowly, as if to say, "you'll never know mine." He's tall and lean, with a chiseled jaw, gray-blue eyes, and lips that make me think about kissing. He reminds me of someone famous, but I can't think of who. I want to keep talking to him, though.

"Has anyone ever told you, you look like a younger version of that actor, what's his name?"

"Um that actor…you got to give me a little more than that. What movie?"

"Oh man, I'm so bad at remembering actors' names. I can't believe I can't think of it! I can picture him, but I can't think of his name, or the movie. Anyway, you're like a way younger version. You could be his son. How old are you anyway?"

"27."

"You're a baby," I say, feeling very old.

But I can't stop thinking about him. On my days off, when I'm doing housework, cooking dinner, at the park with the kids, my mind conjures images of his face and I feel just a little buzzed, like I've had a few glasses of wine. I know I should stop this fantasizing and think instead of *what is lovely, what is pure*, like the Bible instructs. But my mind keeps wandering back to him, and the buzz blurs the edges of my depression, anxiety, worry and boredom.

I look for him on Facebook and see that he shares an account with his wife. They don't post a lot. There are only a few pictures of him. One from a vacation a few years back where he's wearing a t-shirt and shades. The picture shows the long, lean muscles in his arms that I can't see in the shirts and ties he wears to work. A few photos of their new baby. She's very cute. I wonder, inappropriately, if I should offer them some of the baby clothes Alex has outgrown. She has so much cute stuff, a lot of it hand-me-downs from Cadence, Hannah, and friends. But some new stuff too, gifts from her baby shower, many outfits only worn a few times because the seasons didn't fall right, or she grew too fast.

The next week, Brock and I are sitting across from one another at one of the tables, waiting for our next tour. I tell him I just can't believe he's so much younger than me and I don't feel 35. He says I don't look 35 either. Our conversation moves to our spouses.

"How did you two meet?" I ask him.

"We worked at a bar together. I was quite the player until I met her. She tamed me."

"Hmm. Guess you could say that about my husband and me, too. He was innocent until he met me."

"Oh really? What do you mean by that?"

"Well, he was a Christian and saving sex for marriage, and I… wasn't."

"Wow, you corrupted him!"

"Well, not exactly. I waited until we were married! Anyway, it's kind of a long story."

"I think we have time," he says, looking at the clock, which shows we still have an hour before the next tour. So, I tell him the story about how God used James to change my heart. But sharing my testimony, the details of my heart, with Brock isn't the same as sharing it with the girls at CPC. Instead of pointing him toward God, I feel my heart pulling me away.

"Pierce Brosnan, that's who you remind me of!" I blurt out. "But again, a way younger version."

Scrutinizing him through squinted eyes, I add, "Maybe more of a cross between him and Josh Hartnett."

Either way, he's hot.

Another night, Brock's foot nudges mine, then his knee brushes mine, and each time he touches me, I feel electricity course through my body. I don't remember ever feeling such an extreme chemistry. Why am I feeling it now when I'm happily married? *What's wrong with me?* This energy, wrong though it may be, makes me feel alive. Having kids and breastfeeding wreaks havoc on a girl's hormones, so I had resigned myself to the fact that my libido would probably always be sluggish. *Guess not!* But I doubt he feels anything, and I'm a wife and mom, a Christian, for heaven's sake! I need to stop it with these thoughts.

Later that night, I'm in the staff kitchen grabbing a protein bar from my lunch box in the fridge and he walks in and smiles. He makes a joke about playing footsie under the table and looks at me in a way that tells me he does feel it too. *Crap.*

A few days later I catch him appraising me from the back of the room. I get up and walk over to him and he leans in and says, "So there are two things about you that are utterly fascinating to me."

"What are they," I can't help but ask.

"Number one, you're an older woman, and number two, you're short."

"Are you kidding?" I laugh. "Of all my features and benefits, *that's* what fascinates you! To me those would be two huge negatives."

I fascinate him, I think, buzzing inside.

It doesn't make sense. I have this handsome, sweet husband at home, who's still very much attracted to me and always wants to have sex. He's a great dad, a caring husband, a hard worker. But talking to Brock, fantasizing about him is like taking a drug, and the high I get from it is more addicting than alcohol, nicotine, or any other drug I've tried. And I've tried a few. But never been addicted. I didn't think I had an "addictive personality."

This isn't the kind of attack I had been on guard for when I learned that I should *put on the full armor of God* so that I could *stand against the devil's schemes.* I hadn't expected to be vulnerable to this kind of thing. Still. After all these years in this perfect Christian bubble with my Bible studies, small groups and play dates. But the enemy preys on our weaknesses. In my case, my yearning for attention, adoration, acceptance from guys. Even though I'm still getting that at home, suddenly it isn't enough to quench my thirst.

I *know* I should run away from the flames, but instead I reach out and touch the fire with my fingertip, until soon it becomes numb, and this whole thing no longer feels wrong. It goes on like this for a few weeks, until I'm thinking about him all the time, unable to sleep, losing the healthy appetite I've always had. Soon we start giving voice to the feelings we're both having.

"You're the first thing I think about when I wake up and the last thing I think about when I go to sleep," he says to me one day. Another time, "I can't get you out of my head."

We both have families at home. We try to resist the attraction. I tell one of the girls at work how I'm feeling. She's older and not a Christian.

"It's fun to have someone to dress for at work, someone to make it more exciting. Just be sure you never come to work horny, or you may end up in a closet somewhere," she jokes, knowingly. *No way that would ever happen*, I think, embarrassed. But Brock and I agree we should probably never be alone together.

"I'm just a man!" he says to me one day, warningly. And this idea, that he would not be able to resist me, excites me.

"I'm not even all that..." I say, goading him.

"Oh yes, you are. You're like the perfect little package..."

I can't get enough of his compliments and don't mind one bit that they're aimed at my physical attributes alone. I want him.

It's December 2, 2009, the first Wednesday of the month, and my friend Cassidy has asked if I want to go to Continuum, a monthly women's ministry event at church. I accept her invitation, thinking it's just what I need. Maybe I'll have a chance to talk to her about my struggle.

Cassidy was my student ministry co-leader last year when James and I volunteered with the team that helps lead the church's high school youth group. James led a small group of boys with a male co-leader, and together Cassidy and I helped a group of teenage girls wade their way through adolescence, working out their faith in this crazy life. I quit student ministry soon after Alex was born. It was just too much to try to waddle through my own life with two small kids, a business, and a home. I didn't have the time, mental capacity, or emotional space to pour myself into the girls also. I've had to learn that there's a season for everything, and I figured I'd find a way to serve again when the kids were a little older.

The women's events at church are always a beautiful experience, engaging all the senses with pretty table decorations, delicious snacks and coffee, beautiful worship music and great teaching and conversations. I walk in a little late, after getting Cadence and Alex checked into their classrooms. Another great thing at church is the childcare. The women here truly love our kids. You can feel it. And it gives us moms a break, a chance to talk to other adults, learn about and worship God, have some mommy time. I choose a table at the back and save a spot for Cassidy. I recognize several of the other women at the table but don't know them well. I haven't been coming to Continuum regularly this year. Last year, I was a table leader, but I feel a little out of the loop now that I'm working full time. I'll work this afternoon at 2:00. I love that my schedule allows me to still do things like this, play dates with friends, work out at the gym, and mornings at home with the kids.

The subject this morning is *Faith*. A couple of the women's ministry leaders teach from up on the stage, sharing stories of their faith, lessons learned. Their words are insightful and inspiring, as always, and I feel tears spring to my eyes as I consider my own faith. I feel a pang in my heart as I realize that all this thinking about Brock has started to break my faith in Jesus. I had always imagined I could take whatever adversity God - or Satan - would give me, and that it would make me an even stronger Christian, a light to others, an example of faith. I never imagined it would be something within me, my own sin, that would plant the seeds of disbelief and make me doubt everything I had come to believe. But that's exactly what is happening. Because how could I be a "new creature in Christ" and have such thoughts?

One of the ladies who's teaching makes a vague reference to her own life that gives me the sense she has a deep, dark secret in her own marriage. She says something about how God's timing is often different from our own, that things can take a long time to resolve, "like 20 years long, in my case," she says. I file that tidbit away.

It's such an open, honest sharing and teaching that during the designated table talk time, I decide to share my own current struggle with the girls at my table. I tell them about the guy at work who has been consuming my thoughts, the battle that is right now raging within me: part of me loving the attention and excitement, and stoking the fire every chance I get, and part of me thinking I need to run far away from him, even if it means quitting the job I love so much. I tell them that these feelings, this sin in my heart, instead of making me stronger, helping me stand up for what I believe, has wedged doubt in my heart and made me wonder if believing in Jesus and trying to be a good Christian was just a big mistake. Maybe I've been trying to be something I'm not; this perfect, moral person, quiet and meek, submitting to my husband. Because just when I have a chance to prove that's who I am, I'm failing big time.

I remember James' parents telling me about a family friend named Lola Minton, whose name in James' family was basically synonymous with adulterer. She had been his mom Sheri's best friend, but then she had an affair, which, in their opinion, obliterated her life and her family, and proved categorically that she had never really been a believer in the first place. If she was, she would not have done that, they said. *Maybe I'm not a true believer either.*

The girls at the table listen to me, and I can feel their compassion, understanding and love. They remind me that just because I've been stuck in a sinful place for a while does not necessarily mean I'm not a believer. And the fact that I'm confessing it to them is a good sign that God is working within me. They encourage me to tell James what I'm thinking and feeling. And to quit the job if possible. I know they're right. But I don't want to quit.

At the end of the meeting, one of the girls at my table, whom I've never seen before today, hands me a hot pink index card with her name and number handwritten on it, along with a Bible verse, Galatians, 6:7-9: *Do not be deceived: God cannot be mocked. A man reaps what he sows. Whoever sows to please their flesh, from the flesh will reap destruction; whoever sows to please the Spirit, from the Spirit will reap eternal life. Let us not become weary in doing good, for at the proper time we will reap a harvest if we do not give up.*

I tuck the index card into my leather-bound Bible, the one Amanda had personalized with my name and tenderly presented to me when I became a Christian.

At home I tell James I've been having thoughts about someone at work. He innocently tells me it's OK to have bad thoughts if they remain just thoughts. He doesn't take my confession too seriously. After all, he's someone who could think about something for years without ever acting on it. But I know better. Thoughts create actions, especially in someone like me, with my go-getter, can-do-it attitude that can't help itself from going after every goal it thinks up. Thoughts are powerful. I think of that quote from Ralph Waldo Emerson:

"Sow a thought and you reap an action; sow an act and you reap a habit; sow a habit and you reap a character; sow a character and you reap a destiny."

And I feel like it's already too late. I'm on a slippery slope and I don't really want to get off because it feels like the most perfect, powdery ski slope, and I'm just gracefully carving my way down. I sense that I'm coming up to a huge cliff and I'm building up too much speed. I don't know exactly where the cliff is, and if I don't stop in time, I know I'll go flying off it to my death. And the logical thing to do is to avoid death, but I also love the thrill of flying. I already know I'm not going to stop at the top of that cliff. In fact, I'm building up as much speed and power as I can, and I'm going to bend my knees... and jump.

"I would never cheat on my wife," Brock says to me one evening at work. I've joined him outside for a smoke break, despite the fact I don't smoke. Even his smoking isn't a turn off for me.

"Of course not. Me neither," I say quickly. *Does anyone ever imagine they would be capable of doing such a thing until it happens?*

Another night, feeling bold and flirting with danger, I ask him if he thinks kissing would be considered cheating.

"I'm not sure," he says.

Who am I kidding? If there was a line to cross, I'm already so far past it, I can't even see it anymore. Jesus said, "anyone who looks at a woman with lustful intent has already committed adultery with her in his heart." I've already cheated in my mind. I can see no good reason not to bring my fantasies to fruition.

The cliff comes just a week later. After some drinks together with several coworkers after work, Brock walks me to my car.

I haven't had so much to drink that I feel like I shouldn't drive. But still, defenses lowered, boundaries slurred, inhibitions removed by a few lemontinis, Brock gently reaches out to grab my hand as we walk through the parking garage. That electric shock again from his touch. We walk hand in hand like that, pretending for just a moment that we are together.

When we get to my minivan, the one I told myself I would never own, I awkwardly reach down into my purse to find my keys and he grasps my chin and draws it up to face him, then kisses me hungrily and pulls my body up against his as we tentatively touch each other like we've wanted to for months. It's almost impossible to pull away, but I do. It's late and I remember suddenly that I have to get home, and we're standing in a parking garage. And it's that time of the month. As I drive away, I know it would have gone all the way if I hadn't stopped it. There's just so much pent-up passion between us. I'm sure this episode is *to be continued*.

I crawl into bed, still feeling buzzed, numb from the whole thing. But I awake at five the next morning, unable to fall back asleep. I lie there in bed for a few minutes as reality sets in. *Really?* I ask myself, as I finally see the whole situation and my part in it, clearly, for the ugly thing that it is. I'm married. I have committed to love my husband for the rest of my life. And here I am running around crushing over some random cutie who barely even knows me. And if that weren't bad enough, last night I crossed the line from virtual to physical. *I kissed another man. I touched him. I made out with him.* I may not have had sex with him yet, but that has become a legitimate and immediate possibility. *Is that really what you want to do?*

No! screams a tiny voice from deep inside me. And for the first time, I really pray that God would take it away, that He would make me feel for my husband the desire and excitement that I've felt for this other man all these months. And miraculously, immediately, He does, almost like he's saying, "Girl, all you had to do was ask."

James and I make love and I feel a restored belief in God's power in my life that lasts throughout the day. I call Brock on the way to work to tell him it's over. I can't do this. He agrees so quickly and easily that it stings my heart just a little. But that's for the best, I think.

At work, I look at him from across the room and realize he's not even that hot really, just a boy, not worth my marriage. I was seriously going to throw away everything for a roll in the hay? What was I thinking? Why didn't I realize how ludicrous that was? It's OK, I tell myself. At least I realized it now, before it went further. *God, please forgive me.*

It's already done. All you had to do was ask. Ask and you shall receive, He whispers to my heart. And I feel better, lighter. I drive home from work buzzing with a different excitement, amazement at God's power to simply take away such a strong attachment. *I should tell James. How amazing God is*, I think.

It's almost midnight when I get home from work and creep into our room. He's asleep in our bed. I wake him up, breathless, saying, "I have something amazing to tell you."

I tell him about the flirting and fantasizing with Brock over the past few months, culminating with last night's tryst in the parking lot and my realization that it was wrong and asking God to take it away. But I realize he's no longer listening. He's not hearing the good part, the part about God's power and grace to turn it all off in a moment. The part about stopping before it was too late. And I've never seen such a look of pain and anger on his face.

"Fuck, Danielle!" he says, slamming his fist into the tile floor of our bathroom, where we've somehow ended up crouched together.

"You *kissed* another man!" And then softer, sadder, "I thought I would be your last first kiss."

And in that moment, my own heart breaks, too. I've broken two hearts at once. It's like our marriage was a ceramic piggy bank filled with our love. And I've smashed it to the ground. There it lies on our bathroom floor, in a million pieces, all the love spilled out, still there but scattered, unattainable.

You stupid, stupid girl, I say to myself the next day. *Telling him, right there, right then, when he was half asleep in bed and you hadn't even processed it all yourself. That was the second stupidest thing you've ever done. Right behind flirting with, fantasizing about and then making out with Brock in the first place.*

I wish I could go back and undo the whole thing. But if I couldn't do that, I wish I could go back and choose *not* to tell James, to instead just turn around and walk away, quit the job, and forget anything ever happened. I wish I would have thought through the hurt this would cause him. In all those months of struggling with my thoughts about Brock, I spent so little time thinking about James. How could I have forgotten him like that? I feel unbelievably guilty and shameful, not only about what I did, but about what I was on the way to doing. How could I have had so little love for my husband to even go down that path? The truth is I barely considered him. I was selfishly consumed by what I wanted. Even now, I want him to put his arms around me and tell me it will be alright. That he loves me and forgives me and he's so glad I'm his. But he doesn't.

James has asked me to stay home this weekend and we've been talking and fighting. I can feel a huge rift rising between us. There's a company Christmas party on Monday, since Monday is like Saturday for us, a day off. They're doing a casino night. James has agreed to go because I told him *The Guy* won't be there. Brock told me he won't. Thankfully James didn't ask me what the guy's name was.

When we get to the party, I see that Brock has decided to come after all. He keeps his distance, acts like he barely knows me, and I choose not to tell James that he is in fact here. He might as well not be.

A group of us - not including Brock - goes to karaoke afterward, and James looks at me sardonically as I sing, "These Boots are Made for Walking." It's always been just a fun song before, but now it feels prophetic.

We have a two-week break from work for the holidays, which is both relaxing and excruciating. James and I are fighting, trying to work through this. He's a sensitive guy, but at the same time insensitive to my feelings. Maybe it's not fair for me to even think about my own feelings. I try to feel his pain instead, put myself in his shoes. But I want so badly for him to see the positive side: that I stopped what could have been a full-on affair and came back to him. He's treating me as if I actually had an affair. Which makes me feel like maybe I should go back and finish what I started. I know it's messed up and childish to be thinking that. But I feel so alone.

Instead of assuring me that he loves me and that we can conquer this together, that he'll stand by me, that he's thankful I stopped it when I did, he lashes words at me. And who could blame him. He maintained his purity until the day we were married. I didn't. And he married me anyway because he thought I had been cleansed by Jesus. I wasn't supposed to go back to my old sin patterns. I wasn't supposed to betray him *after* I was saved. That wasn't in the plan. That wasn't in the gospel.

CHAPTER 11

The Scarlet Letter

FEBRUARY 2010

Two months later, it's my last day at work. I've finally decided to leave the job and focus on my marriage. James and I have been working through a Bible study on marriage with Marcus and Kayla, some friends from church. He's the worship pastor and she's a brilliant songwriter. They're younger than us, but we have kids the same age. The guys like to mountain bike together and Kayla and I get together with the kids for play dates and occasionally a mountain bike ride ourselves.

We told them about my *indiscretion*, and they want to help us rebuild our marriage through God's word. James and I know we need counseling, but he's insistent that it be good Christian biblical counseling. We went to one free session at our church that was practical and helpful, but afterward, there was no offer for further help or advice about where to go.

I want to believe that the gospel could set me free, but there's a part of me who wants to be free *from* the gospel and the constraints of Christianity that I've squeezed myself into. I've asked God to show me how He could give me a joy that surpasses the feelings I crave. But maybe God doesn't work that way. Maybe my motives aren't right, maybe I'm not fully surrendering yet. Because despite my attempts to emerge from this place of lustfulness, this desire to escape my marriage, I can't change the unsettled, unhappy feelings in my heart. And I also know that James neither forgives nor trusts me.

Brock and I haven't spoken more than a few words in passing since we ended it. I desperately want to know if he still thinks about me the way he did before, but he has refused to engage with me. I know he's smart to do that, protecting himself from that slippery slope. How does he find the power to resist, I wonder, when he doesn't even believe in God? I should have even more self-control than him. This makes me feel even more guilty.

But today, knowing I'm leaving, Brock is sweet, open.

"You know I'm going to miss you," I say as we pass in the hall.

"I know," he says sadly, the words, "I'll miss you, too," in his eyes, but not coming out of his mouth. He says he feels bad that I have to quit. He's one of the only people who knows that my leaving is about more than just my husband not liking the crazy work schedule we all love to hate. This job has been so much fun. And it's nice to be good at something. I know it's just a silly timeshare sales job. It's not like I'm curing cancer or delivering babies. But I love helping my customers dream about the vacations they'll take with their families. I'm going to miss it so much. Things are still tense and broken at home, and I feel powerless to fix it. Whatever was lacking in our relationship to even allow this seed of discontent to grow within me has, of course, been magnified by the emotional and sexual relationship I allowed to grow with Brock. I'm tempted to leave my marriage, which I feel incapable of saving. But even though it feels empty and lonely, and I'm not sure if we'll make it, I've resolved to give it my all before giving up.

After work, a group of us cross the street for one last drink. Brock and I sit next to each other, and we fall easily back into flirting. I forget, momentarily, about Bible studies and God's word, and I choose to be a person I'm ashamed of, the smart and Godly version of myself averting her eyes while the sultry heathen takes over.

Brock and another guy are having a conversation about how they like being married but wish they could have just five days of being single. Brock looks around at the various girls, dressed to the nines for a Friday night out in Scottsdale. His eyes land on a tall redhead in a tight white dress that barely covers her butt, thigh-high boots that *this* short-legged girl could never wear.

"You really don't have a certain type, do you?" I say, thinking how he was obviously attracted to me, a woman who looks totally different from his wife, who looks totally different from that leggy girl.

"Nope. I appreciate all types of beauty," he says, smiling ruefully at me.

"Well, I could keep you busy for five days," I say, half joking. "You wouldn't need to look anywhere else."

"I bet you could," he says, winking.

We continue drinking with the group for a while, flirting the whole time, and then it's getting late, and people start to leave. Before I know it, Brock and I are alone at the table. I can feel the energy between us. He walks me to my car again, and the time apart has not dulled the attraction. I search for the strength to stop whatever is going to happen between us but fail to find it. This time, I let him climb into the back of my minivan and make me, officially, an adulterer. Don't get me wrong, he doesn't have to *make* me do anything. I welcome it, invite it. But a minute into it, I push him off me, coming back to my senses.

"Stop. I can't do this. This is wrong," I say.

But the damage is already done. I have cheated on my husband - by anyone's standard. And this one little choice has given me a new name, a nasty name - whether you're Christian, Jewish, atheist or anything else - *Adulteress*. I remember reading *The Scarlet Letter* in Honors English. Hester Prynne had to walk around with the letter A for Adulteress embossed on her chest. My letter is only inside my heart, but I feel instantly changed by it.

"I can't do this either," Brock says, shaking his head, regret written all over his face. I feel him retreating from me even before he walks away, rejecting my offer to walk him to his car. He barely hugs me goodbye, can't get out of there fast enough. And then he's gone. And I'm left in the parking lot like some heroin addict who's been clean for months, decided to take one last hit, but found that it didn't quite satisfy, didn't give me the same high, and left me both wanting more and feeling horribly guilty, searching for something to assuage the guilt.

I don't mention it to James this time. I already know how that would go. And anyway, I've lied and told him *The Guy* wasn't working there anymore. At the time, it had felt like a half-truth that would make James feel better about my being there. Brock might as well not have been there, I rationalized, since we never talked anymore, and our connection was gone. But now the lie feels like a glob in my throat that I can't quite swallow, exacerbated by my new indiscretion.

I don't know it yet, but James and I have just hopped onto a rollercoaster ride that will last three years. I don't like rollercoasters. They make me sick.

Over the next few years, the one thing that temporarily dissipates my feelings of guilt and misery is the high I get from more male attention and attraction, so I collect it wherever I go. I'm still married, trying to be the very best wife and mom I can be. We have lots of great moments together - the two of us, with the kids, with extended family, friends. From the outside no one would know we are in trouble.

But I get depressed, anxious, lonely, or bored, and need a fix. I seek out my drug: from a guy at a bar, someone at work, a friend on Facebook. I don't have to do any major contriving to find it, and most of the time it's just flirting. I start telling myself that maybe I'm just not cut out for marriage, fantasizing about the single life: where I would live, how I would spend my time. How great it would be to have my girls every other week, with some "me time" on the off days. It's like I have an energy about me or a glow that attracts guys wherever I go. Never in my life have I experienced such power. It's fun, intoxicating, almost as much as when Brock told me how much he wanted me. Almost, but not quite. You can never really find that first high again.

Occasionally I feel a different high when I listen to an inspiring sermon at church, read a book that opens my eyes to something I hadn't seen before, or hear a soulful song on the radio. My hope is restored, and I believe that James and I can survive this.

A few months after leaving the timeshare job, I'm out with Courtney and a few of her friends. We're sitting on a patio across the street from where I worked with Brock. I peer at the doorway periodically, willing him to come out for a smoke so I can catch a glimpse of him. We've had no contact, and the one time I broke down and texted him, he never responded. So now I feel both guilty and jilted. Like a junkie who can't get her fix.

Courtney's friend Jessica is going through a messy divorce after her husband cheated on her with a girl he worked with.

"You look amazing," I say to Jessica. And it's true. She looks lean and healthy, despite the drama in her life.

"Divorce diet. I can't eat. Not necessarily the healthiest way to lose weight, but I do feel good," she says. "It's kind of ironic that I look better than I have in years. Since before we had kids."

"So, do you feel comfortable talking about what happened?" Alicia asks, utterly shocked that something so horrible could occur in our own circle of friends. Of course, she doesn't know my story.

"Yeah, it's ok," Jessica says.

"So, he actually had an affair with a girl he works with?" Alicia prods.

"Is still having, to be more accurate," Jessica replies. "He's seriously gone off the deep end. It's like I don't even know him."

Courtney already shared the whole story with me a few days ago. She told me she was having a hard time not hating Jessica's husband, Derek. (Mom taught us that *hate is a very strong word*. It should take a lot to make us hate.)

Jessica and Derek had been together since college. They were the first of their crew to get married, the perfect couple, always having fun and partying together, even after they were married, Courtney told me.

"My heart breaks for you, Jessica," Courtney says now. "How are the boys doing?"

"Oh, they're fine. And Trey is so little, he doesn't know any better. It's crazy that Derek hardly even wants to see his own baby and his four-year-old son."

"And what about the girl," Alicia asks. "Isn't she married too? Doesn't she have kids, also?"

"Yeah, two. From what I understand, she has left her husband and practically abandoned the kids."

"I don't know how a woman could do that. She destroyed two families, all for what? Sex? I just don't get it," Alicia says.

"Yeah, and she's supposedly this devout Christian. Wakes up at four am every day to read her Bible. Talk about hypocrisy. How does that happen?"

My heart drops. I know exactly how it happens, how a conservative Christian mom becomes *the other woman*. I listen in silence. Horrified at the damage this woman has caused to my friend and her family, as well as the example this makes of all Christians to these non-believers. I know that sin can creep up in anyone's heart, and can even take residence there, unwilling to leave. *I am a true believer, still, aren't I?* I ask God, thinking of Lola Minton.

I ache for Jessica, but I envy Derek. He gets to keep the object of his desire, while I'm still trying to get over mine. But deep inside my soul, despite all the *sinful* feelings crowding my heart, I remember God. I think of that woman at the well, how Jesus knew about everything she'd done and loved her anyway. *Could he still love me too?* I pray that He would make me new again. The beauty of being a believer is that even with this sin still very much alive in my heart, I can kneel at the cross and surrender it to Him. Instead of just feeling guilty about it, I can confess everything, and He can forgive me. Again. I can turn away from it. Again. And *this* is a beautiful thing.

But my heart is deceitful and easily swayed. And dealing with an addiction to love and relationships is tricky. I don't know how to avoid *taking a drink* since my drug isn't a substance but a feeling. If I'm going to kick this addiction, I'm going to have to cut it off in my thoughts, in my feelings, before I ever even say a word. But I haven't quite learned that yet.

I had chuckled to myself on the first day of work as I sat through that mandatory sexual harassment video and training. I thought it was ridiculous that anyone would want to sexually harass me: a 35-year-old, happily married, slightly-too-curvy Jewish/Christian mom of two young kids.

As it turns out, it wasn't a vicious, disgusting, harassing attack I had to worry about, but a beautifully seductive temptation, and my own surprising desires. How ironic that I thought I was protected, untouchable, *a new creature in Christ* who had left that old life behind. I didn't even think I could be tempted, let alone actually act on it. It all caught me very much by surprise, and by the time I realized I needed to be careful, it was too late. I was powerless to stop it. Although I know that sounds ridiculous. No one is truly powerless to stop themselves.

And it's not that I didn't try, didn't think about the consequences. I was simply so caught up in the passion, that I guess I didn't care. Or if there was a tiny voice inside me who did care, it was buried alive each time it crept out, under the excitement and thrill of what was going on in my head. That's exactly where the whole thing started, right in my own thoughts. And I would have been fine if I didn't become aware that the same thoughts were going through his head. It was simply thrilling that a hot, younger guy, someone I viewed as out of my league - especially since I wasn't even in the running anymore - would want *me*. I couldn't understand why he would, but I fell in love with the feeling that gave me.

Looking back over my life, I see it so clearly now. I have thrown away friendships, blown auditions, changed my entire belief system, and now almost lost my family – all for the short-term thrilling high that I get from the only drug I've ever been addicted to. It's not heroin, cocaine or even alcohol. It's love - or rather the emotional and sexual attention that *feels* like love - from whomever is the current spectacular object of my infatuation.

CHAPTER 12

Searching for a Fix

Summer, 2010

James concedes that we need consistent income and agrees I should get a job with regular hours and a salary, even if it means putting the kids in daycare. He recognizes that my desire to work outside the home doesn't necessarily make me a bad wife or mother. I start working as an account executive with a real estate title company.

In Arizona real estate, the title company is a third party that helps close transactions. My clients are my peers: real estate agents and lenders. It's my job to build relationships with them and help them with all types of marketing to grow their businesses, in hopes they will open their escrows with my company. It's a very indirect kind of sale, but I'm good at building rapport, and I've always loved helping people. I begin to see myself as a marketing coach. The job is flexible, interesting and comes with a solid base salary, which takes off so much of the financial pressure we've felt these past few years. We find a home daycare for the girls - a mom who used to be a teacher taking care of other kids around the same ages as her own.

A few months later, I receive an email invitation to a business development "lunch and learn," from Chase, a guy I met at a party more than a year ago, back when I was still happily inside my Christian bubble. James was out of town and my friend John invited me over to celebrate the first anniversary of his new business. I brought Cadence and Alex over to my mom's for the weekend, so she could watch them while I went to the party, which was near her house. Chase and I chatted amiably in the living room until he was dragged away by his group of friends to head to the next party, and I headed back to my mom's house to cuddle into the guest bed with my girls. We had both studied journalism, had some mutual friends, and had a lot in common, personally and professionally.

"We should have been BFFs," he joked. We exchanged business cards since he was in marketing and I was in real estate, and I figured I'd never see him again. But evidently, I had been added to his business database. I reply to the mass email now.

> Hey Chase!
> How are you doing? I'm not sure if you remember me, but we met like a year ago at John's house. I still don't understand exactly what your company does! Maybe we should get together so you can explain it to me! I am now working as a marketing rep for a title company and help realtors and lenders with their marketing, but not sure if this is something affordable and useful for small business owners...
> Call me!
>
> Danielle

> Danielle,
> Of course I remember you! You were the only entertaining person at the party ;-)
> We specialize in high-end, B2B telemarketing and appointment-setting. Not sure if it would be a good fit for what you're doing with realtors and lenders, but we can certainly get together and catch up.
> Thanks,
> Chase

On the surface, there's nothing inappropriate in this email exchange, but it makes me feel giddy, and this alone should be enough to make me end it. I was less attuned to it when I first met him, but there was an energy between us even then. We plan a business meeting at Starbucks, something I do all the time for work, in the name of networking, marketing, building relationships.

The night before we're set to meet, I'm invited by some new Christian girlfriends to a worship concert at their church. The pulsing music makes me feel closer to God again. But there's a restless itch that I can't ignore, and I yearn for something to scratch it. After the concert, we all head back to Laura's house to sit around a cozy fire in her backyard and talk about life, sharing our struggles. Robin tells us about her battle with alcoholism, and the feelings she describes seem so familiar, so like my own struggle.

When I feel depressed, anxious, lonely, or bored, the flirting and fantasizing transport me from my real life and make me feel better, like a glass of wine after a stressful day. It's a more pleasant remedy than the antidepressants I took when Ian and I were together in New York. Those made me feel more even keeled, but less alive. I tell Robin I can relate to her, but my battle seems insignificant compared to an addiction to a real substance. I don't even know what I'm addicted to exactly, and I feel like it's sort of a cop out to even call it an addiction. Maybe it's just plain old sin and I should be able to turn it off, give it to God, and think about the things I'm supposed to think about instead. I tell them about Brock, leaving out the part about that last night at work, when we went all the way, since James doesn't know about that and I'm still trying to pretend it didn't happen.

I'm reaching out, grasping for someone to help me break free. I don't know what makes me tell them about Chase and the coffee meeting we have scheduled tomorrow, because surely there's nothing there. But even though these girls barely know me, they sense something wild in my voice when I talk about him, and they urge me not to go meet him. I know they're right. But I go anyway. *It's an innocent cup of coffee*, I tell myself.

Piece of Work

The conversation at the coffee shop is friendly and professional, but there's an unmistakable spark of something between us, and soon we shift from business to more personal topics. We're talking about life, relationships and believing in God. He tells me he's agnostic and I tell him about my complicated religious story, what happened with Brock and how it's changed my marriage, changed me. How I feel so guilty. How I don't understand it.

"You can't help who you're attracted to, who you fall in love with," he says. We talk about that intoxicated feeling you get with certain people, "like an opiate," he says. But we aren't talking about us, now. We're simply two friends who understand each other. We each return to work, and he emails me the PI personality assessment his company does for clients and employees. We had talked about it at coffee, and I was intrigued. I take the test and a few hours later, he sends the results.

> Danielle,
> So, according to our team leader, you're my 'Evil Twin.' Very high dominance but counteracted nicely by the high extroversion. Low patience and low detail. You are quick to connect with people, very friendly and extroverted, with a high sense of urgency.
> I've attached the report for your enjoyment. The first box is who you are innately, the second box is who you are right now, and the third box is the combination of the two. He said there's such a difference between the first two boxes because you're either trying to change some things about your personality right now, or something is going on in your life externally to cause these changes.
> Let me know what you think.
> Thanks,
> Chase

As I read the report I'm utterly fascinated by its accuracy. It's like a mini essay on all my strengths and weaknesses. I see in those paragraphs all the wonderful and terrible things I am capable of. I read it over and over.

Danielle is an engaging, stimulating communicator, poised and capable of projecting enthusiasm and warmth, and of motivating other people.

She has a strong sense of urgency, initiative and competitive drive to get things done, with emphasis on working with and through people in the process. She understands people well and uses that understanding effectively in influencing and persuading others to act.

Impatient for results and particularly impatient with details and routines, Danielle is a confident and venturesome "doer" and decision-maker who will delegate details and can also delegate responsibility and authority when necessary. Danielle is a self-starter who can also be skillful at training and developing others. She applies pressure for results, but in doing so, her style is more "selling" than "telling".

At ease and self-assured with groups or in making new contacts, Danielle is gregarious and extroverted, has an invigorating impact on people, and is always "selling" in a general sense. She learns and reacts quickly and works at a faster-than-average pace. Able to adapt quickly to change and variety in her work, she will become impatient and less effective if required to work primarily with repetitive routines and details.

In general terms, Danielle is an ambitious and driving person who is motivated by opportunity for advancement to levels of responsibility where she can use her skills as team builder, motivator and mover.

It's like my best friend had been asked to describe me. But Chase's comments hit me in the gut. Who I am innately and who I am right now are very far apart. I'm searching for a way back home. But I keep going the wrong way. Or maybe I've been trying to be someone I'm not and I'm finally going the *right* way, toward my true self? Regardless, I feel *seen*, understood. And that feels nice. I think that the drive to feel seen and understood is a motivating force for much of what we do as humans. And feeling *unseen, misunderstood* is at the root of most of our emotional distress, negative emotions, and harmful behavior.

Chase gets me. He and I are a lot alike, I think. *While my husband and I are nothing alike*. We exchange emails back and forth all afternoon.

"I should let you get back to work," he says.

"But I like this," I say.

"Me too, a little too much," he admits. "We should probably stop talking."

"I know what you mean. It's a slippery slope," I say, finally acknowledging the danger that lurks just underneath our friendly banter.

But never one to let it lie, and still searching for something to scratch that itch, I want to hear him say *why* he thinks we can't be friends. So, I call him the next day. I want to feel the intoxication of his desire.

"Yes, I'm attracted to you…of course I want you…" he finally admits. And I feel the liquid heat of my drug melt my insides. A former alcoholic, Chase has a lot more willpower than I do, so he simply refuses to go there with me. He knows where *one drink* leads.

"It's like a drug that will tear you apart and destroy you," he texts a few days later when I push him into another conversation.

"I just want to be friends," I say. "I'm not going to hurt you."

"No, you don't understand. *I'm* the drug," he says.

Oh, I understand. And I want to get high on that drug. So much more than I'm ready to admit to myself.

We text a few times over the next few weeks. It's always me who initiates it, but, like Brock, Chase is *just a man*, and I'm able to pull him out of his willpower long enough to get him to say he thinks I'm beautiful, he wants me. It's those words, that idea of him needing me, desperately wishing he could touch me, that make me feel intoxicated, and it's that feeling I'm addicted to. We don't send pictures or talk explicitly about sex. It's the hint of it that gets me. If it were more explicit, it would probably make me uncomfortable. For all my exploits, I'm still so reserved in that way, a fact that irks me as much as it assuages me.

"You were right, you are a drug, and I am so addicted," I tell him, flirting. But he's firm, refusing to see me or continue a friendship of any kind. In his last text, he says, "Stop looking outside your marriage for excitement and fulfillment. Create it within the boundaries of your relationship."

Such profound advice from someone I know *wants* to have sex with me. And I was just willing to throw myself and my marriage out the window for a meaningless fling. More guilt. And still that undeniable hunger for more attention. Nevertheless, I recommit myself to making my marriage work. I sign us up for a group vow renewal service at church. I try to focus on all the things we fell in love with about each other. We spend quality time together - mountain bike rides, dinner dates, concerts - trying to reconnect and fall in love again. But it's up and down, and every time we hit a valley, I find myself retreating from our marriage, wanting to be divorced.

Now it's November, and I'm at work when a Facebook Instant Message pops up on my screen. It's from Parker, one of the guys I worked with at Outdoor Adventures in college. I use Facebook to build relationships with our clients, so I often have it open at work.

Parker: How's marriage?
Me: Good...
Me: Well, it's harder than you'd think. Didn't you ever get married?
Parker: Nope. No marriage.
Me: Oh, I thought you and your girlfriend from college had gotten married.

No response. I turn back to my work, my cheeks flushed from the encounter. I always had a crush on Parker. If I'm honest, he's at least 50% of why I applied for a job at OA in the first place, after going on a weekend backpacking trip with the group as a paying participant.

A week later, out of the blue:

Parker: Your kids have the coolest, most amazing and beautiful mom. They are very lucky.

Me: Awe, thanks, Park. That is such a sweet thing to say. Why do you say that?
Parker: You have just always been so fun. And you were so sexy in college. And I look at pictures of you now and my jaw just drops.
Me: Are you serious????!!!
Parker: Yes.
Me: I had such a crush on you in college.
Parker: Me too.
Me: You did? All you ever did was give me a hard time. Why didn't you ever say anything?

Ah. Here it is again, that high that makes me feel like I'm on top of the world. How ironic that Parker had a crush on *me*. I think about how different my life would have been if he had told me he liked me back then. Maybe we would have dated, gotten married, had a nice outdoor adventurous life together. Maybe I wouldn't have had such a messed-up addiction to love and relationships. Or maybe it wouldn't have made a difference. Who knows?

Parker and I develop a pattern of not contacting one another for a few weeks or even months, and then out of the blue checking in again, just to see how things are going, then exchanging some messages over the next few days until we fade away again. He lives hundreds of miles away and it feels like a safer way to get the extra attention I crave. He's always been a man of few words, but each time he writes to me, he manages to say just the right thing to stroke my ego and feed me my drug. And whenever I think about him, it drives an invisible rift between James and me, and I wish I were single. I feel like I have no control. Just when I'm feeling over Parker and have stopped thinking about him constantly, he reaches out again, and I get attached all over again.

I start going to counseling. My therapist confirms that I'm "addicted to love." I begin to learn techniques to cope with it. And I push on, trying to water my own grass instead of always looking for love on the other side.

One day Parker gets a little bolder, tells me what he wishes he would have done back in 1993. For him, I'm a safe fantasy. I'm married and far away. He can look at pictures, imagine being with me without committing to anything. But even though I haven't seen the guy in person in 15 years, I develop a strong attachment. This must be what they call an emotional affair, I think. One more checkmark on my list of sinful choices.

"You are married!" he reminds me, as if I've forgotten. Then he'll stop contacting me for a few weeks or months, but invariably, I'll hear from him again one night when he's lonely or bored, and we'll start up again.

In January, I decide I want to do the 24 Hours of Old Pueblo. It's this crazy mountain bike race they put together in the middle of the desert outside of Tucson each February. The weather is almost always bad: pouring rain, freezing cold. James has done it several times, both as a solo entrant and as part of a team of fit and fast guys, including his brother Luke. They aren't doing it this year, so I decide it's my turn.

My mountain biking skills and confidence have never quite come back after the crash on Twisted Sister when I broke my arm, but I'm feeling fit and determined, so I find a team of girls who need an extra person and I volunteer myself as a rider, and James as our team mechanic and cook. Luke joins us with his pop-up trailer, and everything is light and fun, like a party.

We call our team "The Go-Go Girls." We dress up in 70s garb, and pre-race festivities include dancing and hula-hooping in the makeshift town square erected in the desert. The race starts in Le Mans style - the first rider on each team stages their bike and then runs down the rocky trail to hop on when the gunshot is fired.

I'm the third rider in our rotation. Just before dusk, it's my turn to race the 17-mile lap. We'll keep going through the four-part relay for 24 hours, logging as many laps as we can in that time. I hope to get in four laps.

I didn't have time to pre-ride the course, and by the time I set out, the wind has picked up and it's getting cold. I curse the course and everyone who told me it wasn't that hard. For me, it's miserable and my pace is slow and slogging. I never know what's coming around the next corner and I'm passed every five minutes by a real cyclist going twice as fast as I am. It's hard enough to navigate the narrow trail and rocky desert terrain without also worrying about how I'm going to ease over to the right so that some racer can pass me.

Eventually, I make it to the end. I can see camp, and it's an easy downhill section, so I pick up speed. I'm not sure how I will do this again and again, but at least I've almost completed my first lap. Whizzing down the hill, just slightly out of control, I hit a gully and pop up into the air, careening off to the left and landing flat on my face, chest, and knees. It's a hard blow and my head feels tingly. I get my bearings and sit up. There are people around me asking questions, trying to determine how hard I hit my head.

"Are you OK? What's your name? What happened? That chin looks bad. You're gonna need stitches."

I put my hand to my chin, and it comes away bloody. I feel a chunk of skin hanging down, but strangely it doesn't really hurt. Both knees are bleeding and stinging, but still, I reach for the baton in my back jersey pocket, knowing the next rider on my team is waiting in that tent just a half mile up the trail, and I must get her the baton so she can continue the race. I've already wasted so much time, caused us to fall behind our goals with my slower riding, and now this. I'm relieved that I probably won't have to ride that nasty course again thanks to my crash, but I'm determined to finish this lap and bring the baton in. I stand up and start walking my bike along the trail. A guy I don't know walks with me to make sure I'm OK and I don't pass out. Eventually I even get back on my bike, pedaling in the last few hundred feet. I'm proud of myself for that. As I pass the baton to my new friend, she gives me a worried look.

"What happened?" she asks.

"I crashed, right near the end. It was hard. Really hard. Go get it done! You can do it!" I say, with the best smile I can muster, gently shoving her off to ride her lap. I'm led to a makeshift medical tent, where half a dozen medics tend to my wounds, cleaning my chin with soapy water.

"This will need stitches. We could butterfly it up for now though and you could go tomorrow."

One of the ladies tries to reach James for me, as I didn't bother bringing my cell phone out on the trail. Cell service here is spotty, so it takes a while to reach him. Finally, he walks in. He shakes his head, incredulous that I crashed in the last ten minutes of my lap, just past where he and Luke hiked out to cheer for me on the trail.

As I lay on a stretcher, assessing my pain and symptoms, the fingers on my left hand start tingling. When I mention this to the medic who's cleaning and bandaging my wounds, he frowns. Tingling can be a warning sign of a more serious spinal injury, and they go from merely recommending stitches tomorrow to insisting James take me to the hospital, even suggesting an ambulance ride may be safer than the jostling of a car through the desert. We decide to play it safe and go to the hospital, but James wants to drive. We borrow a car from one of my teammates since James' truck is buried behind our campsite.

X-rays and MRIs confirm that I'm fine, just a little banged up. The doctor deftly stitches up my chin, careful to do it in a way that will leave minimal scarring on my face. Sitting together in the hospital, James suggests that maybe I should quit mountain biking. He says it's because he loves me and doesn't want to see me hurt, but I feel like he's taking away one of the strongest common denominators we have left between us, trying to control me and push me down. It makes me angry, makes me want to escape.

I email Parker a picture of my scratched-up face with the caption, "Not so beautiful right now," hoping he'll tell me I still look beautiful to him. But he doesn't bite. He's in a "staying away" phase.

CHAPTER 13

The Ring

JUNE 2011

The hot summer night mirrors my ornery restlessness. I haven't talked to Parker in a few months and I'm itching for someone to flirt with. My friend Sheila invites me out with some of her girlfriends, and James encourages me to go and have fun. He doesn't understand that I'm like a recovering alcoholic who's too weak yet to go to the bar. *I know*, but I want a figurative drink, and looking forward to a few literal cocktails, too.

It's one of those nights where you're feeling great, on fire. It's not my outfit or hairdo, I just feel good in my own skin, happy with myself regardless of the few extra pounds that have crept back on in recent months. I've learned that confidence really is sexy. I'm 36 years old and feel like I have the power to attract any guy I want. *But I'm married*.

The evening starts with dinner and drinks at a high-end resort in Scottsdale. Sheila's friends are great - a diverse assortment of married and single ladies in their late 30s and 40s - and we talk and laugh about life, love, marriage, and kids. I share with them some of my story, my struggle over the past few years. I tell them that James and I are in a good place right now, but the one thing that's still lacking and I don't know how to fix is the sex and intimacy. I can't get it back, can't connect with him, can't seem to enjoy having sex with him. And I worry that I won't be able to live like this the rest of my life.

"Sexual and intimacy problems are almost always rooted in something else. There must still be some emotional issues you guys haven't worked through," one of the girls offers.

Another tells us her mom had a lover for many years. She simply filled up the part of her marriage life that was lacking with someone else. And she's still married to this day.

"I could never do that," I say, knowing I don't have the ability to compartmentalize, to be in two places emotionally, even if I could wrap my brain around the morality of it. For me it has to be all or nothing. But as the evening wears on and the drinks flow, I start thinking it might be fun to have a boy toy, someone just for fun. And thoughts create realities.

I'm out on the dance floor rocking my hips, feeling the music in a relaxed way that I've seldom been able to do. Dancing usually brings me back to 7th grade, as I awkwardly tried to move to the music in a way that didn't make me look like a dork. But tonight, I don't care. That's one of the nice things about already being married. I'm not desperate. I'm not even looking for anything.

"You are like a man magnet!" April says, glancing around the dance floor. And I'm basking in the delight of my attractiveness, like a power I've never had before.

One guy walks by and our eyes lock. He's very cute: tall and lean, dark and handsome, with bright blue eyes and a chiseled jaw, just my type. When April and I decide to take a break from dancing and go back outside to join the rest of the group, I walk past him and smile. The next thing I know, he and I are out on the dance floor, like I had simply willed it to happen. He either doesn't notice or doesn't care about the wedding ring on my finger. But I'm acutely aware of its weight on my hand, and I guiltily finger it as we dance. It's become a nervous habit, this twisting of my wedding ring with my thumb. Perhaps I'm trying to remind myself that I'm still married, like when someone snaps a rubber band on their wrist to help them break a bad habit. I think of the ring from Lord of the Rings, James' favorite movie. That ring represented a type of temporal and evil power men desire, a wealth that spawns greed and corruption, while my ring is supposed to symbolize a perfect union between me and James, unbreakable.

The boy is behind me, holding my hands. *Can't he feel the ring?* I wonder. I feel his lips on my neck, and then before I can stop him, he spins me around and plants a sensual kiss on my mouth. He's got moves and they are working. But I can't do this! I break away. *I need to end my marriage first,* I think. *Enough is enough. I should not be married.*

"I can't," I say, and walk back outside. Later, he catches up with me and asks what's wrong, but I don't tell him I'm married. I'm too ashamed. And he's so young and carefree that I think it doesn't even occur to him that I'm an almost-middle-aged married woman with two baby girls at home. We exchange numbers and I text him the next day.

"It was fun hanging out with you last night. The thing I couldn't bring myself to tell you is that I'm married and have two little girls. I'm sorry. It's complicated."

He doesn't care. The following week, he meets me at a restaurant where I've just attended a business networking meeting. We have a few drinks together and I tell him about Brock and Parker, and how unhappy I am. I feel a lot like when I first lost my virginity with Kyle in high school the week of my 17th birthday. We did it just that once and then I broke up with him. My virginity was gone, but I had scarcely had a chance to explore my sexuality, and I have chased it ever since. The "affair" with Brock has left me feeling much the same. I've technically committed adultery and therefore will always be considered an unfaithful wife, and yet I stopped before even letting myself go. At this point I've already committed the crime once. I'm already guilty, so I may as well do it again.

We go back to his apartment and as I'm standing there looking around his sparsely furnished living room, my thumb rubs my wedding ring so vigorously that it slips off my finger and onto the tile floor, making the same gentle clinking sound as Ian's ring falling from the note he left me in Rocky Point so many years ago. I hastily bend over and snatch up the ring, putting it away in a zippered pocket of my purse instead of back on my finger where it belongs. I ignore this obvious sign from God to stop, and I proceed with my vile act. *A man reaps what he sows.*

It doesn't take long for him to finish. But I can't get into it, our rhythm is wrong, his room looks like a college dorm. *What am I doing? Who have I become?* I pull my clothes on and leave his apartment as fast as I can, never to see him again. The encounter is a cold reminder that the grass isn't greener on the other side. I vow to water my own grass and stop looking outside my marriage for whatever it is I'm searching for, and I bury the indiscretion deep in my soul, like it never even happened. Except of course that it did.

James is still struggling to forgive me of the sin he knows about, a molehill compared to this mountain. He doesn't trust me, checks my phone and computer when he thinks I'm not looking. I've developed a habit of picking my phone up and carrying it with me wherever I go, which only makes him sure I have something to hide. Most of the time there's nothing there. But James senses I'm no longer all in, and I know he's not either. He's developed a righteous attitude that because of my indiscretion, any squabble or issue we have in our marriage is my fault. And I take it. I believe it. He's good. I'm bad. Obviously. I try so hard to be better, forgive myself and move on. But I can't. And the pain of it is rotting me from the inside out.

The ring - a reminder of a promise, now broken.

CHAPTER 14

Roller Coaster

Labor Day Weekend, 2011

"We need to talk," James says as I set the groceries on the granite countertop, his tone ominously serious. I can't see his face because he's busy stirring something on the stove, but I notice the tension in his shoulders. It's lunchtime, the Friday before Labor Day, 2011, seven months after the 24-hour race. We've been married seven and a half years now. A year ago, we moved into a big, beautiful home closer to the trails we love so much.

We're going camping this weekend with some friends. Alex scurries about underfoot, opening the pantry doors to look for a snack. She's in a sweet and playful mood, a pleasant and unexpected treat from our very spicy three-year-old. No whining or temper tantrums, even though we just came from the pediatrician's office for her three-year-old well check and shots. I was worried she would cry, look up at me with those big blue eyes as if I had betrayed her by letting the nurse give her that shot, not warning her how bad it would hurt. That's what Cadence's brown eyes seemed to say last year when she got her four-year-old shots. But Alex just took it stoically, barely flinching when the needle pierced her little arm. She smiled broadly when I told her how brave she was. She whispered into my ear that she wasn't brave, she was really scared.

"That's what being brave is; when you're scared, but you do it anyway, face your fears. It wouldn't take bravery to do something you weren't scared of," I said, pinching her sweet cheeks and kissing one tenderly.

"Alex, don't eat fruit snacks now, we're going to have lunch," I say now. "Is that what you're making, Babe?" I ask James, glancing over at the splattered stove, the pans and dishes strewn about the countertops. About a year ago, when there were still boxes everywhere waiting to be unpacked, I sat back after the last bite of a delicious dinner James had cooked and jokingly quipped, "How 'bout you cook every night and I'll clean up?"

"Deal!" he said with a delighted smile. He loved getting creative and cooking up gourmet meals like a top chef on one of the cooking shows he was always watching.

"Seriously? I'm serious!" I said, thinking I was getting the better deal since at the time I was doing most of the cooking *and* the cleaning. It's not that I'm a bad cook, it's just not my pleasure, my passion. But cleaning up after James' cooking has proven more tedious than cleaning up after myself, I think now, glancing at the mess all over every surface of the large kitchen.

"Uh, no," he mutters, his blue eyes icy. "I'm making spaghetti sauce for camping. I hadn't even thought about lunch."

"OK, is it financial stuff you want to talk about?" I ask, slightly annoyed and bracing myself for some huge charge he has forgotten to tell me about that will suddenly show up in our account, which already hovers way too close to zero. We've spent the last few days in heated discussions about how we're going to get ourselves out of the financial hole we're in. We've already cut all unnecessary expenses, I've canceled my gym membership, we're short selling one of our rental properties. But we have so much credit card debt that none of that makes much difference. I've tried to convince James that we need to do something drastic, but he's been, so far, unwilling to consider moving or selling our home.

I don't want to move either. I love this house. We got an amazing deal on it and it's like it was made for us. The spacious kitchen with a large granite-topped island, big open rooms, high ceilings. And the views and sunsets from our upstairs balcony are amazing. We can see Red Mountain, the Superstitions and Usery Pass; and further away, Camelback, the McDowells and other mountains whose names James knows but I don't.

But I've already resigned myself to the probability of moving and detached myself from this home. I'm stuck in this in-between place where I don't know what to believe anymore.

Still, it throws me off guard when James says gravely, "No, it's not about the finances." My heart skips a beat when he says, "a few weeks ago, you left your computer open to a story you were writing, so I read it…"

I'm irritated that he was snooping, but I feel like I've lost the right to be angry about any offense my husband has committed against me, when I'm guilty of so much more. I feel guilty all the time these days, despite the confessing, repenting and constantly asking for forgiveness that has become a regular part of my inner monologue.

"I know I shouldn't have been going through your stuff, but I needed to look something up on the MLS and my computer was upstairs and yours was sitting right there, open. I know you hate when I use your computer, but…"

He's right. I do hate it. James is a successful realtor now. I decorated our spacious office upstairs for him, but his laptop, smart phone, iPad, and random yellow legal pads, papers and files are always scattered throughout the house, which also bothers me. Although you'd hardly know it looking at our house most days, I hate clutter and crave order. Unfortunately, both James and I are naturally more in the slob camp than the neat freak camp, despite the lifelong neat freak influence of my dad, who couldn't stand to have anything out of place. My mom was more easy-going, but raised by a single mom, she knew how to get things done. Together they kept our home clean and organized. With James, it's always just me trying to organize our lives, and never living up to my own standards.

I feel a vague sense of panic whenever he borrows my computer. It's like I have no place that's just for me. I feel invaded, trapped.

Parker and I finally ended our thing for good the other day, so I won't have to worry about an email or text from him popping up, and there's no one else waiting in the wings, thank God. I'm determined to turn away from all that permanently this time. My mind flits back to the stories about Lola Minton, the adulterer, as it often does. It strikes me that James' family would think *I'm* an unbeliever, too - if they knew the truth about me. And I have a desperate need to prove that my belief is true and real. *It is, isn't it?*

I start washing dishes and pouring rice milk into a pink princess sippy cup for Alex. I wonder if Cadence will be asleep today when I walk down to meet her school bus at the end of the street in a few hours. That girl. I've never heard of a kid falling so fast asleep on the way home from school that the sweet bus driver can't rouse her when they reach her stop and invites Mom to climb up into the bus to scoop her up. It's happened several times already and we're only a few weeks into kindergarten. Each time, I try to gently shake her awake, but she doesn't budge, so I gather her into my arms and carry her up the little hill to the house, grinning joyfully even as I shake my head in disbelief. Carrying her petite little body up that hill is a secret mommy pleasure. And I love any excuse for a little extra exercise anyway. She almost always wakes up just as soon as I gently plop her down on the living room couch or the red chaise lounge that sits between the fireplace and the corner window that looks out to the pool. I love both of my girls so much. We both do. They're one of the main reasons we're still together.

"So anyway," James goes on, "I read this story on your laptop and I recognized that it was a true story from your past, because I knew the story. The names were changed, but it was still obvious. In fact, I was thinking of telling you that you should be careful about that."

I don't know exactly what he means by that. I have flip-flopped between writing my story as a memoir or disguising it in a novel. I have several starts of chapters that are all parts of my own life story. Sometimes I feel like I could really tell the whole entire truth easier in a novel. I'm also concerned about protecting the people who have played roles in my life but haven't necessarily signed up to be in my book. Every time I've tried to write fiction, though, I realize that the truth really is stranger, more dramatic, and more amazing than fiction. And I'm not creative enough to make up stories from scratch anyway.

"Yeah, I know. I wish you wouldn't go through my stuff, but whatever," I say, looking up at him. Maybe soon he won't have the option because I will be gone. I really don't know if I can do this anymore, this farce of a marriage.

"So, anyway?" I ask.

"Today when you were gone, I was down here and saw your computer sitting open and decided to look and see if you had written anything new since the last time, and I found a new story called *Dear John*."

I feel light-headed and my heart starts racing.

"Is it true?" James asks. "Are you having an affair?"

"No!" I say quickly, wrapping my arms around him and burying my head somewhere between his belly and his chest, where it naturally lands when we hug because of our height difference. I feel him relax and inhale a deep breath.

"Oh, thank you." He says, his voice charged with emotion. "I was so worried that since the other story was true that this one was too, but that this one was about something that had happened… was happening now. And then you haven't wanted to have sex so much the last few weeks, so I thought…"

"Don't worry, Baby, I'm not having sex with anyone else. I just haven't been in the mood," I assure him, hugging him tightly. That much is true.

"It was just written so differently from your other stories and there were a few references in the letter that were very familiar, like recently familiar."

I pull away and walk over to the small built-in kitchen desk where my laptop sits open. As I drop into my pretty brown and beige French damask-patterned chair, I mumble, "Well, it is based on truth. I get ideas from my life and build on them. I think all writing originates from truth."

Thoughts zip through my head like fireflies I can't quite catch. Should I tell him the truth about Parker? But Alex is right here running around at our feet, we're trying to get ready for the camping trip, Cadence will be home from school soon, and I really need to think. Is this what I want? Because I *know* that if I tell him everything, our marriage will be over.

I scroll through the "Dear John" document James has left open on my computer, even though I read it dozens of times before sending it to Parker a few days ago and could probably recite it by heart. I deleted the actual email, just like all the others before it, but I decided to save the body of the letter as a word document. I thought it might be the seed of a good novel about a whole relationship that started on Facebook, even though in my reality, the relationship never evolved past a few texts every now and then and a longing for what might have been.

> I promise I won't keep doing this, but I wanted to tell you how I felt. Although I responded hastily yesterday (in the bathroom after walking out of a movie and seeing your email!) and I said I agreed with you, I want you to know that my heart feels like it's breaking. Ending any relationship is hard for me, even if it is a forbidden one that didn't really happen. It's harder when you can't talk to anyone about it...

James wondered why it took me so long in the bathroom. I told him there was a line - you know women's restrooms - and I had to go number two, but he knows I rarely do that in public bathrooms, and I wasn't sure he bought it.

Parker and I were supposed to talk on the phone this past Monday. I was going to tell him I couldn't do this anymore, this up and down. I was going to end it this time, so he wouldn't suddenly show up in my inbox two months later just as I was getting myself back together again. But instead, he sent an email Sunday night that said he thought it was better we don't talk.

James and I were able to sneak in a rare afternoon date Sunday. His parents came over to watch the kids while we went to see *Crazy Stupid Love*, a movie all about this couple on the brink of divorce who ends up staying together. We've learned to be creative to find time alone together with two small kids. We've had some great times these past two years, despite everything. He's loosened up a bit and we just have fun together - when he's not thinking about my infidelity and I'm not fighting the desire to do it again.

I got Parker's email as the movie got out.

"I need to move on with someone who is available, and I can't do that while being secretly involved with you," it said. "I'm sorry for the rollercoaster. I promise not to contact you when I feel lonely. I wish you the best."

I quickly responded, "I agree. This isn't healthy for either one of us. I wish you an amazing life!"

After the movie, we went home and made dinner with James' parents, talking and laughing about how cute our two little girls are. The next morning Alex woke me up at 5:00, wanting rice milk, and I couldn't fall back asleep, so I headed downstairs to write a little. When I got to my computer, all I could think about was Parker. I just wanted to tell him how I felt. I knew it was a mistake, that we had ended it, said our piece and I should just leave it at that. But I didn't listen to my own voice of reason, or the voice of God within me. I pushed them both aside like I've done so many times these past few years, in order to tell Parker my thoughts about life. As if he even cared.

> I wish you all the best and I do still want to hear about your adventures, whether they include climbing mountains, getting married or having kids. It's all an adventure, and you can have whatever it is that you want. It is not too late. Don't regret the choices you made in the past because you can't change them. Just use the knowledge you have gained to make a different choice today if you want to. (I think that is for me as much as for you!)

Crap. It was a stupid idea to keep this letter. I'm like the worst criminal ever.

"It's not what you think," I say to James. "It's based on something that happened, but I'm not having an affair." Which also is technically true. Because how can you have an affair with someone you haven't seen in 15 years.

"But you can see how I would think that, right?"

I nod. Yeah. I could.

"But let's talk about it later," I say, gesturing toward Alex. "Let's get ready for our trip now."

"OK, I just couldn't handle it if you were cheating on me," he says. Yeah, I know that all too well. And even though I've spent much of my time recently wishing I wasn't married; I truly do not want to hurt James. *He's an amazing father. But does he love me for me?*

I remind myself, once again, not to focus on how I feel, or even how James feels. I've been taught that love is an action more than a feeling. It's a choice. I've read so many books - about marriage, infidelity, love addiction, boundaries, psychology.

"What if God designed marriage to make us holy more than to make us happy?" Gary Thomas asked in his book *Sacred Marriage*. In our culture, we focus so intently on seeking happiness, but as Christians, we're supposed to die to ourselves and glorify God. I try to wrap my brain around this idea of our marriage as a process of growing in intimacy and character, but maybe we're too far gone, maybe I've messed things up too much. And I feel so sad. I simply don't know how to breathe life back into our marriage. I've tried to water the grass. But it's still not turning green. I see a sprout here and there, but I don't know if it's enough to sustain either of us the rest of our lives.

Maybe I should just tell him, I think. About Parker, and everything else before him. Come clean with a full confession and put an end to the burning guilt in my heart. But how? I've already appeased him with my quick and fervent denial that the letter was real. He seemed so relieved, taking my word at face value.

James has always had a naivety about him, an innocence, but I know he's not stupid, and he doesn't trust me still. Yet it's almost like he chooses not to delve into things that might be unpleasant. Instead, he acts stony and indifferent, as if he doesn't care at all. Which makes me feel even further away from him. I wish I could go back and undo it, make a different choice and stay in the beautiful bubble where Jesus' love was enough to cover any lack in our imperfect human relationship. *But I guess it wasn't enough for me, was it?*

The camping spot near Clear Creek in Northern Arizona is beautiful; grassy and shaded with big green trees. It doesn't even feel like Arizona. I imagine how gorgeous it will be in a month or so when the leaves start to change color. We don't see changing leaves in the Phoenix valley.

Our group has every level of camping equipment, from a fully equipped brand-new Class A motorhome; to a sleek toy hauler; an older, but well-cared-for pop-up trailer; one guy's set-up in the bed of his pick-up truck; to our family's brand new four-person tent, which will be a lot "cozier" than the used Class C RV we recently sold to pay off debts.

When we arrive, our friends have all set up their various contraptions in a large semicircle, and someone has already tied a small tire swing from the limbs of a huge oak tree behind our spot. Some of the boys have brought motorized dirt bikes, which they ride round and round the outskirts of the large campground in full protective gear. This isn't the kind of camping I'm used to. I haven't camped much at all since college, and back then, with Outdoor Adventures, it was a primitive, natural style of camping, only packing what you could carry on your back, and never a campfire or a motorized vehicle in sight.

I think about Parker and wish he were here with me now. James is cold and distant. *How did we get so far apart?* I wonder sadly, knowing it's all my fault.

"We would have stayed in our tent and only come out when we had to for our courses..." Parker texted one time.

"Why didn't you tell me or act on it?" I asked. "You had to have known I liked you. I was always pretty good at making my feelings obvious."

"I did. But I was so shy. You would have had to sit on my lap for anything to happen."

"Who would have known that was all I had to do! I just assumed you weren't interested in me. That I wasn't outdoorsy, tough enough for you."

"You were perfect. You were beautiful."

I don't know why I was the last to know. And I wish it didn't matter so damn much to me now. Why do I care so much about what other guys think about me? Why is it so important to be desired by men?

I remember a conversation with my mom, just after I left the timeshare job. After hearing about the affair with Brock and my feelings for him, she started talking about how it was all because I had never received the validation and acceptance that I so deeply craved from my dad.

"Really?" I asked, thinking that sounded like some psychological mumbo jumbo, but at the same time, realizing the truth of her words. My dad was there, in our home. They didn't get divorced until after I graduated from college and was living all alone across the country. But he wasn't truly present. He was busy with work, emotionally unavailable, not really interested in coming to my plays, concerts, awards ceremonies. Like most dads, I guess... though James isn't like that with the girls. He's a wonderful dad. He loves spending time with them, we laugh together at their silliness, and we both make sure they know they are loved, no matter what.

But even if I didn't get every little thing I needed from my dad, why wasn't James enough to fill me up? Why wasn't God enough? Why did this come back to haunt me so many years later and why can't I just get over it now? I had a good childhood. I wasn't abused or mistreated. Why do I have these deep feelings of unworthiness still? Why do I feel so sad and empty? I pick up my Bible and try to read, but the words blur, and I can't feel God's voice in this moment of despair.

After unpacking from the trip and doing several loads of laundry when we get home Monday, I meet my sister-in-law Amanda at Starbucks. We like to meet up every now and then, chat about life married to the brothers and other girly stuff. She knows about the trouble in our marriage, and I think she understands in a way no one else does. I've mentioned flirting with Parker before, but tonight I tell her the whole story, including the letter James found Friday.

"I actually wrote, 'If I thought you wanted a real relationship with me, I would consider leaving my husband for you.' James read those words!" I sigh. Amanda and I decide that I'll just forget about Parker and put all my energy into my marriage. Telling James would only hurt him and slow down the process of saving our marriage.

But when I get home from Starbucks, James is acting funny. He asks me what we talked about.

"Everything and nothing, "I say.

"Was that a real letter? Did you send that letter in an email to someone?" he asks pointedly when we get up to bed, looking me in the eye. The direct confrontation and very specific question surprises me, and I pause just long enough that he knows I did. I can't lie outright to his face. A direct question deserves a direct answer.

"Yes," I say.

"Well, I don't think I can be married to someone who does this," he says.

Part of me is relieved. But the roller coaster ride isn't quite over yet.

CHAPTER 15

Turn Around

September 12, 2011

Our new counselor, Vale sits with his hands in his lap, his soft blue eyes thoughtful as he listens to our story. I can feel his empathy and understanding, for both of us.

I share my story - the half-truth mostly honest version of it that James knows, about the emotional affair and kiss with Brock, and then the virtual emotional affair with Parker. I've been editing out the middle part where I actually committed adultery for two years now, so I can't simply add it back in now.

"If you died today, Danielle, do you think you know what would happen to you, where you would go?" Vale asks.

"No. I guess I don't. I know that if I believe in Jesus and he has saved me, my sins are forgiven and I go to heaven, regardless of what I have done. But I don't know if I do believe in Jesus, if I ever was really saved, and I don't know if I do believe the Bible is true. My actions certainly don't show that's what I believe."

"OK," he says, thoughtful. To James he says, "She doesn't know her place in this world, in her faith, in her marriage. She's lost."

I once was lost, but now I'm found. But now lost again? Maybe. I have confessed my sins to God, but do I need to also confess them all to James? I want to do this right. I have already done so much wrong. I don't want to hurt him anymore. But could we still heal without him knowing the whole ugly truth?

James reaffirms his commitment to forgive me and stay together. Because that's what he's been told he should do. That's the righteous thing to do. And he's the righteous one. But in rare moments of honesty he admits, "I'm not God. I can't just forgive and forget. I see visions of you with another guy, over and over. I'll never be OK with what you did to me."

One night, he says to me, "You're the most selfish person I know."

Nothing could sting me more. I've learned that the opposite of love isn't hate, but selfishness. I don't want to be a selfish person. I don't want to hurt people. It's the very opposite of the type of person I have always tried to be…thought I was…know I must still be…somewhere deep inside.

Sometimes I try to forgive myself every day. And I quickly forgive James every single time he slices me with his insults, hoping my forgiveness of the little daily ways he hurts me will help him forgive the unforgivable way I've hurt him. He has every right to be angry. I accept the insults, which are true. Breathe them in. I deserve it, even more than he knows. I pray for forgiveness even while I don't believe I'm worthy of it.

Reading up on forgiveness, I learn that most of us misunderstand what it means to forgive. When you forgive someone, you don't condone their vicious act. You simply release yourself from the hold it has on *you*. When you forgive, you release a prisoner - but the prisoner isn't the other person. It's you. I try to share my new understanding with James, but my words don't penetrate. In the Bible there's a story about Peter asking Jesus how many times he must forgive someone who has hurt him.

"Should I forgive him seven times," Peter asks. And Jesus says, "Not just seven, but 70 times seven."

My mind flits back to those elementary school times tables. I had to repeat them over and over before I finally memorized them. Math never came easy. I hated the times tables and sevens were the hardest. *Seven times three is 21. Seven times four is 28. Seven times five is....* I can picture my mom calmly drilling them into me, assuring me that knowing times tables would be important in life. *Seven times seven is 49...so seven times 70 is...490.*

"We are all adulterers at heart," Vale reminds James. "In God's eyes, one sin is no worse than another, even though to us humans, certain sins cut deeper than others. God can forgive *anything*."

The question of whether to tell James everything gnaws at me. But I worry that the whole truth would break him. I don't want to reopen his tender wounds and pour acid inside them. Maybe *not* telling him is the more loving thing to do. But then there would always be a lie between us. It's like a cavity in a tooth. If you don't get the whole thing out, you'll always have that decay in there, rotting away. I would always have this horrible truth rotting away at my heart. I have to tell him the whole truth.

A client gave us a gift card to PF Chang's, so we get to enjoy dinner out, even though we're still broke. We sit at the bar - no kids, my mom at home with them so we could go out on a date.

"I want to know everything. I want to have all the cards laid out on the table, so I know how to play my hand," James says. We finish dinner and the last few swallows of our drinks, then drive over to a little grassy area near a lake across the street. I point out the condos I sold the year before we met. I'm stalling.

Finally, I launch into the story of my life, including all the boys before James, from my first time at 17 with Kyle who was 19, to the time Ian forced himself on me in the backseat of my car in the weeks between Rocky Point and our divorce. I didn't call it rape. He was still my husband. But the encounter was quick, hard, punishing. Not a mutual loving act. I guess he felt like I deserved it, he was entitled to me. And I didn't disagree. I didn't hold it against him. I knew even then that hurt people hurt people.

I take a deep breath, as I prepare to tell James the parts of the story that he doesn't already know. I tell him about how I lied to him when I said Brock didn't work there anymore, because I desperately wanted to keep working. Tears sting my eyes and I start hyperventilating. This is a bad idea. I can't say these words to my husband. But he gently encourages me to continue, and I tell him what happened that last day. How I stopped it, but not in time. Another man had been inside me, even if just for a moment. I can almost feel his heart breaking into pieces.

He maintains his composure far better than he did the first time, when I told him about the kiss two years ago. But he's visibly shattered. He quietly demands to know if that is all. I tell him about Parker, our history and how the emotional affair came about, how I almost went to visit him. He's not as concerned about Parker since it was only in my head. But to me, what I had with Parker matters even more than the physical stuff. It's powerful, painful, and fresh.

James wants to know if there's *more*: additional instances of infidelity, other guys. But I can't talk any more. I need a break. We get into his truck and drive the mile or so to Harkins Theatres to see *Courageous*, a Christian movie about fatherhood, family, and love. As I sit next to James in the darkened theater, I see his jaw working, his mind creating film reels of all my indiscretions instead of focusing on what's a genuinely good movie playing in front of us.

Afterward, at home in bed, he asks if I have anything else to tell him, again looking into my eyes and asking so directly that I can't possibly lie. So, I tell him about the brief texting flirtation with Chase that resulted in nothing physical, but more and more breaking of my heart and our marriage. Then, hesitantly, I tell him about the one-night stand with the boy from the bar.

The next day James mopes around the house, broken. He can't work or even eat. I urge him to call his friends, lean on them for support, and he follows my advice.

In the afternoon we're in the kids' room, sitting on the carpeted floor watching them play. The girls start bickering and Cadence hits Alex, right in front of us. She looks at us and quickly apologizes to her sister. Alex, without any encouragement from us, leans over and hugs Cadence and says, "I forgive you." She looks over at James and me and says in her sweet three-year-old voice, her blue eyes huge and adorable, "When someone says I'm sorry like that, you don't say 'I *don't* forgive you.' You say, 'I forgive you.' That's what you say."

James and I look at each other, incredulous. It's like a message from above. I will think of her sweet voice each time I utter or hear that three-word phrase, "I forgive you." Such simple words. But so hard to say when we've been truly hurt.

Later, James and I are in the hallway, arguing softly, and Cadence walks up.

"What are you guys fighting about, Mommy?" she asks.

"We're not fighting, just talking."

"Well then what are you talking about?"

"Well, you know how you sometimes disobey and do what you are not supposed to do and then have to ask God for forgiveness? Well, grown-ups do that too. Nobody is perfect. Remember the story of the forbidden fruit in the Garden of Eden? God had told Adam and Eve not to eat it, but they did anyway, and then they had to leave the perfect garden, and ever since then, we all have sin. But Jesus forgives us. That's what we are talking about."

"Oh," she says, walking away with a smile on her face.

"Wow," James says, "You just shared the gospel with our daughter, completely naturally."

"Guess God can use any circumstances to accomplish His goals," I say, thinking of my favorite Bible story, Joseph and the Coat of Many Colors, where Joseph's brothers sell him into slavery and many years later, he says to them, "You meant it for evil, but God meant it for good."

I believe in this moment that God could turn even this mess into something good, and we hold on some months longer, trying desperately to put back together the pieces of our shattered marriage.

I fill pages and pages with scenes, letters, and journal entries about our roller coaster ride, up and down, up and down, up and down. I furiously write the first draft of my memoir as I'm living it, trying to conclude it in some sweeping dramatic way, like a Disney movie where love and faith conquer all. But every time I think I've reached a good ending point, and we really are going to make it, we hurl down another drop on the track and my heart falls along with the speeding, rickety coaster car. I want to scream at myself to just get off the damned ride already.

James writes me a letter about the feelings he was having right before the thing with Brock started, when I was first working that job with the odd hours that I thought fit our schedule so perfectly.

"I have been 'engrossed' in your actions and have not been able or willing to look at my own actions during that time. I know that if I had tried harder to be supportive of you and your desires, and meet your needs better, things would have been different."

"I stopped praying for you," he confesses. "In fact, I kind of stopped praying all together. I intentionally made it as hard for you as I could...My resentment turned to bitterness and those feelings were never dealt with. They were buried under alcohol. At night when I got the kids to sleep, I would have a drink, alone in our house wishing you were sitting next to me..."

It's nice to hear him finally taking a bit of responsibility, but I feel mournful as I read his words - if only I had seen how he was hurting, if only we had *really* talked back then, when the first cracks in our marriage started appearing. I wish I had felt comfortable talking to him about my feelings and doubts, too. But that's just not the way he was raised, the kind of faith he had. He has such a black and white way of seeing things, that I was afraid if I told him the truth about my doubts, he'd think I was an unbeliever. So, I buried those feelings deep in my heart. If we had both been more honest, maybe we wouldn't be here. Maybe I wouldn't have looked for attention outside our marriage. We could have together created a field of protection around us that nothing could penetrate. But instead, we walked around one another, not really seeing the other at all. Engrossed in our own feelings was a good way to put it.

After an emotional conversation that ends with me praying fervently for us both and our marriage, I lay on top of James and hold him. Our bodies start responding and it's like an invisible force takes over. Maybe other people experience this all the time, sex as a deep spiritual joining of two people, but not me. I have always inexplicably held back, especially with James, I realize now. Maybe I was self-conscious about being so much more experienced than him.

"That was God," I say to James when we finish together, mesmerized.

"Yes, it was."

I decide to try Celebrate Recovery, a Christ-centered 12-step program for people struggling with hurt, pain, or addiction of any kind. It meets at a nearby church, so I show up at a meeting one night and they separate us into groups based on what kind of addiction we struggle with.

But I find myself checking out a cute guy across the room during the large group meeting before we break up into smaller groups by gender, and I realize that most of the guys I've been attracted to were addicts themselves. I decide that Celebrate Recovery isn't the right place for me to work through my issues right now. Not going back feels brave, a turning away, a repentance. Instead of focusing on myself and my addiction, I learn to turn away from it, focus instead on what is good and right - my kids, my home, my husband, my God.

I start to break the cycle of my addiction and run whenever a situation crosses the line or I feel myself getting high. I have to say no a surprising number of times. A chiropractor that brushes up against me just so during my first adjustment. I don't go back for a second one. Another friend on Facebook who starts chatting me up and telling me I'm beautiful and he should have dated me in high school. I cut it off immediately and tell him thank you, but I'm married. There are a hundred different ways you have to say no to your drink of choice when it's attention you crave and it's coming at you from every angle. It's not always easy and I don't succeed every time. It's hard to know where the boundaries need to be when you encounter attractive men everywhere - at work, the gym, even in church and Bible study. My mind can think inappropriate thoughts about anyone, anywhere. But I can redirect my thoughts and my heart. I can become a new person. Again. And again. And again.

On a family vacation in Brian Head, Utah, in the Summer of 2012, James and I head out to ride together while my mom stays with the kids at the timeshare condo.

As we ride along the rocky crest, I think about all the ways mountain biking is a metaphor for life. You can't go back, you can only go forward, and you have to look where you *want* to go, not where you *don't* want to go. But you also can't look ahead too far, or keep your eyes fixed too high, or you'll miss the rocks coming up in your path. You have to see the obstacles coming your way and head straight toward them. That way you gently roll over the rocks and gullies, quads and hamstrings flexed, prepared and strong rather than caught by surprise.

"You're such a good climber," James says, when I make it up a short, steep incline without having to get off my bike and walk it. But it's the long, hard, boring stretches where I falter. "You need to push through it, past the threshold," he encourages, knowing I want to stop halfway up the steep two-mile uphill portion. It feels good when I finally get to the top without stopping. I'm glad I didn't give up. I need to do that in my life too, I think, instead of always looking for a different trail, a better path I should have taken, or could possibly switch over to now.

It's nice when James is in a hopeful, happy mood instead of an angry, punishing one. I never knew words could cut so deeply. *Sticks and stones may break my bones, but words will never hurt me,* my mom's chant reverberates. But it's not true. Words sometimes hurt even more than broken bones.

After dinner, James and I grab a blanket from the truck, thinking maybe we'll go have some fun beneath the stars. It's the blanket they gave me after my crash at the 24-hour race. It still has a sticker on it that says, "disaster blanket." The name makes me laugh ironically.

"Danielle's disaster blanket," I say, "for Danielle the disaster."

"More like Danielle the Destroyer," James says, a lightness in his voice despite his words. We have sex after that, in our comfortable hotel bed, not under the stars on the disaster blanket, in the bed of the truck, or on the front seat. It feels like neither a sweet lovemaking nor a carnal fuck session, but more a disconnected going-through-the-motions kind of sex. And I don't know how to fix what I have destroyed, or if it was even there to begin with.

One day James and I are discussing divorce and he says, "But there are just so many reasons to stay together: the kids, what would people say?"

"Why do you care so much about what people say?"

He doesn't answer, so I do.

"We already know what they say. They all say we should stay together. But none of them is in our marriage, here with us. Only we can decide what's right for us. In all your reasons why we should stay together, is any one of them because you love me so much you can't imagine your life without me, you want to grow old with me, you don't want to lose me?" I ask, knowing the answer.

"No," he admits.

"Well, there you go."

"You know, even if we didn't have this big, huge thing between us, there would always be ups and downs…"

"Yeah, but we do have this big thing, and I believe with every part of me that it will happen again if we stay together. I believe, *once a cheater always a cheater*. It's evident everywhere. I never understood why people who cheat on their spouses end up marrying the person they had the affair with. You know it's going to happen again!"

I swallow any argument I may have against his logic, stay calm.

"I think you should talk to a therapist, regardless of what happens with us," I say.

"I don't need a therapist. I just need to ignore the bad feelings. The only time it goes away is when I ignore it and feel nothing. Any emotion I feel, good or bad, brings it back."

"But you can't live like that. No matter what happens with me, you're going to be around people. You got to live. You need to learn some coping mechanisms."

"Coping mechanisms. I shouldn't need coping mechanisms," he mutters angrily.

"Everyone needs to find ways to cope with the hard things in life. Did you think your life would just be perfect, easy, that you'd never have to deal with anything hard?"

"No, I didn't think my life would be perfect. I just didn't think my wife would fucking cheat on me!" he says.

"I know. I didn't either, believe it or not. But I can assure you, that whether I am married to you or not, I will never cheat again," I say confidently, stepping into the truth and strength of these words. "Because it's not worth it. It doesn't feel good. There is nothing good about it. I broke my heart, too, with the choices I made."

I used to believe in living life with no regrets. But this I truly, completely, regret. But I'm tired of being in limbo. Three years. That's a very long time. I've tried everything I know how to do. I stopped the destructive behavior, confessed it to God, confessed it to James, repented. I have tried to be the best wife I can be. But he doesn't want to live with someone who has been unfaithful. And that simple fact underlies everything else. Even when things between us seem to be going well, the slightest thing sets him off and his true feelings come lashing out.

This week we got in a fight about sex. He got angry because I wasn't into it. And all I could say was, "I'm sorry." Because I can go through the motions and try, but I can't make myself feel what we both wish I would. Many times, I have tears in my eyes when we have sex. I want good sex, too. But our bond is broken, despite all the work we have done to repair it, and it comes out in the bedroom. It's like Humpty Dumpty who has fallen off the wall. All the king's horses and all the king's men can't put Humpty back together again.

We're in our bedroom a few days before Christmas, the ninth anniversary of my becoming a Christian. I've just gotten home from an early morning marathon training run, cold and sweaty at the same time, getting ready to hop in the shower, and he's just woken up. He's telling me about a nightmare he had last night. In the dream we kept running into all these different guys and each time, I introduced them as someone I had "fucked," a word I almost never say and certainly would never use in that context, even if his dream was true. But that's beside the point.

He says he kept waking up and going back to sleep and having the same dream over and over, like Groundhog Day. And it sounds so familiar, just like our life. We keep going over and over the same ups and downs and never really getting anywhere, like running on a treadmill.

"I'm so sorry," I say, squeezing my eyes shut. "It's just a dream. It's not true. I'm not doing that," I try to assure him.

"But it is true!" he snaps. "You did cheat on me. You did fuck other men," he reminds me, once again, as if I could have forgotten.

Only two, and only one time each, I want to say. But I know it doesn't matter. It only takes one time to make it official. And yet I'm ready to move on from this identity as *Adulterer*, put on the cloak of God's righteousness, and become a better version of myself. Something snaps open inside me, like a caged bird breaking free, and I just let go - of all my explaining and rationalizing and striving.

"You are never going to forgive me, are you?" I ask. "You are never going to let me live this down, never going to see me as anything more than the woman who cheated on you, who shattered you."

He stares at me, unable to deny it.

"Well, I am truly sorry. I wish I could undo it. I've said that a thousand times. But you know I can't. I have confessed. I have repented, and I am doing the best I can. But it's never going to be good enough for you. *I'm* never going to be good enough for you."

"I don't know," he says.

"Let's just stop doing this," I say.

"You're just giving up? That's a harsh reaction to my nightmare."

"This is not a reaction to your nightmare. I am very sorry about your dream. I'm sorry for *all* I have done to hurt you. This is something I've been thinking and feeling for a while now and your dream just brought it to the surface," I say. "I just can't do this anymore."

I'm no longer hopeless in my brokenness. I have found redemption and freedom in God's forgiveness. But I must get down off this roller coaster that our life has become. And I truly don't believe James will ever again see me as anything more than the woman who cheated on him, *The Adulterer*. And I am ready to be more than that. I'm ready to let it go.

PART TWO

Growth and Resilience

CHAPTER 16

Chasing Butterflies

FEBRUARY 2013

*"Just when the caterpillar thought the world was over,
he became a butterfly."*

The butterfly - majestic, colorful, fluttering from bloom to bloom - is considered a symbol of transformation across cultures and religions.

Even as I'd cuddle in next to each of my baby girls over the years to read the beloved children's story, *The Little Caterpillar*, I'd contemplate the butterfly's impressive metamorphosis: from tiny egg, to growing caterpillar, to cozy cocoon, to its eventual emergence from darkness, becoming the beautiful, graceful, free-flying creature we know.

But it doesn't get there easily. I've read that it's only through the perfect timing of the butterfly's eclosion - emergence from the chrysalis - and the chemicals released during that slow, deliberate struggle - that the butterfly can fly. If you were to try to help it along prematurely, it would emerge weak, dull, its wings useless. Newly emerged butterflies must also hang upside down for a time so their wings can expand and dry properly. If they don't have room to do this, they will be grounded for life by deformed wings.

The struggle and the timing are key to the butterfly's development and freedom. And I suppose this is true in our own lives, too. We often resist hard work, try to take the easy way out, do the minimal necessary, look for shortcuts. We want a quick fix. I wonder how much we stunt our growth and clip our own wings when we do this.

James and I are in the process of divorce but still living under the same roof, getting ready to list the house for sale, working out the millions of details and loose ends that must be tied up in order to dissolve our marriage and our life together. We haven't told the kids yet. We'll do that this weekend. We're committed to sharing custody 50/50 and making sure they know they are loved by us both.

We've already told our families the news, and James' family has stopped talking to me completely. I've always known that the way my family stays connected even in divorce is unusual. But I've been part of his family for almost nine years, and even though I knew my relationship with each of them would change, I didn't expect them to cut off all contact. I was naïve. Maybe my mom did me a disservice in teaching me unconditional love. Maybe regular people can't forgive when they've been hurt so deeply. I feel hopeless, broken, and sad.

So, I run. Running has become my therapy, my social life, my chrysalis. I'm training for a full marathon - 26.2 miles. And I feel like I've finally mastered the long hard slog, pushing past that threshold to stick with and finish this monumental task I've started. I was never a runner - running was yet another thing I told myself I wasn't good at as a child, until eventually I believed it. But amazingly and quite unexpectedly, now in my late 30s, I've transformed myself into a runner - one of the hardest and most rewarding things I've done yet.

As for the rest of my metamorphosis, that's still a work in progress. The butterfly's entire life cycle is only 28 days long, its metamorphosis complete in just a month. One lunar cycle. We humans have much more time than that to screw things up, but also more time to learn and grow from our mistakes, and eventually emerge from the rubble. I'm learning to be patient with myself and others.

Piece of Work

Sitting outside the Starbucks near our house after a 15-mile marathon training run with my running group, sipping cold water and warm coffee, I feel good. They talk about a runner's high, but for me, running isn't so much a drug, not in that desperate, needy way that the attraction and attention was. It's more like a safe harbor, a bridge, easing me gently away from even needing a drug to feel better.

The running group provides a built-in health-conscious social life. We meet at Starbucks several times a week for early morning runs followed by coffee and conversation, get together for happy hours and even a book club. I fell into the group about a year ago when I decided I wanted to become a triathlete and started taking baby steps toward accomplishing that enormous goal. My whole life I had believed that God just didn't create me to run. My boobs were too big, my hips too wide, my legs too short. I had never felt a runner's high or learned to love the feeling of my heart pounding out of my chest. In elementary school, I was not only the shortest kid in the class, but also the very slowest runner and the last one picked for every team in PE.

But last year, I decided I wanted to become a runner. And sometimes all you need to do to make something happen is believe that it can, then take one step at a time until you get there.

I gathered up my nerve and showed up for a group run, and four or five ladies singled me out and inducted me into the "JV Group."

Since then, I worked up to a half marathon and now I'm grinding toward a full one. I'm constantly amazed by the athletes in this group, many of whom are 15 to 20 years older than me and could easily outrun me. I didn't know that regular people could continue to improve their fitness and win races in their 40s, 50s, 60s and beyond. They're an inspiration.

Running, for me, is about striving for the next goal that's just a little out of reach, like fireflies you can't quite catch in your jar, or butterflies that you'll never fully capture. Butterflies *look* like they're just fluttering aimlessly, yet they're powerful symbols of resurrection, transformation, and celebration - reminding us to keep the faith as we undergo change in our lives. I want to be a butterfly.

A few weeks later, I'm feeling exhausted but amazing as my friend Zoe and I make the final push toward our unofficial Starbucks finish line after a 20-mile training run. The fact that I have just *run* 20 miles with Zoe - a real runner, gorgeous with her long, lean legs - astounds me.

After several hours together, we've gotten to know each other well. I've shared stories about my family, divorce, infidelity, struggle, and faith. I'm maybe a little too candid about all that. But it's important to me that people know right up front that it's my fault James and I are getting divorced, that I was unfaithful to him. I want to offer this, at least, to him: taking all the blame for our failure to stay together forever like we promised God we'd do. I know at some level that nothing is ever completely one person's fault; but taking all the responsibility instead of trying to pin part of the blame on him is freeing, healing even. And if I'm already blaming myself, sharing the whole sordid tale with anyone who will listen, then I don't have to worry about what they may hear from someone else.

As Zoe and I turn the corner and jog the final feet to the patio, where cyclists lean their bikes against cement pillars and couples and families enjoy a relaxing late Saturday morning coffee break, I catch sight of two achingly familiar faces sitting there - Luke and Amanda. It's been several weeks since I've seen them, when before we'd get together for a family dinner, a pool party, something at least once a week. I nudge Zoe and tell her that's my brother- and sister-in-law, and I start to move toward them quickly, automatically, to say hello.

The scene moves into slow motion as I forget for a moment that we aren't talking, that they no longer consider me their sister. I walk up to their table, breathless, exhilarated, proud of the run I've just completed, and genuinely happy to see them. Amanda looks up, gives me an awkward smile, but Luke - Luke does this thing that absolutely stops me in my tracks. He stares right through me, as if there is *no one* standing in front of him. He's stone-faced. I'm not even sure how he's able to display such an emptiness of expression. No happiness, anger, sadness - just nothing. It's the most shocking treatment I've ever received, to be so completely ignored by someone I love, really love. Until this moment, I thought he would always be my brother, no matter what happened between James and me. Just like I told Amanda that I'd always consider her my sister when she and Luke were contemplating divorce years ago.

I back away, stung. A few months ago, when James told him we were getting divorced, Luke told me he was angry with me, but he didn't hate me. Apparently, he's changed his mind.

There's really nothing to do but move on with my day, shaky with shock as if I've just been in a car accident. I try to drink my coffee and chat with my friends. But I can't stop thinking about Luke and Amanda. I want to fix things, explain to Luke all the intricacies of our marriage and divorce, tell him that it wasn't just me who decided one day to give up on our marriage. That James could not forgive me, and I could not live in that unforgiven state. Even though I said the words that finally put our divorce into motion, James had been telling me for three years - in so many ways - that he no longer wanted to be married to me. I finally let him off the hook.

Eventually, I work out that there is nothing I could say that would make them understand my point of view in this. So, I will just keep on loving them, even if they have no love left for me. That's, I think, what Jesus would do.

It's hard not to explain myself. My deepest need has always been to be understood. I think again of the butterfly, full of lightness, brightness, joy, and bliss. Maybe it's time to just be wholly myself, honoring the successes I've had, living in the moment, without worrying quite so much about how others perceive me. Time to embrace the changes and complete my metamorphosis. Into what, I don't know.

Standing next to the king-sized bed in our large bright master bedroom, I'm deep in thought as I fold laundry while watching HGTV. It's one of those shows where they take half an hour to get through

10 minutes of footage, but I find it relaxing to watch people on TV fix up homes. James and I have fixed up a few houses together over the past few years - new paint and flooring, fixtures, a good cleanup. And now here I am tearing apart our own home.

I pull a small pink cotton shirt up to my face and breathe in the clean scent, pushing away the thought that I'm making a horrible mistake. It's the Sunday before Easter, Palm Sunday. I always feel reflective on Sundays. It's usually a day off from running, after a long run Saturday. I'm still in recovery mode after completing the marathon on March 2, getting ready to head to Carmel, California with a few friends to run the Big Sur Marathon next month. As I fold the never-ending pile of little girls' shirts and flowery dresses, my own jeans and lacy underwear, James' boxer briefs and t-shirts, I wonder if he remembers how to do his own laundry. I've been doing it for almost nine years. Our divorce will be final in a matter of weeks, just a few days before our anniversary, then Cadence's birthday, then James' birthday. We always did have a lot of important dates in the spring. Now I've added one more. Divorce: April 18.

But I feel compelled to continue right up until the end - folding his shirts and neatly piling them on our bed, only to be unfolded again and hung on plastic hangers in our closet. Our closet. I'm not even sure where to begin to separate what's mine from what's his. The clothes, of course are easy, but what about pictures, music, memories from nine years of marriage? The house is under contract and my lease on the new townhouse starts May 1, so we're all under one roof until then. But I'll have to start packing soon.

I don't really feel like going to church today. Am I even a Christian still? Am I still Jewish? Am I saved? Was I really forgiven? Maybe I should just watch a movie - a nice, fun, easy chick flick. James is taking the girls to "his" church, which was "our" church up until a few months ago. I know without anyone telling me that I won't be welcome there now, and it would be awkward anyway.

We met with Vale a few weeks ago for one last counseling session at the church, and he was a gracious and understanding as ever. I let him read the seething letter James' father, Glenn wrote me upon learning of my infidelity and our impending divorce. It was full of hateful words that cut to my core, but I had wanted to keep it, if for no other reason than to remember his words. But Vale encouraged me to destroy it. He said those were *not* Godly admonitions, and my sins were *not* unpardonable by God. I was *not* too far gone for God's grace. I burned the letter unceremoniously and threw away the ashes. That felt good. But I do still wish I had kept it, despite the pain that reading it caused me - or maybe because of that.

It's James' week with the girls. Even though we're all still living together, we've decided to start separating our time with them, to practice for divorce. But I don't really want to be alone today. James walks into the room to get dressed for church.

"Do you think I could just go with you guys today," I ask quietly, my voice high-pitched with emotion.

"Absolutely not," he replies with a steely stare. He's so angry, so hurt. I did that to him. To us. To me. I feel unbelievably guilty, sad, and lonely as he leaves for church with my babies. Maybe it's at least partially hormonal - that time of the month, but I feel like tears could erupt at any moment. It's like I've lost my place in this world. The thought reminds me of that soaring Michael W. Smith melody, one of the songs on the cassette tape Lewis burned for me in college, planting a seed of Christianity all those years ago. A seed that took root many years later, until I uprooted it, along with the strong foundation of my marriage and my life. And now I'm completely unmoored.

Even though I don't want to go alone, I feel a stirring in my heart to go to the neighborhood church we stopped by a few times over the years and that I've visited several more times now that James doesn't have a say. He didn't like the teaching, the music. But maybe God has something for me there today. I could use a sign of hope.

I walk in and stand hesitantly at the back of the sanctuary, scanning the rows for a familiar face. When I don't see any of the few friends I know who come here, I walk straight to the front. James never liked to sit up front, but I was always a front sitter before James. In every class or meeting where there were rows to sit in, I'd be right up front, ears perked, ready to soak up the learning. So now that I'm all alone, I decide I will be a front sitter again. I look over to my right and notice I'm sitting a few seats down from the head pastor and his wife. They don't know me yet. I give them a shy smile as the worship music begins. Tears leak from my eyes as I sing the beautiful words about Jesus, salvation, peace, and love. I wipe them away, trying to keep my emotions in check.

Carl, one of the associate pastors, walks out onto the stage as a large photograph on the screen behind him takes my breath away. An orthodox Jew, maybe a rabbi, complete with prayer shawl - *tallit*, and head covering- *kippah*, stands between one man who looks like a Catholic priest and another who appears to be a Muslim religious leader. I smile. This is either the beginning of a joke - a rabbi, a priest and an imam walk into a bar - or a message meant just for me.

Carl has recently returned from a trip to Israel and preaches a message about peace amid chaos. And with every word he speaks, I can feel God saying, "Thanks for coming. You were right. I have prepared a message specifically for you, Danielle. You are *my child*. Jewish, Christian, it doesn't matter. *You* are my child. And this is for you. Church is for you. *This* church is for you. Keep coming here and you will be fed."

The sky is bright blue and cloudless as James and I walk into the Mesa courthouse on April 18, still married, then walk back out divorced an hour later, the blinding sun bright despite the melancholy in our hearts.

It's too easy and doesn't feel real yet. Joint custody of our babies, our assets neatly divided, the proceedings quick and formal. James unfriends and blocks me on Facebook, and I post: "Sad day for me, but it's the first day of the rest of my life and I am optimistic for this next chapter."

I receive 83 encouraging comments, but one hits me in the gut. It's from Amanda, my now-ex-sister-in-law, who's been one of my best friends for almost 10 years.

"Don't really know what to say…this is all very sad and difficult and I'm not ready to jump on the 'next chapter' bandwagon. Praying for you, James, and the girls. Praying for all of our extended family too as this affects all of us. May God be near when we're hurting and fill our hearts with peace and hope."

She unfriends me soon after. She doesn't understand that looking forward to the next chapter is the only way I know how to live. It's who I am. It doesn't mean I'm not ashamed, broken, repentant, and sad. I am. But you can't go back. You can only go forward.

Later that night, I receive a private message from Josh, a guy I dated briefly between high school and college, a carefree summer spent with my best friend Mae. Josh and I were part of a small group of kids who hung out at Mae's so much that summer that her mom joked about putting us to work to earn our keep.

"Hey Danielle, saw your post but didn't want to post publicly. Sorry to hear what you're going through, I'm in the middle of mine myself. Surround yourself with positive people and remember it's ok to feel bad and mourn. It gets easier. If you ever need to talk, I'm always around. Good luck," Josh writes.

"Thanks, Josh. Sorry to hear that. Marriage is hard! Would love to catch up. Feel free to call me sometime…"

I hope he will. It would be nice to reminisce about old times and be comforted by someone familiar from my past, from a time long before I created all this heartbreak.

CHAPTER 17

Where do I Belong?

May 2013

Five weeks later, lying on the carpeted floor of my new bedroom in the townhouse I've rented a few blocks from the home we've just put on the market, I pound my fists and stomp my feet into the scratchy gray carpet, feeling panicky and fragile.

My dad has agreed to pay the rent, and in exchange, I will take care of Nana, who's 91 now and starting to show signs of dementia. The downstairs master will be hers. My room is the second master, directly above hers. And, separated from my room by a long hallway and a small loft area, is a third *en suite* bedroom that will be for Heidi, our German foreign exchange student. She's been with us since January, when our first student, Kiana went home to Brazil after spending the fall semester in our home, just as our marriage was imploding. Cadence and Alex, now seven and almost five, will sleep in the open loft area between the two upstairs bedrooms. The movers will be here tomorrow with my furniture and the boxes that contain my half of our stuff.

But tonight, it's just me. All alone in this empty house with my thoughts and feelings. And they don't feel good. I want to take something, do something to drown out these negative emotions. I understand how someone could consider suicide. It would be easy to slip into the thought pattern that I can't deal with this pain - this pain that *I* caused, to wonder if maybe the world would be better off without me in it.

I've been banished from the big house tonight. It's Thursday, Daddy Daughter Day, and I can tell I'm going to hate Thursdays. Sitting at an inside table at the Las Sendas patio restaurant a few months ago, James and I carefully worked out a schedule for splitting our time with the girls: We'd each have them every other week, but with a midweek switch and sleepover: Mommy Daughter Day on Wednesdays and Daddy Daughter Day on Thursdays, so that neither of us is apart from them for a whole week. It's a good, reasonable, flexible plan.

I could feel James beginning to erect an angry wall between us when we first began to negotiate the terms of our divorce, but I refused to fight him on anything. We were able to avoid lawyers and trials. We simply hired a mediator to help with the paperwork and negotiations, just like Ian and I had. I know how ugly divorce can be. I know that hurt people hurt people. I remember how Ian smashed every picture frame in our living room and cleared out our shared bank account less than an hour after we agreed in our mediation session to leave the money there so I could pay our bills. Being divorced from someone can be 15 times harder than being married to them, and I simply refused to let James and I fall into that horrible game, those court battles I've heard so much about. My mom taught me that when someone is mean to me, I should *kill them with kindness*. Just as Jesus advised us to *turn the other cheek*. Not that James was ever outwardly mean. I just knew that if I wanted him to be flexible and gracious with me, I had to be flexible and gracious with him. So, we don't fight. And the girls seem OK.

What I didn't anticipate was how *not OK I* would feel, how empty and quiet my house and my life would be when the girls were with James and not with me, how it would wrench my heart to know that I was missing half their lives, the little everyday moments that you barely think about until you don't get to be there for them.

I spent the earlier part of the evening with Caleb, who's in the running group and has become a good friend. He's more than just a friend, technically a lover. But that word doesn't feel right either. We certainly care about each other, and we are involved physically, but we're each going through our own things separately and neither of us truly lets the other one in. We're comfortable companions, but it's a no-strings-attached sort of relationship that soothes but doesn't satisfy. For both of us, I think. His mom is dying of early-onset Alzheimer's, and I've been over at their house a lot the past few weeks. I watch his mom dancing in circles on the Saltillo-tiled kitchen floor, in her own world as her brain shuts down a little more each day. His dad patiently cares for her, continuing to sleep next to her even though she's mostly already gone. But I don't feel like I add anything to the equation. I guess just being there is something, but I wish I had more to offer, more help or comfort to give. Caleb is both soulful and cerebral, and so am I, despite my bubbly personality, but we lack a true connection. Maybe it's just a question of timing, but we both know the relationship is what it is for right now but isn't going anywhere. He's not ready to be saddled with a twice-divorced broken older woman with kids. And for me, sometimes being with him makes me feel lonelier than being by myself. Tonight, we were watching a movie at his house, and I just felt so sad that I left and came here, letting myself into the empty house with the key I picked up this afternoon from the landlord.

What have I done? Why did I throw everything away for this? Why couldn't I just make it work, stick it out? I wanted to be free, but this doesn't feel free at all. I gave up safety and comfort and a whole extended family, for...nothing. I'm all alone. The divorce is final. Our marriage is over. And it's all. My. Fault.

A sob and a scream fight each other in my throat, and I'm grateful no one can hear the guttural, animal sound that finally erupts from me as I sob-scream into the vacant house. Normally carefully composed, smiling, joking, always looking for the good in every situation, never allowing myself to focus on the negative, moving on quickly from pain; in this moment I feel all alone in the world. And I cry out. To God. To myself. To everyone and no one.

I allow myself these few moments of misery. Allow myself to feel the pain. And then I take a breath, feeling better already, like when you're sick to your stomach and finally puke. I breathe. In and out. And I know it will be OK. I will be OK. I can choose joy, even in sorrow. And I will fly again. And there are people who need me: Nana, Mom, Cadence, Alex, Heidi… I have more life to live. I can't let this valley define me.

I pour myself into running, CrossFit and dating to keep myself busy on the weeks I don't have the girls. I start training for the Berlin marathon. Heidi's dad works for BMW in Berlin, and when Heidi told him I had completed my first marathon in March, he said, "Your host mom is a runner? The company gave me three entries for the Berlin marathon and didn't know who to give them to since no one I know runs marathons. Do you think she and a few friends would want to come to Berlin to run a marathon?"

Uh, yes please! Three free entries into the coveted Berlin marathon in September and a built-in family to show me around? I'll take it!

Meanwhile, Nana's dementia is worse than we thought, and every morning feels like Groundhog Day as I answer the same questions over and over.

"I live here with you now? This is your house? How's your mother?" She asks in her familiar accented voice. Some days I have patience for it all and answer brightly, infusing my responses with humor and smiles. Other days, I grit my teeth and impatiently tell her I've already answered these questions a million times. I'm ashamed of my impatience on those days, grateful she forgets it within minutes.

It's early June when I message Josh: "Hey, how are you doing?"

He responds a few hours later: "I'm good…moved into my own place this weekend. How are you?"

Soon we're flirting, and a few weeks later, I book a flight to go visit him in Philadelphia. I'm single now, I tell myself. I'm allowed to fly across the country for a fling with an old flame rather than just fantasizing about it like I did with Parker. I push away the nagging thought that I'm a Christian now and shouldn't be having sex outside of marriage. *That was fine for James, but I'm too old for that.* Josh and I have a great weekend together: Authentic cheesesteaks, dinner and drinks, tourist sites, even some shopping. And of course, the physical stuff that we didn't quite get to in high school. He's fun and attractive, and I'm comforted by our shared history and current experience. I've always had this desire to hold onto friendships and romanticize the past, trying to recreate something that in fact never was. I can feel my heart falling for him even as I feel him pulling away, afraid to develop feelings when neither of us is in a place to begin a new relationship.

Beyond the fun, the weekend serves as a sort of informational interview for a new career. Josh is an employee benefits producer and I'm looking for something outside of the real estate industry, so I don't have to compete with James or run around in his circles.

True to form, when I get home, I email the president of a large insurance brokerage and tell him I'm going to be his next star producer. He hires me and I start working right after the Fourth of July weekend. The insurance business is surprisingly interesting, in the wake of Obamacare, the Affordable Care Act. I like helping companies navigate the ins and outs, and having my hands in healthcare, at least on a peripheral level. If I had it to do all over again, I would become a nurse, obstetrician, a naturopathic doctor or maybe a midwife. But that ship has sailed, so this is a good way to feel like I'm helping people indirectly with their health.

On August 15, I'm at work when I receive a Facebook friend request from Mike Tantone, another blast from the past. He's yet another guy I had a crush on, once upon a time. But in high school, he was in love with Mae, just like all the guys were. They dated for a while and then he hung around her like a puppy dog after they broke up. He and I went to one dance together as friends and hung out at Mae's house or backstage during theater productions, but he was more her friend than mine. I didn't know him well. Even so, Tantone was one of those names I tried on once upon a time, wondering how it would sound as my own - Danielle Tantone.

Today is Mae's birthday. Mike must have seen my happy birthday post and decided to connect. His profile picture is a newborn baby, so I assume he's a new dad. I message him later that night:

"What's up! Did you just have a baby? Well, not you, but did someone else just have your baby? She's beautiful."

"I'm good! She is beautiful isn't she! She's my brother's second. I don't have any kids. (Sad Emoji) You have a beautiful family as well! Looks like I really screwed up in high school! You look amazing!"

He assumes I'm still married since so many of my Facebook photos show happy family scenes. I wonder if I should delete the pictures of James now that we're divorced. But our life together is part of who I am. It produced my two beautiful children. I'll take new pictures, make new memories, but I won't delete my life, I decide.

Once Mike and I have sorted out that we are both in fact single, we start talking, but by now this Facebook flirting thing has gotten just a little cliché. And he lives in Nashville, a city I'd move to in a heartbeat if it were up to me, being a music lover, a wanna-be-singer and a fan of Southern architecture, front porches, green grass, and big trees. But James and I have agreed to stay in Mesa to maintain joint custody, so moving out of state won't be an option for at least the next 13 years, until Alex is 18 and off to college.

Mike and I start messaging back and forth, despite my reservations. After a few days of chatting, we decide to try a phone call. I discover that he hasn't set down roots in Nashville. He's there for a job - business manager for a friend's small landscaping company, but his family and friends are here in Arizona. He was only briefly married while in the Navy a few years after high school, and he doesn't have kids of his own, though he's been a father figure to a few former girlfriends' kids and absolutely loves his role as Uncle Michael to his two nieces.

But he informs me that I probably won't want to keep talking to him when I hear what he's been up to the past 20 years. He's had some dark times.

"Try me," I say. "I'm not as much of a goodie two shoes as you may think."

He launches into a story that involves overcoming meth addiction and serving time, and I feel my heart open to him. *This is someone who will understand forgiveness, grace, struggle, and growth.* I recount all my struggles these last few years and he tries to calibrate this fallen Christian version of me to the bubbly Jewish girl he knew in high school. I feel like I can tell him anything and I won't be too much for him. I'm not too Christian, too Jewish, too experienced, too loud or too passionate. I can just be me. All of me. He may not always get me, but he *sees* me. And I want to let myself be seen by him. We talk and talk, and by the time we finally hang up, it's been four hours. I find Mike passionate, real, romantic, and funny. He obviously loves kids and I bet he'd get along great with Cadence and Alex.

He needs to be a dad...Could I have another baby? I ask myself after hanging up.

Are you crazy? I respond. *You just got divorced! You wanted to enjoy the single life! What are you thinking?*

Slouching into a white rocking chair in the Charlotte airport Friday, September 13, a week after my 39th birthday, I'm on a layover on the way to Nashville to visit Mike. I pull out my phone to a text from Mae, "Are you going to Nashville to see Mike Tantone?!"

He must have posted about my visit on Facebook. She's got to be shaking her head. First Jack and now Mike. It's like I'm determined to create that high school sweetheart romance 20 years later.

In Nashville, Mike is there in the airport with flowers and a quick kiss, and we hop into his truck, a reddish-brown Ford F150, clean and vacuumed. I can tell he takes care of his things. We've been talking and writing for weeks, like an old-fashioned romance with the modern benefit of video chat. He takes me out for sushi the first night, then to the Brewhouse to hear his friend's band play. We dance to the music - a combination of Country and Rock, snapping a smiling selfie of us on this "second first date."

The next day we meet his boss, who's also a good friend, at Wine on the River, a fun fall festival event. The day is warm, and I wear a black sundress, my hair blown straight, dyed dark. I feel vibrant, healthy, and happy. On Sunday, he drops me off at a beautiful forest-filled park so I can get my training run in. The Berlin Marathon is just a few weeks away. We visit the Grand Ole Opry, stop into bars on the famous Broadway strip to listen to live music, stroll through museums, and get to know one another. This time, I think, there is a possibility for something more, and I'm ready.

My week in Berlin is magical. The marathon is so much fun. It's surreal to run through the historic city, hopping right over the foundations of the fallen Berlin Wall. Chilling to consider Germany's violent history, the Holocaust that killed six million Jews. The 26.2 miles pass easily in the balmy weather, so different from the Arizona summer heat I've trained in. I laugh incredulously when I learn that I've come in 4000th out of 40,000, top 10%.

Heidi and her family show me all over the city. The night of the race, my friend Carise and I go out for fondue with my German friend Andreas, who I dated during my Paris semester. On my last day, I coast across the gorgeous country by train to visit Munich for the real Oktoberfest. It's a bit of a letdown. I arrive at 10:00 PM on the last day of the historic celebration, and it feels like the end of a frat party, no one even noticing the beautiful authentic *dirndl* that Heidi and her mom helped me pick out at a posh department store in Berlin.

Throughout the trip, Mike and I message back and forth, building a relationship through snippets of modern love letters. The first time I write "I love you," it's in German. "Ich liebe dich." He jokingly responds "Uh, Lieberman?!!" And it becomes an inside joke. Each night while I'm in Berlin, we sign off our texting conversations, "Lieberman," accompanied by little emojis with hearts for eyes. *He loves me. And I love him.*

Mike comes to visit me in October. It's a trip home he had already planned for his 40th birthday. During the long weekend, he decides to move back to Arizona. I'm the catalyst, but not the only reason. He wants to be close to family again and he's one of those weirdos who truly loves the dry heat. I return to Nashville to visit him once more the week before Thanksgiving. In December, he loads a trailer to move to Mesa. He won't live with me, of course. Even if James would allow his kids to live with someone I'm not married to, I don't want to rush headlong into anything.

James stipulated in our divorce negotiations that he be allowed to meet anyone I'm dating before I introduce them to the kids, and I get the same courtesy. I agreed to this and anything else he asked for, refusing to let us fight over trivial things when I know we both love those girls. Since I'm ready for Mike to meet the girls, I set up a meeting between him and James. A few weeks before, James calls me, freaking out. He tells me he pulled a background check, and do I know who this guy is? He sends me a copy of the report and I understand how seeing Mike's criminal record in black and white without knowing him as a person or hearing the details behind the legal sentences would be alarming. I plead with him that they are nonviolent crimes, and he should meet him in person before making judgments. Mike writes James a letter explaining that he comes from a good solid family, spent many years making bad decisions, but that he has changed. He loves me and wants to create a life with me and my girls. It's my first taste of the reality of being married to someone with a felony on his record. Mike corrects me. He's not just "someone with a felony on his record," but a "felon." "Once a felon, always a felon." *Just like once a cheater, always a cheater?* A felony is like a life sentence, even after you've served your time, I come to know. *So, in some ways they are the same, even though my sentence is less visible and doesn't have to go on job applications. I don't wear my Scarlet Letter on my chest, but I still feel it there.*

James reluctantly gives his approval for the girls to meet Mike. The four of us go out to the movies, and by the end of the evening, they're climbing up on his lap and his back, laughing and playing like he's the Pied Piper. He's like a big kid himself, playful and easy-going. The girls start calling him Mikey and I think he will be an amazing stepdad.

Coincidentally, James has also reconnected through Facebook with someone he knew in high school and now they too are dating. I assume she doesn't have a criminal record, but I don't run a background check. I schedule a meeting with her at Joe's Farm Grill, down the street from the church where I'm singing Amazing Grace at the funeral of a friend of a friend. Singing at funerals, offering my voice as a comfort to people mourning the loss of a loved one, is a strange joy for me.

Maybe it's just that the funeral has made me emotional, grateful to be alive, but I instantly love Leah. She's my opposite in appearance and temperament: sweet and subdued, tall and blonde. An elementary school teacher with no kids of her own, I imagine she's the kind of girl James' family always wanted for him. But I don't feel threatened by her. I'm happy for him, glad that he's found someone more suited to him, and confident that I couldn't have dreamed up a better stepmom for my girls if I tried.

CHAPTER 18

God Blessed the Broken Road

February 2014

A gorgeous strapless wedding gown with a corset-like beaded top that laces up the back then flows down into a silky skirt and train hangs on a molded dress form. It looks whimsical and just a little sad up there, its tags still attached, having never fulfilled its purpose of being worn by a girl on her wedding day.

"Would you wear that?" Mike asks, winking. "No one has bid on it yet."

"I guess, if I had a reason to," I say. "It looks like it's just my size."

Mike puts his name down on the silent auction leger. Starting bid: $50.

"You're crazy," I say, shaking my head!

"You're crazy and I'm out of my mind," he sings in a little falsetto.

I break into the chorus of John Legend's hit song *All of Me*, grabbing his hands in mine as if to dance. Taking my cue, he leads me into a dance that is all our own, a haphazard combination of Swing, Two-step, Charleston, and Waltz. We laugh as we sing loudly together, not caring who hears us, and half hoping everyone does.

He leans me back into a little dip and I reach down to make sure I'm not flashing the room as my silky flowy strapless dress moves with me. James never wanted to be the center of attention. But Mike and I both love to be.

There are so many things I love about Mike. He's fun and funny. Hardworking and loyal. Sweet and sensitive and romantic. He tears up when I sing, or when something touches him in any way. And he flies off the handle when something rubs him wrong. He admits when he's wrong, albeit hours later. Where James was stone-faced and unemotional in almost every situation, you always know exactly how Mike feels.

I believe I can love him despite his hurts and hang-ups, just like God has loved me despite mine. In fact, perhaps there's no one in the world more suited to love him than me. Maybe God had him in mind for me all along, and my struggles have prepared me for him. Two broken people trying to find a way back home. James and I always held back from one another, but with Mike, I feel like I can be honest in a way I wasn't able to with James.

I sense some underlying issues - an abrasiveness that peeks out from beneath the playfulness, a desire for control, a demand for attention, validation, and respect. And I know I'm pushing toward marriage for a combination of reasons that I never say out loud. An intense desire to create a *happily ever after* - for me and for Mike. I want to be all the things he wanted when he dreamed of marrying his high school sweetheart like his parents did. He just turned 40 and I'm only 11 months behind him. I don't want to waste any more time. I want Mike to be able to move in with me and the girls. And the one reason I'd never admit: I want to redeem myself, prove James wrong about all the things he said and didn't say about me - that I can't stick with anything, that I'll always be a cheater, that I'm a failure at marriage.

The first time Mike tries to propose, we're at Disneyworld in Orlando, the day before a Spring Break Disney cruise with the kids. We're staying with Sabrina, a cousin on my dad's side who was the very first baby I got to hold and change and carry around like she was my own. It's hard to believe she's a working adult now, a college graduate. Age is funny like that. As a child, someone eight years younger than you is a lifetime away, but as an adult, that time is like nothing.

After a 12-hour day at Disneyworld, full of rides, junk food, sun, and so much walking, we stop to watch the electric parade. We find a decent spot, the kids curled up in the rented double stroller, Mike and I crouched on the ground. When it's over, I stand up, exhausted and sticky, the girls starting to whine, people everywhere. I'm ready to be done with Disneyworld, take a warm bubble bath and curl up in the comfy guest bed at Sabrina's.

Mike starts to get up, moves from his butt to his knee and reaches up toward me as if he wants a hand to tug himself to standing. I grab his hand absentmindedly, but instead of letting me pull him up, he turns me toward him. He gets a serious look on his face, reaches for the ring in his pocket, and starts launching into a romantic proposal with a tender, loving look in his eyes.

"Oh no, no, no," I say, interrupting him. "Not here, not now."

I don't mean to hurt his feelings, but I'm in no place for a proposal right now. I knew it was coming and I do want to marry him. We already have that gorgeous dress he won at the auction (he was the only bid), and we picked out the ring together at Jared a few weeks ago. He knows I've never had the romantic big gesture type of proposal and I secretly want that. But this is not what I had in mind. He feels rebuffed, annoyed that I'm trying to control even his marriage proposal. But still, he gives it another try and hits the nail on the head two days later, on the ship.

The girls and I are all wearing pink princess dresses. Mine is an 80s style full-length prom dress in bubblegum pink that I found at Goodwill, and Mike has a matching cummerbund and bowtie beneath his suit. We bought the outfits for my running friend Zoe's birthday party a few weeks ago, an 80s prom theme, but we figured they'd be perfect for the elegant dinner the second night at sea.

Mike has pre-arranged for the entire wait staff to present the rings - mine as well as a plastic one for each of the girls - hidden within our desserts. It's romantic and dramatic, and I say yes this time. I glance over at Cadence, who sinks into her seat just a little, not a fan of being the center of attention. She's like her dad in that. Alex seems happy and they both dig into their desserts. Strolling back to our cabin after a long fairy tale evening, Mike and I bicker about stupid inconsequential stuff, and I know this next chapter will be different from my calm easy life with James. But maybe that's a good thing. He'll keep me on my toes.

After disembarking from the ship in Orlando, we're driving a rented car down the freeway toward Ft. Lauderdale to visit some cousins. I call James to tell him we're safely on land, and I share the news of our engagement. I hear him draw a breath before announcing that he and Leah also got engaged during their own spring break trip. I think he's a little irritated by how our paths are running so parallel to one another.

By the time I tell him some weeks later that we've picked a venue, the Las Sendas Vistas Pavilion, I think he's ready to slap me - surely, I must be doing this on purpose. He and Leah have settled on the exact same venue, six months later, in January. Our lives are interconnected, even in divorce, despite his efforts to separate himself from me. I think having similar tastes, similar views about what we want for our lives and our kids is a good thing. I guess we aren't quite so different from each other after all.

If it were up to me, Mike and I would do a destination wedding somewhere tropical instead of all the hoopla I've already done twice. But this is Mike's first real wedding, and he wants all our friends and family there.

We argue all the time, about small, stupid things, and I wonder how we will weather the inevitable hard stuff in our marriage. We start premarital counseling with Carl, the pastor who beckoned me back to Christianity with his Palm Sunday message of peace and hope when I so desperately needed it. The fact that Mike is willing to be vulnerable, to work on us, talk through things, and express his feelings, gives me hope.

At our wedding, Mike cries happy tears as I sing to him, *God blessed the broken road that led me straight to you.*

We head to Cabo for our honeymoon, staying at the timeshare James and I bought when I was selling them. The place is gorgeous, with an enormous infinity pool overlooking the vast Sea of Cortez beyond. Mike and I enjoy an idyllic week, swimming, and sunbathing during the day; dining, dancing, drinking at night, making love at all hours. I wake up early in the mornings to write, still trying to complete my memoir called *Believe*, the story of my faith journey. I feel conflicted about where to start and end the story, and how my current life fits into all the chapters I wrote before. This is my third marriage in 15 years. I never saw myself as the kind of woman to be married three times. And yet here I am. On my honeymoon. The third honeymoon in this jam-packed little life. It's been quite an adventure, a rocky road, but I've always believed that everything happens for a reason, that everything I've come through has uniquely prepared me for today.

As I sit writing in our gorgeous suite, I'm also checking Facebook because we only have a few more minutes of Wi-Fi. Someone we went to high school with died last night. A friend posted this beautiful sentiment: "Count your blessings, live in the moment, love everything and everyone around you like it is the very first time, be grateful, be ever so grateful you were given another day. Forgive and forget. Live in the happy and embrace the not so happy as an experience you will learn from and take away what you will work on. Life is truly a gift. Breathe it in and always believe in the things you cannot yet see."

A perfect manifesto for my life.

Mike and I are in bed, just waking up one morning shortly after returning from our honeymoon when I receive a random flirty text from an unknown number.

"Who is this? I don't have your number programmed in," I text back.

"It's Chase!" comes the quick response.

I can't help but laugh out loud at the crazy irony that now he's ready to start something up with me. I tell Mike the story of our brief flirtation while I was with James, how I reached out to him right after James and I were divorced, but he was in a new relationship then. Now here he is reaching out to me days after I've remarried. Like a little test. I quickly respond.

"You're never going to believe this, but I just got back from my honeymoon and I'm in bed with my new husband! Guess our timing is just a little off."

"Ha. I'm so sorry. I wish you all the best, Bad timing indeed," he says, and I never hear from him again.

Many times, over the next few years, I feel like a failure for giving up on my marriage to James. I keep him on a pedestal, remembering him as this perfect, easy husband - and all our problems as my fault. My relationship with Mike is complicated. He's emotional and reactive, demanding and particular, which is especially jarring after James' calm and steady demeanor. Mike's past has left him scarred and he's more difficult than either of my previous husbands. But I am more persistent and resilient than I ever gave myself credit for being.

Each of our lives today bear little resemblance to the picture James must have imagined for us, but I believe there is beauty, love, and happiness for us both. And our kids are truly blessed to be part of two loving households, loved by four parents instead of two.

I believe God puts people in our lives for a reason. I believe I can do and be anything I set my mind on. I believe that God is good, even when people are not, and that He loves and forgives us, even when people cannot. I believe in loving my enemies, just like Jesus - *and Mom* - taught me. I don't like being despised by James' family, extricated from the lives of Hannah and William, whom I loved as my own precious niece and nephew.

But I decided that if I want love, I need to be loving, and if I want forgiveness, I have to be forgiving. I try to show them all love by reaching out at birthdays and anniversaries. Glenn and Luke finally tell me to stop, so I do, realizing that it isn't loving to do something they don't want, and knowing that I can still love them, even in silence.

I've realized that how people treat you when the going gets tough, when they're hurt and angry, has very little to do with you, and everything to do with them. I continue to treat them as well as I can, given that I have almost no contact with either of them. I haven't seen Luke again since he looked right through me at Starbucks. He simply avoids coming to events where I might be: concerts at school, birthday parties, awards ceremonies, baptisms. The rest of the family shows up and waves politely from a distance, even stopping for some small talk after the event is over if I put myself in their path and leave them no other choice. Glenn makes sure to avoid eye contact and leave before the end to avoid this possibility. Once I call him out on it in an email, about his lack of forgiveness and the example he's setting for the kids, but Amanda calls me out for calling him out, and I realize that I don't need an outward display of Glenn's forgiveness. I need to stop living my life to please or impress him, which I was never able to do anyway.

The divorce has been harder on me than I thought it would be. All my emotions came crashing down and I suffered from depression even after I thought I had worked through it all. I regretted my actions. I regretted throwing away my marriage for nothing, just because I pursued a thought pattern that felt like it gave me joy, made me feel alive and beautiful. I used to believe in a life of no regrets, but I have made some choices I truly do regret now.

And yet, I have learned that I'm worthy of God's love, and that I can change. I can be the kind of person I want to be, get better and better.

We can create that high any time we want, with our own thoughts. Chase said that you can't help who you are attracted to, who you fall in love with. But in fact, we have more power over our thoughts and feelings than we can possibly imagine, and when we "can't help but fall in love" with someone while we are married to someone else, it's only because we *decide* to be powerless to stop it. We don't really want to. And there are so many better ways to feel good.

I believe God is real and He wants what's best for us. He's given us a framework for how life is supposed to be, and He knows that we will mess it up every day. But He expects us to fight for righteousness and goodness.

Jesus dying on the cross is a strange choice from an all-powerful God. He could have just forgiven us, knowing we would never be perfect. But I think He knew we needed an example, not an example of how to follow every rule, but an example of the kind of people we are supposed to be: not afraid to sit next to the adulterer, the dirty homeless guy, the tax collector. Looking for the spark of humanity. Seeing someone's pain and struggle and seeking to speak into their life.

The grass is only greener on the other side because it's new and well-watered. But you can water the grass wherever you are, create a beautiful life, a well-watered garden. You can throw away the camera and look at life through a new lens. Life is beautiful if you decide it is, if you see it that way. You only have one life to live, and it is yours. That doesn't mean you should seek comfort and selfishness in every moment, but rather true joy, which truly exists when you are loving and serving and focusing on others.

Still, I wonder how long it will take before I stop looking at my life through James' lens…

CHAPTER 19

Give us Grace

June 2015

Early in the morning, the day before Father's Day, we're a month shy of our second anniversary. The girls are at Daddy's house and Mike is on his way back from California in the big semi he drives for work now. I've been feeling bloated, and my period is a day late, so I take a pregnancy test.

When those two lines appear once again, I jump up squealing, then run a few laps around the empty house. Our dog Magnus stares at me like I'm crazy, and I decide I can't keep this news to myself until Mike gets home. I call my neighbor Margaret, and she walks over for a celebratory cup of coffee in my kitchen.

When Mike comes in the door, sweaty and road weary, I hand him the most amazing Father's Day present I could possibly give this childless 41-year-old man - the positive pregnancy test, pillowed in a little jewelry box and wrapped in a colorful gift bag. Tears fill his eyes and run down his cheeks as he registers the meaning of the test strip he holds between his fingers. He sets it down gently on the granite countertop to pull me into a tight hug.

The next day, we go to his parents' house for Father's Day dinner. We decide to tell them the news right away. At our age, it's no small feat that we were able to conceive naturally. We had even met with a fertility specialist, thinking we might need some help. But here I am pregnant without any outside help. I'm sure this one is a boy and I'm thrilled. Maybe we will name him Jesse, after Mike's grandpa on his mom's side, or Joseph, after my mom's father who died long before I was born.

When I start bleeding three days later, it's like an extra heavy period. Back before early detection was possible, I might never have even known I was pregnant. But we knew. And we're both sad. We mourn the loss of the life that might have been, but I'm thankful the miscarriage happened so early in the pregnancy, and I'm hopeful that if I was able to get pregnant this time, I'll be able to do it again, maybe in a few months.

I get pregnant right away, in my next cycle. We're cautiously optimistic and it's hard not to panic each time something feels strange in this pregnancy. My body isn't quite as resilient as it was 10 and 8 years ago, with Cadence and Alex. Mike and I are both convinced that the baby is a boy, but the ultrasound shows us otherwise.

During the last two months of my pregnancy, I get to see our daughter every week on the ultrasound. At the "advanced maternal age" of 41, I'm considered "pregnant elderly," so there is extra monitoring to make sure everything is OK. I assume she'll be early, just like her sisters, but the day before her scheduled C-section, I realize she's going to stay put and show up right on schedule. I post on Facebook:

> I've been having contractions for months, have been to the hospital twice, convinced I was in labor. But no, this one appears to be quite content to wait for her scheduled arrival time, despite our impatience!

> Can't wait to welcome Baby Grace into the world tomorrow. The name Grace has a lot of meaning for us. On one hand Grace is simple elegance, refinement of movement, poise, finesse. And on the other hand, in Christian belief, grace means the free and

unmerited favor of God. It is something we don't deserve and cannot earn, and one of the hardest things to give to another person, especially someone who hurt us, an amazing blessing… Can't wait to hold my amazing blessing from God tomorrow!

Grace is a delightful baby. She smiles and laughs, nurses well, and sleeps in later than any baby I've ever seen, allowing me to have some precious mommy time in the mornings. Ten years younger than Cadence, and eight years younger than Alex, she fits right into our family and we all love having a baby around. And Mike thrives in his new role as Dad.

It's November 3, 2016. I awake with a start, feeling panicky and overwhelmed, unsure, and anxious, the way I seem to wake up most mornings lately.

I open my eyes and squint to see the digital clock a few feet away from our bed. 5:20 am. Still dark outside, a light rain shower pattering the house. I hadn't planned on running or going to the gym this morning. My alarm is set for 6 am. I ran yesterday and felt like I needed a little extra sleep more than the exercise today. Plus, the girls are here, and I have a lot to do this morning. My heart starts to race, and I force myself to lay quietly, close my eyes and just breathe, listening to the steady hum of seven-month-old Grace's white noise machine through the video monitor on my nightstand. I lean over and tap the button on top which illuminates the video display. My baby is still fast asleep. She woke up at 2:00 am wanting to nurse, so she won't need her usual 5:00 am feeding today. I feel eight-year-old Alex's little body squeezed up against me and remember that she came into our bed about an hour ago after a bad dream, and promptly fell back asleep cuddled between Mike and me, our dog Magnus no doubt curled up in Mike's legs.

I run through an inventory of what I need to accomplish this morning. Get Cadence and Alex up by 6:30 to get to school on time, get myself showered, the baby fed, and do at least some lead-generating, money-making work before I head to a real estate industry event at 9:00. Women of Strength, it's called. I left employee benefits just before getting pregnant with Grace and now I'm weaving my way back into real estate, trying to build up my own business again, almost 17 years after I first got my license in New York City. I've had many starts and stops since then, small successes and diverse experiences. But after all these years, I sometimes feel as unsure as ever, shattered and broken despite so much to be grateful for. I'm insecure in a way I never expected to be, lacking belief in myself, trying to find direction and purpose. I have such a big *Why* for my business: my family, my girls, so much to live for. But it's hard to start again. I've zigzagged so much in my career, tried many things, pushed brazenly forward in different industries, projecting a confidence that was usually only surface deep.

I know life is a series of seasons, ups and downs, choices that lead us down a path, sometimes a path we never meant to go down. I know everything that has happened in my life, every choice I've made, has brought me to exactly where I am, where I am meant to be. And I can't go back. I can only go forward. But even now, at 42 years old, I sometimes feel so scared of moving forward. I've made too many mistakes already. There's no more room for error, no more chances left. I've used up my nine lives, my three strikes. This is how I feel about work, but also about my marriage and my whole life. No one would know this from social media or even seeing me in person. I almost always project a genuine warm smile and a confident posture, even when I'm all torn up inside. *Maybe this is my superpower. Being able to be both truly joyful and completely broken at the same time.*

I take a deep breath and hop out of bed to face my day, pulling on the pajama pants I took off during the night because I was hot. It's that wonderful time of year in Arizona where it's still hot enough during the day that the air conditioning runs, but at night it cools down enough that it doesn't click on. It gets stuffy, even with the ceiling fans. I quickly brush my teeth, grab the baby monitor, my phone and water bottle, and head downstairs, switching on the light in my office before heading to the kitchen to make coffee.

At 6:30, I climb the stairs to wake up Cadence, reaching up to tickle her foot on her high loft bed. Then I walk down the hall to our bedroom to wake Alex.

"Time to wake up, baby," I sing. Mike stirs and I add, "Big baby and little baby!"

The morning is drama-free and not too chaotic, which is rare with three girls and a high-strung husband. Alex especially can be moody, particular. I often wish her school had a uniform like Cadence's, so that every morning wasn't a struggle to find an outfit that meets both Alex's standards and mine. Sometimes I'm struck by how much Alex and Mike are alike in the way they react with strong emotions and can be mercurial in their moods. Mike should be particularly empathetic toward her, but he struggles to understand her, and there's a constant tension between them.

The rain starts up again as I'm getting ready to take Alex to school. I grab a sweatshirt from the neat stack Mike made in the car. He's so much like my dad in his desire to have everything in its place, and having a husband who's a neat freak is not without its benefits. We pick up Margaret's kids on the way down the block to the elementary school. Cadence goes to a different school and will take the bus today. Grace turns her head from one side to the other looking at the neighbor kids. She's such a happy, amazing baby. A delight. The glue that holds us together.

On the way to the event, I listen to my recording of a book called *The Power*, by Rhonda Byrne. She's the same author who wrote *The Secret*, which came out in 2006 when Cadence was born. I didn't read it at the time. The Law of Attraction was a "worldly" idea that didn't jive with James' conservative Christian worldview that I was trying so hard to embrace as my own. Our pastor preached that you could be "so open-minded your brains fall out." We needed to protect our minds and our hearts from these wrong ideas. Satan could use them to turn us away from God.

Growing up, I was taught that being open-minded and worldly was a good thing. Learning about other cultures, religions, races had always turned me *toward* God, not away. But I was trying so very hard back then to be the perfect Christian wife. Coming to Christianity from Judaism as an adult was like a backwards fall from innocence. It required me to narrow my beliefs and understanding of the world rather than broaden them, to re-examine history, science, and culture as I had known it. I felt compelled to do so, but I never stopped questioning, contemplating, learning, and seeking to understand viewpoints different from mine. *The Power* reminded me that the greatest and most powerful force in life is *love*. And there is nothing unchristian about that. Listening to the author's lilting Australian accent as I drive down the freeway reminds me to think about what I love, rather than what I don't love.

I take a breath and feel God's love embrace me. I'm OK. I'm good. I have much to be grateful for and much to look forward to. I grab my breast pump and my packed purse and walk bravely into the ballroom. Less outgoing and bouncy than I used to be. A little worse for wear. Wearing glasses because I had pink eye the other day and it's a little red and sore.

I recognize familiar faces but have to strain my sleep-deprived mommy brain to remember names. I used to have an amazing memory for names and faces, but I've been so many places and met so many people at different times in my life that my brain is a little overcrowded. Like one of those old card files at the library that has too many cards packed in, all a little out of order and jumbled up. I can imagine how Nana, now 94, feels as she struggles to recover a memory. It's there somewhere, but you can't quite grasp it. At times I think there is nothing sadder than losing your memories, but other times I think it would be a blessing to forget a few of mine.

Even though it's called Women of Strength, there are many men here. I see the tables are sponsored by different real estate companies, many of whom I have worked for at one time or another.

There's James' company. I see the owner, Dan and the broker, Sue, but either they don't notice me or choose not to acknowledge me, and I don't try to make eye contact and then walk up boldly and say hello, the way I normally would. Instead, I avert my eyes, look for less hostile people, people on my side or people who don't know there are any sides to be on. I knew the day would come that I'd run into James at work. I knew it would be hard. But it's worse than I thought it would be. I feel afraid. I feel less than. I want to shrink up in a little ball and hide. This is so not the person I am, the person I've always been. Getting in the buffet line, I make conversation with a lady whose last name is *Sans Soucie* - which literally means "without worry" in French. *There are signs everywhere if you look for them.* I compliment her beautiful red dress, take a breath, and tell my heart to beat again.

I finally see James, but he doesn't look my way, probably on purpose, so I don't say hello. I see him regularly to exchange the kids, but this is the first time we've run into each other at a work event. This is partially why I left the industry immediately after our divorce, and one of the reasons I'm struggling to get back into it now. If I thought I was insecure before, unsure, unworthy, misunderstood, now it's 100 times worse.

The first speaker is Jon Jorgensen, a young guy who performs a dramatic interpretation of an original poem called "What are you afraid of?" It's like he's speaking directly to me. It's OK. Just breathe. Shattered. Broken. Not by things that were done to me, but by my own actions. Even all these years later. Even with so much to be joyful about, I can't seem to put the pieces together.

The next speaker is Robbie Parker, whose daughter was killed in the Sandy Hook elementary shooting in 2012. December 14, 2012, he tells us it was. I think back to my own life and what I was doing at that time. Cadence was in first grade, and I remember hearing about the shooting and all the schools adding extra security at that time. But what hits me as I recall the date is that it was the exact week James and I decided to get off the rollercoaster and end our marriage. I can feel him sitting just a few feet away and I wonder if he remembers, too. Maybe not. He seems to have shut off his brain and heart to anything associated with me. I guess that's what he needed to do to move on.

Tears spring to my eyes. Not just because this man's story is so heartbreaking, but because in my story, I'm the perpetrator, the bad guy, the wicked witch, evil sorceress - the shooter who destroyed lives. In my favorite Bible story about Joseph and his coat of many colors, I'm not Joseph or Pharoah or even the brothers, but I'm Potiphar's wife, the one who seduced Joseph. And that's not who I ever wanted to be. I was selfish, stupid, short-sighted.

In the car, I weep and cry out to God. What do I do with this? How do I go on? How do I claim joy when I sometimes don't feel like I deserve it anymore? How do I show the world that I've felt remorse, accepted my guilt, but then move on from it? How do I forgive myself and become new? How do I live? How do I connect with people? How do I move forward?

After the event, I head to Cadence's school to see her perform in the Battle of the Books. She's so smart and sweet. I pull in just before James. My instinct is to wait for him and walk in amiably together, but I know he wouldn't want that. I'm feeling shaky and out of sorts, but when I see my daughter's smile and give her a big hug, it's all right. My heart is full. Nothing else matters. She still thinks I'm wonderful, even though she knows the story of why her dad and I got divorced, or at least a basic child-appropriate version of it. Being a mom is the best and most important job I have ever had. *Give yourself a little grace, just like you do everyone else in your life.*

Later that night, I pick up my Bible. The same one Amanda gave me when I became a Christian, just before I married James. I unfold the magnetic flap of the brown leather, open it up, and a bright pink index card tumbles out. I'd forgotten about the card that woman gave me at Continuum as I was struggling with my attraction to Brock but hadn't yet acted out. I look at its curled edges and the handwritten scrawl of the verses from Galatians she had been led to speak into my life. I think about how strange it is that I had never met her before, even though everyone else at the table was familiar. I've never seen her since, either. Her name is on the card, but when I check Facebook, she doesn't come up. Of course, not everyone is on Facebook, but *could she have been a real-life angel?* I read again the words she had wanted to share with me:

Do not be deceived: God cannot be mocked. A man reaps what he sows. Whoever sows to please their flesh, from the flesh will reap destruction; whoever sows to please the Spirit, from the Spirit will reap eternal life. Let us not become weary in doing good, for at the proper time we will reap a harvest if we do not give up. Therefore, as we have opportunity, let us do good to all people, especially to those who belong to the family of believers.

It had felt like such an inappropriate verse for me. All doom and gloom. And I had stubbornly ignored the warning. I had sowed to please my flesh and I had reaped destruction. I had broken so much: James' heart, our marriage, our family, my own heart, my own faith even. But in these verses, there was hope, too. God had welcomed me back like the prodigal son, and I know now that I will have other chances to sow to please the spirit. God never gave up on me. At the proper time, I will reap a harvest if I do not give up. It is not too late. It is *never* too late. My story is so far from over. And it is going to be a glorious unfolding. And I am never alone.

That's the bottom line. God is there. To catch us when we fall. To carry us when we can't walk alone. To convict us, guide us, forgive us even when no human can. To give us another chance. Just like Amanda had said to James when he met me, "God is a God of second chances." And third chances. And fourth chances.

CHAPTER 20

Generational Trauma

Summer 2018

It's the week after Memorial Day 2018 and we've rented a private house right on the beach in Rocky Point. A few years back, before Grace came along, we came down this same week with Mike's whole family. We all stayed together in a huge villa with a bunk room for the kids at Las Palmas resort.

This time we're in a more secluded area, away from the high-rise condos of Sandy Beach, and we brought my mom along with the five of us. It's early morning our first day here, and I'm the only one up. Reclining in a faded denim chair, I gaze out the open sliding glass door toward the beach and the vast ocean beyond. The waves crash softly, endlessly against the sand. Low, white crests along the vast turquoise of the ocean. I love the beach, always have. Just like both my parents do and my grandparents did. It's in my blood. And I love my quiet time in the morning before anyone else is up.

Rocky Point – Puerto Peñasco – is an easy four-hour drive from our house. Closer even than San Diego, the most popular US beach destination for Phoenicians. And you can't rent a 2000-square-foot home on a private beach for $175 a night in San Diego.

The dusty town feels simultaneously rundown and unfinished, as it has for at least the past 30 years. But our view out the back door makes me forget about all that. Watching my girls frolic on the beach, ride the waves, collect seashells, and build sandcastles is priceless.

The house is comfortable, with unfinished travertine floors, even on the long staircase that leads to two large bedrooms upstairs. It's solid, but not. You can see an expansion seam in the drywall under the wall-mounted air conditioning unit, as if there's a constant leak within the wall. The kitchen cabinets are blonde oak, haphazardly thrown up in the kitchen, the stainless-steel fridge smudged and scratched, the home's exterior corroded from salt. But it's clean, bright, and spacious, and will make a great home base for our four-day stay.

A cool breeze wisps into the room and I hug the sleeves of my soft faded cotton sweatsuit, a hand-me-down from my sister. Dozens of seashells spill over the tiled railing of the back patio, thanks to the girls and their Gigi - the name Cadence gave my mom when she learned to talk. My mom liked the sound of Gigi better than Grandma, so that's what all the grandkids call her now. All the tension between us has melted, and she and Mike are close, too. She's amazing with the kids. No surprise there.

The girls selected the very best of the millions of shells that scattered the beach yesterday when the tide was low. Now it's low tide again and I stare out over the vast expanse, thinking about life and love and family.

I wish Mike would talk nicer to my girls. I know he loves them, but I think he sometimes forgets they're my precious babies. On the beach last night, he was so sweet with two-year-old Grace, proudly helping her discover the joys of the sea. But when Alex tried to playfully join in the fun, he got angry with her for pushing in. She was fine and went on playing with Cadence and Gigi, but I'm sure she felt hurt, rebuffed, deep in her soul, and that makes me feel so sad. I wish I could protect my babies from pain.

I think I know where this comes from. Mike has shared stories about his childhood. I know he was eight years old when his parents realized they weren't going to be able to have another child and adopted a baby boy. I know that he loved his new brother, wanted to protect him like a third parent. But I think he felt pushed aside, displaced. He had been an only child, a perfect son. With a new baby, Mike had to find new ways to get attention. Maybe that's why he got into so much trouble later. I think there's a little boy inside him who still feels hurt and jealous, and he subconsciously offers Alex - who was also eight when her baby sister arrived on the scene - the same subtle punishment he felt as a child.

I love that little boy inside of Mike, but I also love my own baby girls, so I watch carefully, like a mama bear, ready to stand up for them whenever I feel they need me to, and prepared to leave him if it comes to that. There are moments of such sweetness between Mike and the kids. But he always has to press his opinion and dictate his way. I know I express my own opinions boldly, too. I talk too much to try to explain my heart and be understood. But where I fight to see the bright side, the best in people and situations, Mike has a negative realism that pulls us down. I wish I were impervious to it, but I'm super sensitive to the people and moods around me, even my children's. And once I'm in a bad mood or a negative frame of mind, I have a hard time snapping out of it.

I ask God to help me know what's right to do. It would be easy to just leave. I can make my own living and I don't need Mike to take care of me. I can't deny the underlying tension that colors our life. But I have this deep knowing that instead of running away from this difficult situation, I should stay and fight, for my kids, and even for the little boy in Mike who just wants to feel loved. I keep myself grounded and push through where I once would have run away. I trust that I'll know if it's ever time to leave.

I think maybe most of us have a little child inside, who acts from a place of pain and fear, inadvertently causing us to hurt other people. I wonder how much of our hurtful adult behavior stems from childhood and generational traumas, big or small, that cut us more deeply than we realized.

I've been thinking a lot about my dad lately. I've always felt hurt by his lack of emotional attachment - to material things, homes, but especially people, especially me. I grew up hearing the story of how he and his family were forced from their home and their country with practically nothing when my dad was only nine years old. But lately I've been reading books and watching documentaries about the Jews of Egypt, pondering my family's Egyptian history and how much I didn't learn about their lives before Papi died and Nana got lost in her dementia.

Mike and I had lunch with my dad a few weeks ago and I asked him to tell me more about Egypt. I wanted to really understand that part of his story, my ancestry.

I can picture my dad at the *Lycée Français*, strong and stocky, his naturally olive-toned skin tan from so many afternoons at the beach. He could have passed for an Egyptian, but even though the bustling seaside city of Alexandria had been home to his family for generations, they were never considered Egyptian.

I see him emerging from the cool Mediterranean Sea, wiping the foam and sand from his brow as he pulls himself up, smiling. He loved everything about the beach: the sand, the water, the people, the colors. He told me he could spend all day there, watching people, surfing the waves, munching on his favorite *Caca Chinois* candy. His family's private *cabine* served as a home-base filled with his extended family - *cousins*, *tantes* and *oncles*.

I imagine Nana there too, hurrying toward him with a multi-colored Egyptian towel, her shapely bare legs tan and olive-toned like my dad's.

My dad was an only child, and more than a bit spoiled, *un enfant gaté* by anyone's account. He would hide his toys so he didn't have to share. One time he went so far as to dig a hole in the ground and bury a toy he didn't want his cousin Yves to play with. He got a taste of his own medicine when he later went to dig it up and couldn't remember where he had buried it. But he was charming and sweet, a golden boy with a good heart, so his brattiness didn't keep his cousins from loving him.

Nana tended to coddle him a bit, not in a modern indulgent way, but in an old-world protective way. The only daughter of a wealthy Italian businessman, her family was part of the fabric of Alexandria.

Papi courted her, they married, and once he had his son, he felt no need to further procreate. Nana would have liked more children, but she didn't argue with her husband. That just wasn't done.

They lived an upscale life in a gorgeous apartment. Papi was a bank executive at *Banque Belge* and spoke six languages fluently. He also worked at the racetrack on weekends, helping with the spreads, the charts, the numbers. The only boy in a family with seven children, born right in the middle of his six sisters, he was the family's patriarch, making sure everyone was taken care of and everything was under control. He was also a charming ladies' man, the life of any party, and there were many in the cosmopolitan Alexandria of the 1940s and 50s, an international hub of activity, life, and culture.

Jews and non-Jews alike, the Europeans were welcome guests in Egypt. They ran the banks, the shops, the cinema, the racetrack. They spent their leisure time at the cinema, cafes, French *patisseries,* and the beach. At the Alexandria Sporting Club, they played squash, tennis, cricket, and golf, and enjoyed horseback riding and gambling. But even though Egypt was their home, their passports were French, Italian, British. Some of them were *apatride* - stateless. They were not Egyptian, European, or even Israeli. They were children of the world. At home and school, my dad's family spoke mostly French, but they lived in a multireligious, multicultural and multiethnic environment.

My family was among some 80,000 Jews who lived in Cairo and Alexandria, but they were not particularly religious. They followed the traditions of their faith quietly alongside their Muslim and Christian neighbors. Each of them worshiped with their families - Muslims at the mosque, Catholics at the cathedral, Jews at the synagogue. But they would wait outside for their friends from the other religions to complete their mass or service, then gather at someone's home to sing and dance until late at night.

Kids rode their bikes in the streets. Everyone knew everyone, and they all respected one another. They were integrated, but not assimilated. Each group kept their unique identity, even though they

---

They could each take only one *valise*, so I[...] ing onto herself and her son, despite th[...] valuables in their pockets. Papi hollowed[...] hide whatever jewels and money wasn't co[...] to my dad to hold onto.

For my dad, it was all a fun game, an e[...] oblivious to the violence and fear, but h[...] their safety, and he had no idea of the h[...] even some of his close family members en[...]

They boarded a big ship called *The Yu[...]* many people, but my dad didn't underst[...] anything but a glorious adventure. When[...] the locals threw bread and olives up to the[...] ship like sardines.

"Why are they throwing us food?" my [...] "We play at the beach and have a membe[...] We are not peasants."

They eventually landed in France, sta[...] the south for a few months, then moving to[...] to secure a new position with his old con[...] family was among the lucky ones. Despite[...] they landed on their feet and began to re[...] comfortable lifestyle they had enjoyed in [...]

After about a year in Paris, Papi moved [...] to New York City and then to the suburbs[...] ing a brand-new tri-level on a quiet street[...] loved my own childhood summers spent [...] day with all the children on the block. T[...] an Italian family, a Jewish family from Br[...] out of each other's houses grabbing fresh [...] sausages or Nutella. I loved mothering the [...] than anything.

Three of Papi's sisters stayed in France[...] there. The other three settled in New Yor[...] and broad Jones Beach, also a staple of my[...]

were friends. Intermarriage among the di[fferent groups was common,]
but the Europeans didn't feel like foreigner[s.]

It was a beautiful life in Alexandria, a g[reat place for children and]
older people alike, the perfect playground [for my dad as a young]
boy. My dad was blissfully unaware that Ale[xandria had been changing]
for years now, that the peaceful coexistenc[e the Jews of Egypt]
had enjoyed with the Arabs for so many ye[ars was ending.]

Politically, the Jews of Egypt had alway[s been involved]
with Zionism, socialism and even commun[ism, especially after]
the oppression of World War II. Egypt wa[s part of the Arab]
coalition that attacked the newborn Jewis[h State of Israel in 1948,]
and an anti-Zionist movement began to fo[rm. Some Jews]
connected with Zionist groups were arreste[d and even kicked]
out of the country. The political climate [worsened and many]
families decided to flee, knowing they we[re not welcome. My family]
never talked about politics, but I get the i[mpression they were]
more moderate. Eventually, though, that d[idn't matter.]

Fires burned through the city as Egypti[ans attacked foreign-]
owned stores, and the beautiful cinemas a[nd hotels from the]
British occupation. The new President, Nas[ser, started nationalizing]
Egypt, claiming ownership of all major asset[s and foreign hold-]
ings, even privately owned companies. When [he took over]
the Suez Canal, it started the 1956 War. Fran[ce and Britain attacked]
Egypt, and Israel alongside them, so Egypt [expelled all French]
and English residents, and all Jews, regardless [of nationality. They]
placed restrictions on importing and exporti[ng goods and travel per-]
mits. They tapped telephone lines, screened [mail. Bank accounts froze.]
Soon people couldn't even access their own b[ank accounts. Businesses]
closed, and families left Egypt to head to Bri[tain, France, America,]
or Israel. There were rumblings among my [family members.]
Il faut partir, they'd whisper. And one night [my grandparents were]
evicted from the home they owned, the only [home my dad had known.]

But even when authorities showed up at [their door to confiscate]
artwork, collectibles, antique furniture, china [and jewelry, my grandmother]
shielded her little boy from the harsh reality [of the situation.]

it was a far cry from the Alexandrian coast. My dad had an array of cousins spread out over two continents. The family would always remain close, with a fierce love and a strong bond that I didn't know was uncommon in families.

My dad practiced speaking English for hours in front of a mirror, trying desperately to erase all traces of his Egyptian French accent so he could be just like the other kids.

"That's an interesting accent," people would say to his parents. "Where are you from?"

They would respond vaguely that they were French, rarely mentioning Egypt, because it was too complicated to explain that they were from Egypt, but not Egyptian.

"Malka, such an interesting name. Is that Italian?" others would ask.

They usually avoided explaining that in fact, Malka is the Hebrew word for Queen. It wasn't that they were embarrassed to be Jewish. They were proud to be Jews, but it had always been a quiet and personal faith, even before it had become a crime just to be Jewish in their home country.

Papi was all about picking yourself up and starting over, focusing on the good. Focusing on your family and their health and safety. He knew that you can't go back. You must move forward. The Jews of Egypt are one of the best examples of resilience, surviving and adapting, even after they were humiliated. This resilience and strength, tempered with tolerance and understanding was ingrained in me from childhood. But I never fully realized the drama and the trauma in my family's expulsion from Egypt.

My dad remained particular about his toys, or really anything that was his. In college he'd hide a quart of gourmet ice cream inside a huge tub that had once held some hideous flavor he knew his roommates would overlook in the freezer. On the surface, he hadn't changed a bit from the adventurous *enfant gâté* he had been in Alexandria. But if you looked closely, you'd notice he had no emotional attachment to the things he seemed to prize more than people. Whether electronics or cars, houses, or boats, he always held them lightly, happy to sell if he got the right price, excited to move on to the next shiny object. He took meticulous care of his things but said goodbye to them without a second thought. Because he was always eager to try something new and never one to set down roots, we moved every few years as a kid, which made it hard for me to form attachments and deep friendships, too. My dad has always avoided emotional life events, anything that might make him feel sad or scared. Though he was married to my mom for more than 20 years, and even still remains close to her after more than 20 years of divorce, he always seemed emotionally unavailable. I knew he loved us, but I rarely caught a glimpse of his deepest thoughts and beliefs about life and love.

I wonder, after all these years, if his quirky personality is a result of the trauma of being ripped away from his home at nine years old. And as I think of that, I want to give him a big hug and let him know that it's OK to cry. Sometimes life just really sucks. But it can get better.

I wonder, too, how many of my own strengths and struggles stem from this thread of my ancestry running through my own life. My tendency to delve right into the messy emotional side of life, contrary to my dad. My constant search for community and connection. My desire to build a bridge between any two opposing parties. Always moving quickly toward joy and silver linings, never resting too long in sadness. It's as if the story was passed on in my genetic code, as clearly as my brown hair and eyes, and the cleft in my chin.

I wish I had embraced my own family heritage sooner, instead of spending so many years trying to fit into everyone else's. I was so quick to shed my weird Hebrew last name that no one really knew how to pronounce to take on Ian's exotic French name, then James' simple English one. By the time I married Mike, I was tired of changing my name. It felt like with each new name came a new identity - someone else's. I changed it, nonetheless. I'd always thought it was a cool Italian name. And I love being a Tantone. But I'm finally ready to step into the truth of my own royal name - Malka, queen.

CHAPTER 21

Reconciliation

March 15, 2019

"Some people come into our lives and quickly go. Some stay for a while, leave footprints on our hearts, and we are never, ever the same."

—Flavia Weedn

It's my first night working as a server at the Las Sendas Patio restaurant at the top of the hill in our gorgeous desert foothills neighborhood. I've recently started nursing school and realized there's a reason that actors and students work as servers. It's flexible and the tips really add up.

I peer out over the deck toward the green grass of the golf course against the rich browns of the desert. Gorgeous mountains, setting sun, city lights starting to twinkle in the distance. It's strange to be working here, in the same restaurant where James and I once enjoyed sunsets, then sat and worked out the details of our divorce. Later, Mike and I would listen to live music, sip pear martinis and gaze at the view I never get tired of. We held our rehearsal dinner here, the night before our beautiful wedding at the Las Sendas Vistas Pavilion just across the parking lot. Now I'm here serving food to my neighbors, friends, and real estate clients - 44 years old and working as a waitress. I chuckle.

Tonight, I'm shadowing Marta, a no-nonsense career server who doesn't want to hear about my sentimental memories, appreciation of the view, or connections to the restaurant's owners. She only wants to teach me how things should run and how to be an efficient and successful server. I'm following her as deftly as my short legs will carry me, feeling not so different from a 16-year-old working her very first job, when I look out over the tables and lock eyes with Amanda, sitting at a two-top with Luke. His back is to me, but I feel my heart race as I point them out to Marta incredulously.

"That's my ex-brother-in-law and sister-in-law."

"Cool," she says, continuing her work. I follow her, nonplussed, serving martinis and margaritas with my heart pounding inside. A heat rash spreads out over my chest. I feel a complicated combination of emotions: fear, excitement, and dare I say, love. I haven't even seen Luke in six years, but he was once my brother. It may have been a love-hate relationship. He may have driven me crazy a lot of the time. To say I was grateful to be married to James instead of him would be an understatement. But I truly considered him family. That day he looked right through me at Starbucks was so shockingly unexpected, like a slap in the face when I was going in for a hug. And now he's here, on my first day of work as a server at 44 years old.

I wonder if they're celebrating - or mourning - William's engagement to his longtime girlfriend Jacie. I texted Will this morning after Cadence told me the news.

"Hey Will, it's Auntie Dani. Just wanted to say congratulations on your engagement. I have really missed seeing you grow up but I'm so proud of the man you have become, and I know you will be a great husband. Please know that I will always consider you my nephew and I'm always here for you. Wishing you an amazing life full of love, laughter, and joy. Hugs and love to you and Jacie."

She has practically grown up in their home from what I've heard. But they're so young, not even old enough to drink alcohol at their own wedding. Luke and Amanda were just as young when they got married, and they're still together after all these years, even though I know they've had their problems, too. I wonder how they feel about Will and Jacie. I only get snippets of their life from Cadence and Alex.

But I don't have time to ponder it now. Marta is on the go again. I peek at them out of the corner of my eye, wondering if they'll acknowledge me or just ignore me. I decide to ignore them and focus on my work, learn this new job. But I keep stealing glances in their direction. I *really* did love them, despite everything. I fight back tears the whole evening, reliving memories of my time in their family - birthdays and pool parties, movie nights, and so many family dinners. A film reel of family life plays through my head as I shadow Marta like a puppy dog.

Even when people forgive, reconciliation - the process of regaining trust and restoring a relationship - doesn't always happen right away, or ever. In 12-step recovery programs, steps eight and nine have to do with making amends with the people you've hurt. It's more than just saying "I'm sorry." It involves the effort of returning something that was stolen or repairing something that was broken.

I couldn't fix my broken marriage, or even return James unscathed to his family. I had forever changed him. He was no longer that innocent boy I had met in a sunburned grass yard of a high school in Gila Bend.

James and I have closure. We both remarried, we see each other every week when we exchange the girls, and we communicate regularly regarding their education and parenting. We have a nice, easy relationship that's more amicable than that of any other divorced couple raising kids that I've ever seen. Even though we'll never be best buddies, I truly love James and Leah, and they have shown Mike, Gracie, and me love, too. More importantly, we all fiercely love those girls - Cadence and Alex. And that makes my heart happy.

I wanted to make amends with James' family, and I tried in all sorts of ways. The rupture from Amanda and Luke, Hannah and William, has eaten at me for years. I adored my niece and nephew, and it breaks my heart that I missed seeing them grow up.

I'd love to hear the words "I forgive you," but what I'd love even more is to build a new relationship with each of them. I wish it didn't matter so much to me. I wish I could just let them go. I have my own family, and Mike's too. But God used James' family to change my heart, and they are part of me, whether they want to be or not. There's an anonymous poem - *Reason, Season, or Lifetime* - about accepting the impermanence of relationships in our lives. I've never been good at letting people go, especially the ones who have made footprints on my heart.

Once, when Alex was sick a few years ago, vomiting uncontrollably, James and I decided together to take her to the hospital. His dad, Glenn met us there, and as we waited in the ER lobby for them to call us back, he talked and joked with me, just a little, as if I were a human being, and it made my heart swell. It was just a small thing, but after years of desperately reaching for anything warm from him, it was enough.

When Cadence got baptized last year, James and I stood on either side of her in the baptismal bath as the pastor dunked her back into the water, symbolizing her own faith in Jesus. Mike and Leah each stood just outside the tank, and Glenn and Sheri, Amanda and the kids, Mike's parents, and of course my mom, who never misses any important event in her babies' lives, cheered on from the pews. Even my dad showed up. It was so very meaningful, to me and to Cadence, to be surrounded by her family like that; our battles, our personal beliefs, our discomforts set aside to show her love. But I couldn't help but notice Luke's absence. *Why isn't he here?* I wondered. *Is it me? Does he find my presence so despicable that he can't even be in the same church as me all these years later? Do I remind him of his own sin and shortcomings? Does he just not care?* I don't know because he didn't tell me. He never talked to me. And I wish I didn't care, but I do.

On Hannah's 15th birthday last year, I texted Amanda, asking her to wish my baby niece a happy birthday from Auntie Dani and remind her how much I love her. She thanked me for always remembering. And later that day, I received a text from an unknown number that took my breath away. "This is Hannah. Thank you for the birthday wishes."

"Oh, thank you for the text, my sweet girl. That means so much. I have tears in my eyes! Love you!"

"Love you too."

Amanda taps me on the shoulder while I'm filling water glasses at the server's station set up near the restrooms. I whirl around and see her sparkling blue eyes and wide smile, and I gather her into an embrace. I tell her how wonderful it is to see her, and Luke, too, but that I didn't know if I should come say hi. She looks into my eyes knowingly.

"He wants to say hi," she says. "He feels bad about how he treated you."

"Ok, I'll come to the table when I can."

But I get busy with serving, so instead they come up to me, on the way out after they've finished their meal. Luke looks down at me with a warm smile, and I can see the love in his eyes. I reach up and wrap my arms tightly around him.

"It's OK. You're still my brother. I *never* stopped loving you," I say.

"I don't know what to say," he says, choked up.

"You don't have to say a word. This is enough." And it is. Restoration. Reconciliation. Healing. Closure. Love.

Three miraculous things happen the weekend of Cadence's 13th birthday the following month. The first is James and Mike hosting her birthday party together on Mike's parents' boat at Saguaro Lake - eight giggling girls, two dads and one very happy daughter and mom. The next is James and I standing together with Alex this time in the baptismal bath, all our family there. The third is Luke finally showing up to an event where I am.

Right before the service, as James and I take our seats on either side of Alex, I gaze out across the sanctuary, searching for the familiar faces of all our special people. My parents and Mike's, and James' entire family: Glenn and Sheri, Amanda and Hannah, William and Jacie, and Luke, finally Luke.

"Uncle Luke is here!" Alex exclaims.

"Yes, he is," I say, smiling as I wipe away tears. He catches my eye from across the room and smiles back at me.

The day is a joyful celebration of Alex's faith. James and I together with her in the tank an outward symbol of an inward reality and commitment to being together in raising our children, despite our hurts, anger, and history. Just like the baptism itself is an outward sign of an inward spiritual transformation. When I post on Facebook about it, a Jewish friend asks me if a baptism is like a Bat Mitzvah, and though it's a much smaller life cycle event in terms of fanfare, money spent, preparation involved and all that, I would say that baptism can be a monumental event for individuals, families, and communities.

The sermon, preached by Pastor Matt, who always touches my heart with his extensive understanding of both the Hebrew language and the Jewish context of the Bible, talks about how we come to God afraid, unprepared, inadequate. But He simply says, *Shalom* - peace be with you. God can make dead things alive, and He never gives up on us.

By the time I receive my breast cancer diagnosis a few months later, I know exactly who I am, standing in the park with my baby girl. I no longer care quite so much what anyone else thinks of me. I have less need for approval, validation, and attention.

CHAPTER 22

Fight Song

Friday, September 20, 2019

As it turns out, the very first person I tell that I have breast cancer is my three-year-old daughter. Which isn't all that surprising if you know me.

It's one of those glorious early fall days in Arizona, where the blazing heat is finally starting to lift, and it's cool enough to be at the park in the middle of the afternoon, after months stuck inside air-conditioned rooms. I feel a special kind of joy that reminds me of the spring semester I spent in Paris my junior year of college in 1995. The city came alive in April as the sun came out. It's reversed here. We cocoon ourselves during the harsh, dry summer heat, and when it breaks, it's like an awakening after a long, damp winter. Windows open, breezes blowing, birds chirping, picnics, campfires, cool glasses of wine on big front porches. But we don't really have front porches here, not the kind you see on farmhouses and Victorians. In the Arizona desert, we have flat, stucco homes, and people sit in their walled backyards, under covered patios or poolside. That's always made me feel a longing tightness in my chest. How I wish we sat out front and had neighbors who just stopped by to chat, a close-knit community who looks out for one another, instead of individual families who pull into their garages and then shut themselves tight. Their own worlds with only their own beliefs and viewpoints, insulated from the outside world. I crave the kind of community my family enjoyed in Alexandria. Different people from different worlds coming together to eat and drink, dance and play.

As Gracie and I swing lazily together on the pseudo tire swing, a momentary reprieve from the dizzying preschool playing and the swirling hurricane motion of my very busy life, I can almost imagine us on a broad southern porch drinking sweet tea and lemonade. I gently stretch back, close my eyes, and turn my head up toward the soft sunlight streaming through the sail shade that sweeps over the playground to protect the kids from the scorching Arizona sun. I breathe in the fresh air and listen for a moment to the birds chirping softly in the distance.

We still have half an hour before we'll need to go pick up 11-year-old Alex from school, and then a few more hours before it will be time to pick up Cadence, who's 13 and in junior high. I'm scheduled to work the night shift at the hospital at six. But for this one moment in time, I'm not thinking about nursing school, night shifts, my still unfinished book, or my never-ending to-do list. I'm completely present with my baby girl.

Opening my eyes again a moment later, I catch a sideways glimpse of a hummingbird hovering in a nearby tree. A few years ago, I made a conscious decision that flying creatures – butterflies, birds - and particularly hummingbirds, would be my personal symbol of love. Whenever I notice one, I make it a point to focus on what I love, and to remember that *I* am loved – at least by God if by no one else.

Hugging Gracie tightly to my chest, I kiss her sweet soft cheek. Then I pick up my phone and snap a selfie of our smiling faces against the backdrop of green grass and blue sky. My reddish-brown hair windswept across my face. The transition lenses in my glasses darkened from the bright sun. A few wrinkles visible on my forehead and by my mouth. A full smile revealing straight white teeth - the product of four years of braces in high school. The tanned olive skin on my *perfectly healthy-looking chest* slightly pink from the sun's heat. Our hands gently grasping the swing's chain. My IPhone's live mode even captures our gentle swinging in the breeze on this perfect, perfect afternoon. The snapshot mirrors how I'm feeling in this brief slice of time – full of joy, hope, excitement; looking forward with great expectation to whatever may be coming, even though, on some level, I already know it's cancer.

You can't even see my underlying anxiety in the shot. Maybe I hide it well, or maybe I've become an expert at focusing on the positive, even when it's surrounded by negative. It's how I cope with life. *Focus on the good. Focus on what you love. Find the silver linings. Think about what you want to happen rather than what you don't. You get what you expect. If you want love, forgiveness, and grace; then you give love, forgiveness, and grace; you live love, forgiveness, and grace. You become love, forgiveness, and grace.* I repeat these phrases over and over in my head, like a mantra.

My 45th birthday was three weeks ago. We invited friends and family for a casual low-key celebration. My mom and Courtney catered the event with a taco truck that a Mexican *familia* parked on our driveway. Everyone raved about the delicious authentic tacos and salsas, and I loved practicing my rusty Spanish with the owners. "*Entiendo bien espanol pero no hablo muy bien,*" I explained. I understand Spanish well, but don't speak it so well. It's the same way I open the conversation when I take care of Spanish-speaking patients at the hospital. Sets the bar nice and low, so they're ok with my very basic language skills.

The night of the birthday party, I wore a strapless white cotton eyelet dress, strappy sandals, and a colorful Egyptian beaded necklace that Nana gave me a few years ago, before dementia took over. I blew my wavy hair straight, and looked well-rested and happy, even though I had worked the night before. A year into pursuing a nursing degree more than 20 years after the first time I graduated from college, I've enjoyed a rich and varied career in sales and marketing. But I always said if I had it to do all over again, I'd go into nursing, and one day a few years ago, I said, "Well why not do it all over now?" I started taking steps toward this new goal, and here I am.

Piece of Work

Now I'm working full time night shift as a nursing assistant to get some patient care experience. I like to joke that it's literally the "shittiest" job I've ever had - I basically wipe butts for a living. It's strange and hard to be in my 40s and starting over at the very bottom of the professional ladder. But it's rewarding in surprising ways. I once saved a guy's life by charting the color of his poop (black - which indicated blood in the stool, internal bleeding). Overall, I'm enjoying the journey. It's good, honest, meaningful work. Not that all that I've done before wasn't. But I really like doing something with my hands and body, not just my mind and my words. I love caring for people in this very basic and physical way. Even though some nights really are just poopy. Period.

I'm still doing some real estate work on the side, and I can't help but notice that the two jobs are more the same than they are different. In real estate, too, I'm responsible for cleaning up crap, even if it's the proverbial kind rather than the literal kind.

I'm doing my best to manage my home, finances, three kids and husband, each with their own breed of moods and messiness. Though I rarely admit it, I'm eternally exhausted, vacillating between the night shift schedule and a regular human schedule. Staying up all night after getting the kids and myself to school in the morning is hard enough. But sleeping during the day isn't easy either. I catch as many hours as I can in the cozy sleep chamber I created in our closet. I go to class, try to cram complicated scientific knowledge into my already-stuffed old brain, drive the kids around, make breakfasts, lunches, and dinners, and do loads and loads of laundry. Like an endless treadmill.

Just before coming to the park, I stopped by the nearest SimonMed imaging clinic to see if they had the results of my breast biopsy back yet. I know from experience that they won't give me results over the phone, but if I stop in and show proof of my identity, they will print me a copy of the radiologist's report. As a nursing student, I'll be able to decipher the medical verbiage well enough. But the report wasn't in yet. The waiting is always the worst. I really hope I'll know before the weekend whether I have breast cancer.

My phone rings. A local number that's not in my contacts. I answer immediately, thinking maybe it's SimonMed calling to let me know I can come get the report now. The moment of calm is gone and I'm back to obsessing over the biopsy.

"Danielle? It's Dr. Tanaka…"

She's the high-risk breast specialist I've been seeing since my first biopsy two years ago. That one revealed only a benign mass of hardened milk from breastfeeding. But nobody called me with those results. They don't call you personally to tell you that you *don't* have cancer.

"You have DCIS – ductal carcinoma in situ," she says now. "The earliest form of breast cancer."

I take a breath as my mind races. I ask whatever questions I can think of as I stand incongruously on the wood-chipped playground with my cell phone to my ear. We talk for a few minutes about next steps. She says she'll work on getting me an appointment with a surgeon in her group and call me back a little later. She's calling from her personal cell phone, and I can call her back with any other questions I think of. The fact that I have the doctor's personal cell number, that she's working late on a Friday afternoon to make sure I get in with the surgeon first thing Monday morning, makes me feel special and just a little scared. Suddenly everything has changed, even though I'm standing in the same park from just a moment ago, the same busy, crazy life. Now I have cancer. Will I keep going to class? Will I keep going to work? Will I be able to take a break from it all?

I know in an instant that if it's a choice I'm given and covered by my insurance, I will get a double mastectomy. My double D's have served their highest purpose – breastfeeding my three baby girls. They have also entertained Mike, my two previous husbands, and more than a few other boys. I was blessed with really good boobs. But I have no qualms about kissing them goodbye. I've heard too many sad stories of women who take care of one type of breast cancer only to get another one a year later, five years later, 10 years later. I've seen too many women *die* of breast cancer. I'm not going to mess around with it. I won't take that risk. I don't need my breasts to live a long, healthy life, and I won't let them kill me.

It's been almost exactly 10 years since the day my mom called to tell me her biopsy had revealed early-stage breast cancer. I was working in timeshare and right in the middle of all that fantasizing about Brock. She said it would have been a full five years before those microcalcifications that showed up on her mammogram would have formed into a mass large enough to feel under the skin. That struck me. Since they caught her cancer so early, she had choices in her treatment. She could do just a lumpectomy to take out the cancerous chunk, a single mastectomy, where they take out all the breast tissue from the affected breast, or a double mastectomy, where they remove all breast tissue from both breasts. I told her if it was me, I'd chop them both off and get a brand-new set. But it wasn't my choice to make 10 years ago. Now it is. And my mind hasn't changed. I'm ready to say goodbye to my 45-year-old, saggy, cancer-hiding boobs and replace them with a smaller, perkier set. I'm tired of monitoring for this hidden danger. I want to be done with it. I'm almost grateful that the uninvited guest has finally arrived to the party, so I can be done waiting, start fighting, and kick that cancer out so fast it won't know what hit it.

I end the call and look over at my little girl, now gleefully gliding down the slide.

"It's time to go get Alex, Sweetie."

"OK, Mommy," Gracie says, running toward me. She isn't always so compliant, but I promised her a trip to Bahama Bucks for shaved ice after we pick up Alex. I feel guilty for being so busy, and I try to spend quality time with my three girls whenever I can, since so much of my time is spent working, studying, and then sleeping since I work three nights a week. I've never worked so hard in my life. I wish I didn't have to, but the hard work feels good - like penance.

I scoop Gracie up in my arms and start walking toward the car, still reeling from the news. Mike is on a coaching call, so I can't call him. I'm happy to see him focused and driven, and I don't want to interrupt that. Plus, this isn't the kind of news you want to deliver over the phone. Even so, I try calling my mom, but she doesn't answer, so I leave a quick voicemail asking her to call me back. I try Courtney, but again reach only her familiar voicemail.

My mind tries to put together the appropriate sentence to share this news with the important people in my life. I'm outgoing, talkative, and direct, but the phrase "I have cancer" doesn't roll easily off the tongue. Some people ruminate for weeks over how to tell loved ones, particularly children, their cancer news: how best to word it, how to protect them. For me it would be easier to write about it on Facebook or my blog than to say the words out loud with my voice. But I know there are people I will have to tell personally before I can even think of posting anything publicly. My mom always tells me I share too much anyway.

For the moment, though, it's just me and Gracie. And I can't keep this inside. This little girl takes baths with me regularly and is constantly asking questions about bodies and how they work. I think for sure she'll be a nurse or doctor someday. I've never seen a kid so fascinated with the human body. She's seen my boobs a million times. She came with Mike and me to the biopsy appointment two days ago. She knows I'm waiting for the results about the "ouchie in my boobie."

My tone is serious but optimistic as I tell her that the doctor just called to tell me that the ouchie is in fact, *cancer*, the bad stuff we were worried about. I quickly reassure her that it's good they caught it early and that they will take it out with a surgery, just like the hip surgery I had a few years ago, where they fixed a torn labrum arthroscopically; and the three C-sections where they successfully delivered my three baby girls into the world.

"Mommy's going to be just fine," I say brightly, to reassure us both.

She listens intently and takes in the news with an appropriate frown of sadness, a few questions, but no reason to believe this will dramatically change my life or hers. *You get what you expect.* Did I get breast cancer because I was expecting it, monitoring for it? I can't help but wonder. Was it working the night shift that threw off my circadian rhythm and caused the cells in my breast to mutate? Just last week I learned the specifics about how cancer cells are formed in the human body in my pathophysiology class. And now the black and white terms from the digital online textbook have become personal, invading my own body. *Necrosis. Mutation.* My cancer is non-invasive, contained in the duct. But that could change quickly. Cancer doesn't like containment.

Neither Grace nor I shed a tear about the cancer that's decided to settle in my right breast. And even though my mind races forward with plans to mount an attack against this most unwelcome invader, I also feel a very large wave of something that feels like relief rolling over me. It's like I can hear God's voice saying, *Relax. Take a breath. Take a break. This is your chance to stop running and stressing and striving for just a minute and focus on what's really important. You don't have to turn away from everything you want to accomplish, but you have a damn good excuse to sit down for just a minute. And maybe you will even find some time to write your story.*

He makes me lie down in green pastures. He leads me beside still waters. He restores my soul. My mind whispers verses from Psalm 23, which has been in my head a lot the past few weeks since I signed up for a seven-week Bible study at church where we're going through the psalm verse by verse. It's one of those Bible passages most people have heard, even if they've never stepped foot in a church and have no idea it's called Psalm 23. *The Lord is my Shepherd. I shall not want...*

I remember hearing the psalm at Temple, perhaps as part of a Friday night Shabbat service, a wedding, funeral, or Bar Mitzvah. I think of my own Bat Mitzvah service at 13. I was proud to stand before our congregation and recite the prayers and Hebrew Torah portion that symbolized my becoming an adult in the Jewish tradition. The party at Pinnacle Peak Country Club afterward was fun too. I got to invite all my friends from school - the vast majority of whom were not Jewish and had very little understanding of Judaism - to celebrate with me. Picture a wedding reception filled with Junior High kids, complete with DJ, decorations, even a life-sized poster board glamour shot of me framed in a mauve colored border that everyone signed. It's one of those kitschy keepsakes that you don't quite know what to do with afterward. Just recently my mom was cleaning out her garage before moving and gave it back to me. Mike and the kids and I got a good laugh. We commented on how I looked like Cadence with darker hair. My unlined teenage face framed with a wave of 80s bangs staring dreamily into the distance. Mike hung it up in the garage so we could all see my soulful smile and big bangs each time we pulled in. Fabulous.

At home an hour later, when Mike hangs up the phone from his coaching call, I'm there waiting to deliver the news.

"I have it. It's positive. Dr. Tanaka called," I stutter. I still can't say the word - cancer. It doesn't seem real. He starts darting question after question at me in his pointed and anxious way, then notices the look on my face, stops himself, and folds me into a tight hug. I pull away and tell him I'm fine. Everything is going to be fine. But I'm antsy, agitated, and impatient for him to catch up with my processing of the situation.

He insists we sit all three girls down as a group and tell them the news before I head to work, and I comply. It's an awkward few minutes on the couch where they don't really know what to say and I try to give them as many details as I know, while also reassuring them I'll be fine. They don't seem too concerned and I try not to let their disinterest bother me. They're kids. They've been through a lot lately. Just a few weeks ago they found out their grandpa, Glenn, had some type of cancer in his leg and didn't even tell them about it until after he had taken care of it. They didn't understand why he would do that, and I found myself trying to defend a man who has largely ignored me for years now.

"The truth is, Sweetie, even adults don't have it all figured out. Even parents and grandparents. We all do the best we can with the knowledge and understanding we have. He probably thought he was protecting you," I told Cadence, curled up in her bed as I tucked her in one night. "I came up with a quote, a sort of truth, recently:

Piece of Work

We are all a piece of work, a work in progress, and a work of art, all at the same time."

"That's really good, Mommy," my little poet had said to me, making my heart swell.

"Give him grace," I encouraged her. "Talk to him."

I move through my shift at the hospital and the rest of the weekend in a sort of dazed stupor. Outwardly, I smile and laugh and joke. But inwardly I scream: *Don't you know I just found out I have breast cancer?! How can you expect me to still clean up poop, study patho, act like everything is normal?*

I wish everyone could see that I desperately need a hug and someone to listen to me without having to say the words, "I have breast cancer." *I wish I wore a sign on my chest.* And there is also an underlying thought that I have a minor kind of cancer anyway. I'm not in danger of dying from it, and it's relatively easy for me to feel optimistic. I see the silver linings, but I still feel panicky and confused - and so very tired. I wish I could curl into a little ball and go to sleep for a long time. At the same time, I feel led to shout a message of hope from the mountaintops. I have this vague sense of excitement about what's to come. And I pray that God will use this challenge in some amazing way.

On Monday morning, my mom and Mike accompany me to my first appointment with my new breast surgeon, Dr. Sommers. Walking into the office, I feel like it's the first day at a brand-new job, school or adventure. As I prepare myself a cup of tea at the cozy drink station set up in the comfortable lobby, I can't help but notice the little wooden sign on the table: *Cancer touched my breast, I kicked its ass.* It makes me smile and I snap a photo of it. Cursing isn't really my style - never was, even before I was a Christian. My mom raised me to choose my words carefully and use positive, uplifting ones. But I like the strength of these words, the past tense of the phrase, like it's already done. I'm ready for battle. But calm and almost joyful.

Consider it all joy when you encounter various trials... I reach into the recesses of my brain to recall the verse from James that I almost memorized during a summer Bible study a few years ago. Something about the testing of your faith producing a perfect result.

After everything in my life leading up to this point, this diagnosis is nothing I can't handle. I'm determined, surrendered, exhilarated, and even prepared to die if that's what it comes to. I'm ready for that "testing of my faith," aching to be an inspiring example of how to face life head on with faith and love. I want to point people toward God with my life. Like I've failed to do in the past.

CHAPTER 23

Surrender

October 28, 2019

Five weeks after my breast cancer diagnosis, it's another perfect Arizona fall day. Now it's October - Breast Cancer Awareness Month. How uncanny the timing of my own journey feels smack dab in this time of year when everyone's thinking about tatas. I can't go anywhere without seeing that cute little pink ribbon symbol, a pink T-shirt, or a breast cancer promotion of some kind.

It's Monday. My surgery - which will include the double mastectomy and the first stage of breast reconstruction - is scheduled for this Wednesday, October 30, 2019 - the day before Halloween. I'll be recovering on the couch rather than trick or treating with the kids Thursday night. It had seemed like forever to wait, and now it's here.

I'm getting ready to meet my friend Anne, my mom, and her mom for an al fresco lunch at Arcadia Farms when the plastic surgeon's office calls and says I need to come in for a pre-op appointment they neglected to schedule. They're able to squeeze me in at 1:30, so lunch will be more rushed than I'd hoped, but Anne will have to get back to her office anyway, so it is what it is. My own schedule has opened up since I decided to take a break from nursing school to take care of my cancer. Even though it's Stage 0 and not life-threatening, I was too consumed with my diagnosis to push through the semester and put off treatment.

As I walk from my car to the restaurant in Old Town Scottsdale, every patio is packed and I'm thinking again of Paris in April. I'm wearing a different coral-colored sundress than the one I wore to the park the day I got the phone call from Dr. Tanaka. Coral has always been one of my favorite colors. I decide to Google the meaning of coral and I smile at the first entry to catch my eye:

"Coral represents the ability to fill ourselves with light and life, expand without ego, to trust our community, to embrace togetherness and oneness, to build something beautiful and bigger than ourselves."

Wow. I laugh. Google is so cool. And God is cool too for creating the people who created Google and the ones who wrote that little description, part of some ad copy for a brand using coral in its color scheme. Or maybe I'm just really cheesy, looking for meaning in every little thing - license plates, butterflies, hummingbirds, Bible verses, songs that happen to come on the radio at just the right time...

But that description is just exactly how I see myself and what I desire most in this world: to fill myself with love and light, and help others do the same; to connect people, and to build something beautiful, bigger than myself. Turning my energies outward, even as I navigate this very personal internal health journey, feels so much better than engaging in secret forbidden fantasies ever did. And it's a true joy that's sustainable instead of a short-term high I can never quite catch. So maybe there's a reason I like coral besides that it looks good against my skin tone.

I smile at my reflection in the window of one of the shops as I walk by. I am forgiven. I am loved. By God. And by myself. And for the first time in my life, I realize that I actually *like* myself. I'm comfortable in my own skin. I know who I am, and I don't need anyone's approval. I know that I have a beauty that comes from inside, that *nobody* can take away. I don't need breasts, and I certainly don't need superficial sexual validation from random guys, or even a marriage from the pages of a romance novel. True love is deeper and more complex than that.

I'm finally beginning to look at my life through my own lenses. They aren't as rose-colored as they once were, but they aren't clouded either. They're clear, clean, unbroken. I can see clearly now.

We enjoy a delightful lunch and then I head to my 1:30 appointment with Dr. Petrov. It's the first time Mike isn't with me for one of these appointments. He's been really great. It's the second time I've walked into the sleek modern plastic surgeon's office, all hard surfaces in white, gray, and black. They specialize in breast reconstruction surgery, but the office lacks the feminine energy and cozy warmth of Dr. Sommers' office.

Dr. Petrov is not as warm and fuzzy as I wish he were either, but Dr. Sommers highly recommended him and I trust her, so I trust him too, even though I wish he would share the specifics of the reconstruction process in more detail. He's not unpleasant as he speaks to me in clipped lightly accented sentences, but I get the impression that he only tells me things on a need-to-know basis, and he doesn't think I need to know much. I've reminded him that I'm a nursing student and I really do want to know all the medical intricacies, his thought process, rationale, and concerns. I loved the way Dr. Sommers explained everything about my cancer and my options in detail, using a life-sized model of the breast as a visual. She let me record the entire hour-long consultation on my phone to listen to later, just like I do with my nursing lectures. Dr. Petrov was much more concise and business-like during my first appointment with him. And I have no idea what today's visit is about.

By 2:30, seated on the high leather adjustable exam chair and clothed in nothing but the black silky robe that almost succeeds in making this feel more like a spa than a surgeon's office, I'm feeling slightly annoyed at the wait, even though it has given me time to make a dent in my never-ending email inbox. Dr. Petrov walks brusquely into the room with Isabel, his assistant, apologizing for the delay. He gestures toward my chest, and I open the robe so he can examine my breasts once again. He appraises them like they're mounds of clay he's about to sculpt, with the keen eye of an artist, but the serious demeanor of an engineer. He cups each one gently to feel its weight, then softly pinches the skin at the top of each breast just like he did last time, furrowing his brow in concern over how thin the skin is. While some women have a thick layer of subcutaneous fat that remains even after all the breast tissue is removed with a mastectomy, I apparently don't have such a layer. It's all actually breast tissue. I guess God decided to place my fat disproportionately in my lower body, like a classic pear. Petrov will use a small amount of that lower body fat to fill in the thin skin over the breast implants he will place, so that the rippling of the silicone sacs is less visible, and they look more like real breasts.

He pulls out a purple marker and draws a thick line down the center of my body, starting from my sternum and going down to the bottom of my ribs. Then he pokes and prods around my nipples before drawing a messy parallelogram around each one, presumably to mark where they will cut.

Wait, what is he doing? I didn't realize I would be all marked up like this!

I consider stopping him. I have a photographer coming over in a few hours to take what I envisioned would be some cool artsy "before photos," showing my breasts before their massacre, and sharing my journey from *before* to *after*, whatever that will look like. I wasn't going to be nude or anything, but these thick markups will surely show through the sheer pink sports bra I was thinking of wearing to show the contours of my natural breasts. Now, instead of my original God-given unadulterated breasts, the photos will portray them already marred - by kindergarten shape drawings.

I want to cry, but instead I shake my head and laugh, realizing these markings could be symbolic of so many things: My breasts blighted by cancer. My life blighted by sin. A Scarlet Letter on my chest. Broken and beautiful.

In the end, Marie the photographer splatters black paint across my chest to represent the cancer against the pink. You can still see the purple marker underneath if you know where to look. But it becomes part of the artwork. My body is a piece of art, a symbol of my own life, a beautiful and rich history, even with the messiness underneath, even with a Scarlet Letter on my chest. *We are all a piece of work, a work in progress, and a work of art, all at the same time. We are all a masterpiece - a piece of the master.* **I am a masterpiece.**

A few days following my diagnosis, after I had called my family and close friends to tell them I had breast cancer, I posted a photo of myself with Grace on my hip, wearing a t-shirt that said "No Limits" and an expectant smile, and I shared the news in detailed bullet points outlining all the reasons I was grateful. The post garnered more than 300 comments. People told me I inspired them with my bravery and resilience, and several friends told me they were finally getting their first mammogram thanks to my story. But even with thousands of Facebook friends, I still sometimes feel so alone.

When I run into people who I know saw my post, they rarely say anything. Maybe they don't know what to say, or maybe they're too consumed with their own life to remember what they read on Facebook three weeks ago.

I feel a dull twinge deep within my breast whenever I remember I have breast cancer. I'm sure it's psychosomatic. There isn't even a true tumor yet, just a build-up of mutated cells rapidly reproducing themselves in the milk duct. I always thought I would try naturopathic methods if ever I was diagnosed with cancer, but in my real-life situation, I've never wavered in my decision to get the double mastectomy. Some people wondered why I would choose the most invasive option, but the bilateral mastectomy offers me peace of mind and feels like a powerful choice, a "no-brainer."

A lumpectomy would cut a large chunk from my breast, and then I'd have to get radiation and hormone therapy. A single mastectomy would remove all the breast tissue from the cancerous side but leave the other breast behind – its cells available for mutation at any time. It would also require hormone therapy that would force me into early menopause, and possibly radiation that can cause all kinds of damage. And it would leave me lopsided, with one natural breast and the other either flat or fake. All that doesn't sound less invasive to me! The double mastectomy will take away *virtually* all risk of future breast cancers and leave me with multiple options for reconstruction.

The weeks have passed quickly, a jumble of nights and days that tumble along like a bumpy ride in an old, tattered wagon. I feel like a zombie, never quite catching up on sleep, despite my comfy closet sleep chamber. Even before this new thing - breast cancer - came into my life, I was hardly getting used to night being day and day being night. I walk through my life feeling drunk with exhaustion, but I hide it well, like a functional alcoholic hides his drunkenness.

I feel like I *should* feel…something…more than I do, like fear, anger, insecurity about the choices I've had to make, and the many more that are coming still. Instead, I feel just a tiny bit numb, but also resolute, strangely calm, with a bubbling excitement underneath, like I know a thrilling secret or I'm looking forward to something big: a vacation to an exotic land, the first day of school in a new place, a new job, a project that's just a bit over my head, or even a new love. The excitement feels positive rather than negative, which is disconcerting. How can I be *excited* to face cancer?

It's like I'm back at the start of my first marathon race, in the dark at 6 am at the top of Usery pass, not far from home. I'm in familiar territory, but everything is different now. I'm standing in the middle of the desert street, squeezed between hundreds of people. There's noise and fanfare and fireworks. I'm a bit sick to my stomach, surrounded by a crowd, yet all alone, poised and ready, knowing I have to pace myself despite the mounting energy coursing through me. I'm ready to go, prepared for this.

Just like the marathon, I know intuitively that it will be beyond hard, that there will be moments when I want to crumple into a pile on the floor and give up. But I feel like everything in my life up to now has prepared me to run this race with courage and faith. Just keep putting one foot in front of the other, over and over and over.

The next day, at Women's Bible study, I make a short speech from the stage before we break up into groups. My voice is shaky. But I've done this before, and I love the feeling of speaking in front of people, inspiring them. I feel confident in God's love. Despite everything. I'm never alone.

"When I signed up for this Bible study, I knew Psalm 23: Green pastures, still waters. I hoped God would use it to show me how to find just a little rest amid my chaotic life. But I had no idea just how relevant, timely, and comforting it would be to me," I begin.

"This isn't the hardest valley I've walked through, and I know many of you are facing deeper valleys than this one. But David uses the words 'walk through' because valleys have a beginning and an end. We don't live there forever. I'm at God's mercy, not entirely sure how He will use this in my life. But knowing that He *will* use it. In the valley, I hold onto my loved ones. And I sing. I look for the door of hope. And more than that, I seek to become a door of hope to other people. I look for the gift in my grief…I breathe in deeply and I feel at peace. I cannot fix or control a single piece of this situation. So, I give it all to Him to take care of. I surrender all."

CHAPTER 24

Silver Linings

November 4, 2019

It's Monday again and I haven't done much besides eat, sleep, read, and catch up on the Netflix shows I rarely have time to watch. My double mastectomy surgery was five days ago. Friends and family pamper me, bringing food or coffee, sweet gifts, sitting and spending time with me in a way we rarely make time for in the busy throes of life.

He makes me lie down in green pastures…

The pain is different from when I had my C-sections, a searing, cutting feeling without the beautiful bonus of a healthy baby to cuddle, and all those feel-good hormones that come along with giving birth. But it's starting to dissipate.

I can feel the expanders, these hard plastic place holders that create pockets for the implants they'll place in a few months. They dig into the tender injured tissue of my chest wall. It feels like they smashed a coconut bikini - one of those ridiculously impractical little things that people bring you back as a souvenir from Hawaii - right into my chest.

The pathology came back and there was no additional cancer besides the area they already knew about. This means no chemo, no radiation and no estrogen-blocking pills that would have brought on early menopause. This is very, very good.

I return to work six weeks after my surgery, on day shift now, which makes me feel more like a normal person. I feel OK physically. I can even forget about the strange expanders in my chest beneath my scrubs for stretches of time. And my own recent experience as a patient adds a depth to my empathy.

One day I walk into the room of one of my patients in response to his call light, smile and ask how I can help, as usual. Overcome with emotion, tears spring to his eyes as he tells me he feels anxious and overwhelmed after his surgeon told him he'd be amputating his big toe today. They hadn't mentioned the word amputation until now.

"It's silly," he says, "to cry over a toe."

I step closer and place my hand gently on his shoulder, look into his eyes and tell him that I understand and I'm sorry. I share with him that I've recently experienced an amputation, too, and it's OK to be sad.

I know that breasts are not the same as legs, arms, feet, or toes. In some ways they seem less important, and in some ways even more. Breasts are perhaps the most defining characteristic of the female body, but outside my clothes, no one can even tell I no longer have mine.

Another day, one of my patients is a young man who tried to commit suicide by jumping in front of a bus. I wonder what he was thinking as he stepped out into the street, how he felt the moment before getting hit. He seems quite perturbed to still be here instead of wherever he believes he would have gone if the bus had successfully killed him.

"Maybe you were spared for a purpose," I say to him. "Maybe there's something on this earth you are meant to do, someone you are meant to be."

I don't know if my words make it past the haze of his suicidal ideation and deep depression. There's a side of me that remains bright-eyed and optimistic, and wants to believe I could make a difference, even when I've known too many wonderful people who have chosen to end their own lives, quickly or slowly.

I try to make him laugh, and finally I say something funny or dorky enough to get him to smile. But the first smile doesn't quite reach his eyes and I tell him so, which makes him laugh slightly and then a real smile lights up his whole face.

"You have to find the things that make you do more of that," I say. "What would you do if you didn't feel so depressed?"

"Go to trade school, become an electrician," he says.

"Well that sounds like a wonderful job. You'd get to light things up. I believe that every person on this earth is unique and special and has a purpose, even you."

I hope that getting run over by a bus and surviving becomes a catalyst to turn his life around. And I do believe that's possible.

In January, I'm taking care of a patient with Influenza. As I place the blood pressure cuff on his upper arm, I chat with him, and he seems so full of life. Some people just have a light in their eyes, even when they're sick. I tell him he looks like a healthy guy, other than his current plight with the flu. He says, "I do? That's funny. I have Stage 4 cancer."

"Wow," I say, taken aback. "You really do look healthy."

I tell him about my own recent diagnosis, and we talk about my decision to have the mastectomy and how I didn't do it out of bravery or fear, but rather because it seemed like the smartest, most logical choice for me. I didn't want to have to ever deal with this again. And even though breast cancer has become commonplace in our world, people do still die from it.

He shares a bit about his cancer and tells me he joined a support group, which at first had seemed silly, but turned out to be a wonderful experience. He tells me he hates the expression "fight cancer" along with all the rah-rah cheerleader talk that comes along with it. While having a great attitude and a fighting spirit certainly helps in the "battle" against cancer, it's not a battle that anyone can win.

"I'm not fighting anything," he says. "I'm just sitting there while doctors inject me with poison and radiation and hope it kills the cancer before it kills me."

I nod my head in agreement, realizing I've felt the same way, particularly since my cancer was non-invasive, I was never sick, and my only fight is recovering from a few surgeries. I really didn't do a thing but lie on an operating table while surgeons removed my breast tissue, which happened to include a tiny fleck of cancerous cells. My fight did absolutely nothing to kick the butt or any other part of cancer as a whole, cancer as a disease. It's a war fought by individuals, and does each individual's plight make a bit of difference in destroying the collective enemy? Does killing my fleck of cancer help anyone else's cancer? No. This is where I feel helpless.

But a few weeks later, a friend posts about how she's not a fan of the whole "colors for causes" thing, and I realize that even though I deeply respect her feelings, I don't agree. She says that every time she sees purple, she feels distressed because it reminds her of her dad's pancreatic cancer, and she imagines that breast cancer "victims" must feel the same each time they see pink. As if they had forgotten they had breast cancer and seeing the color was a harsh reminder. But seeing pink has never made me feel anything other than solidarity against a common enemy. The pink doesn't represent the cancer, it represents the fighters. It represents *our* team, not the other team. Kind of like if we were in a war against another country and we saw the colors red, white, and blue, it wouldn't remind us of the bad guy, but of our team that is fighting. I've never thought of myself as a "victim," but rather as a draftee. I was chosen to fight. And not just against my own little speck of cancer, but for others, too. I've become part of a team that I never wanted to join. The colors are obviously a commercial idea that earns lots of money for the industry. Maybe most of it doesn't even go toward cancer research and treatment. But for me, as a cancer survivor, seeing pink makes me feel strong, not weak. It reminds me how many people are fighting with me, even if just in spirit.

Another friend says, "cancer is a disease, not a war campaign." And while I heartily agree with her, I'm starting to understand that if thinking of it as a war helps get more people caring, sharing and learning, then perhaps the war verbiage is something I can live with. Tomorrow I'm attending a cancer awareness day at the state capitol as a representative of the American Cancer Society's Cancer Action Network. This is my first step toward doing something more than just trying to figure out my own plan for my own little cancer and sharing my thoughts to my friends through my blog.

A few days before my second surgery in February, I'm in the theater watching the new *Little Women* movie and I'm struck by the fact that I never really grieved the loss of my breasts or celebrated their life. There's a scene in the movie where Jo has just cut off her hair and sold it to give her mother some money to take care of her ailing father. Jo, who's generally more concerned with books and writing than beauty, nonetheless sits sobbing on the stairs as she intensely grieves the loss of her beautiful locks.

"Your one beauty!" her sister Amy proclaims dramatically. And I sit there in the theater with tears running down my own face as I empathize with the profound grief the actress so perfectly portrays. Until now, I hadn't felt it. I moved so quickly to triumph and silver linings, as I always do.

Just as Jo chopped off her hair for a reason and a purpose, a bold expression of life and freedom, taking control in her own small way over a situation she had little control over, so did I with the bilateral mastectomy. And just as Jo was left with a new perky hairstyle, I boldly announced to my friends that I was excited about a new set of perky, smaller breasts. And I was. But Jo's hair would grow back and be just as beautiful as before. And though perhaps my new set of boobs might also eventually be something someone might call beautiful, I've come to understand that the reality of recreating a set of breasts after a radical bilateral mastectomy is a far cry from a "boob job."

People have told me they're impressed by my openness, my positivity, my courage, even if some of them think I'm crazy for blabbing about my personal business to anyone who will listen. But it's easy to be positive when I feel so lucky, when my cancer was so minor, when I really wasn't sick and didn't have to sacrifice anything. They have told me not to minimize my pain, my experience. Facing cancer and getting both your breasts amputated actually is a big deal. But I have felt so guilty, when others die from this disease, and I was prepared to suffer but didn't have to. Yet I realized, after connecting with an old friend at a party recently, my first social event since the surgery, that this is about more than just me. She shared the terrifying experience of her own recent biopsy and we laughed about how barbaric and uncomfortable that procedure was.

"You need to write about that," she said. And I recognized that I've glossed over some of the negative aspects of my experience because they just didn't seem like that big of a deal to me, and I wanted to jump right away to the positive. I have seen friends die - from breast cancer or liver failure, accidents, suicide, even murder. Who am I to talk of pain?

But who I am is someone who can give words to my experience and the experiences of others. I can tell the stories of the struggles and triumphs that make us human. People have started reaching out to tell me of their diagnoses or struggles, impressed by my courage and positivity. Even though not everyone's prognosis is as positive as mine, the attitude we bring to the table – our faith, joy, and love, can make a huge difference in our healing process, or in the process of navigating any tough experience.

We are all a Piece of Work, a Work in Progress, and a Work of Art, all at the same time. And we are all just trying to figure out and make it through this thing called life. I want to inspire people to live their best life, be their best self, love with all their heart, and find beauty in their darkest days.

CHAPTER 25

Paradoxes

2020, Coronavirus Time

The timing of the completion of my breast cancer surgical adventure on February 25, just weeks before hospitals everywhere canceled any non-emergent procedures to preserve PPE and brace themselves for the onslaught of COVID-19, is providential and a huge blessing as far as I'm concerned.

A few weeks after my second surgery, back from the Spring Break trip to Disneyland we were able to squeeze in just before the park closed indefinitely, Grace dubs this era, "Coronavirus Time." Everyone is home for an extended spring break, life slows down just a bit and there's lots of togetherness - baking and hiking and playing outside. March in Arizona is glorious, and it's nice having the girls home to enjoy it. I tell them this is how summer is in other places where you don't have to stay inside to avoid the heat.

In April, I return to work at the hospital, and everything is different. I'm a float CNA now, so I go to different hospitals, depending on the need. At first, I'm annoyed that my first day back I'll only be a patient sitter for a non-COVID patient. I want to fight Coronavirus on the front lines. But I don't get to choose where I go or what I do. I take what I'm given. And sometimes just sitting and being with someone, listening to them and talking to them, is the most important thing you can do. I know my family will be happy to hear I'll be in just one room all day rather than exposed to all those germs. I resolve to make it a great day, to bring love, joy, and light into that room and to make a difference in that patient's life.

The hospital's halls are paradoxically empty and suddenly everyone's wearing masks. The last time I worked, just six weeks ago, you weren't even allowed to wear a mask outside a patient room, and even then, we only wore them for specific disease processes. I walk into the room not quite knowing what to expect. The night sitter stands up from his perch on the couch by the window and walks over to greet me and give me report.

"He's comfort care only, so the nurses don't even really need his vitals. Just check his oxygen saturations every now and then."

Comfort care only. That means he's dying, there's nothing they can do to save him. I glance over. He looks so young, and in the dim early morning light, he looks healthy.

"What's going on with him?" I ask.

"Liver failure. You'll be able to see how jaundiced he is when it's lighter in here."

"Oh," I say, my heart breaking just a little. I've lost three precious – and so very young - friends to liver failure over the last few years. I feel an immediate connection to the patient who's about my age and could have been a friend. I feel a sense of gravity and honor in my job. I am the very lowest of healthcare providers in the hospital, but I'll be the one who will care for this patient most closely today, to see his progress, even if any progress moves him away from life rather than toward it.

When the nurse comes back to check on him a while later, she tells me she's never cared for a comfort care patient. This is normally an ortho floor. Her usual patients are recovering from knee or hip surgery, not dying of liver failure. But everything's different in Coronavirus Time. With elective surgeries canceled, an ortho floor takes all different kinds of patients.

I spend two days with that patient and his parents, learning about his life and being there with them as they prepare for his death. It's a meaningful experience I won't soon forget.

A few days later, I awake in the middle of the night with a tightness in my belly, a heaviness in my chest. I've been working on identifying negative emotions and sitting with them for a while, rather than simply trying to stuff them or numb them. I ask my body what's wrong, why I feel this way. I take some deep, cleansing breaths.

This week has been tough, draining. Two emotionally wrought 12-hour shifts in that one little hospital room caring for a dying patient in the middle of a pandemic. Though his illness had nothing to do with COVID-19, it was juxtaposed against its backdrop, which has become all-encompassing, especially at the hospital.

But as I sit with my emotion and feel my heartache in the wee hours of the morning, I realize my insomnia and stress have more to do with a different juxtaposition, one which is always poignant to me personally but feels even more so this year. Easter and Passover. Christianity and Judaism. Social distancing and virtual services have made it easier for the two sides of my faith to collide in a way that isn't nearly as harmonious as I wish it were.

It's Holy Week, the week leading up to Easter. Yesterday was Good Friday.

But it's also Passover, the Jewish holiday which commemorates the liberation of the Israelites from Egyptian slavery. As both a Jew and a Christian, the rich shared symbolism of the two holidays, to me, is too obvious to deny, the Passover story God's perfect foreshadowing of the Easter story. They are intimately related and inseparable.

In French, even the word for the two holidays is almost identical. (Almost. But not quite. The subtle differences themselves strikingly symbolic and utterly interesting to me, a bit of a linguistic nerd.) Easter is *Pâques*. Passover is *Pâque*.

Many of my Christian friends are fascinated by my Jewish background. They love hearing the details of the Passover Seder that the Jews have celebrated for thousands of years. They immediately recognize the history of the Easter story and the symbols that correspond directly to the tenets of the Christian faith. It helps give context to what Jesus, a Jew, would have been celebrating during the Last Supper, and the significance of what was happening in Jerusalem leading up to his execution on the cross.

But for my family and friends who are Jewish-and not Christian, it's not that way at all. They see it as putting a Christian slant on something that happened thousands of years before Jesus was even born. A festival that Jesus may have celebrated as a Jew, but that had absolutely nothing to do with the story of his life, death, and supposed resurrection.

And I'm caught in the middle between two sides of a coin, both of which I see and understand so clearly.

I usually bite my tongue and refrain from tying the two holidays and faiths together at our family's Passover Seder out of deep respect and empathy for my mom. Her heart was broken when I became a Christian 16 years ago, but she loves me anyway and supports me even when it hurts her. I generally keep my mouth shut about anything Christian when I'm around my family, even avoiding mentioning church or Bible study too much. I compartmentalize for their sake. Though for me there is no compartmentalization.

The other night our church did an online Passover Seder led by another member of our church who was raised Jewish and became a believer later in life. It was on Facebook Live, and I joined the broadcast a few minutes late, on my way home from work. I had almost forgotten about it, and I texted Mike to see if he and the kids were watching. He said, "Yes, and your mom is too!"

I felt a wave of hope and happiness that she was watching. I desperately want her to be able to see my perspective, even if she never adopts it as her own. But when I asked her the next day what she thought of the service, she said she only watched a few minutes. She was turned off by the suggestion that the items on the symbolic

Seder plate could have a double meaning, that the Passover story could have signified even more than what the Jews had been celebrating for thousands of years. She told me that the fact that Christians could look at these Jewish symbols, at "her" holiday, as having a Christian significance offended her. At first, I was sad and even a little angry when she told me she was offended.

"How could you be offended by hearing someone's perspective that is different from your own, by listening to someone else's beliefs?" I asked her. "*You* taught me to be open-minded and tolerant of others."

She didn't really have an answer for me. But I soon understood that this is personal. She feels robbed, like Christians have stolen what was hers and tried to make it their own. Both the holiday - and her daughter.

Mike, who loves to loquaciously discuss anything and everything, came up with a perfect metaphor as he tried to decipher and describe what made her feel that way.

> Imagine you write a book. It's a memoir, your life story. You write it and you publish it, and it's done. Read and studied by millions of people around the world. Then someone else comes around and writes another book. But they don't call it another book. They call it the second half of your book, your very own life story. And they try to call the whole thing their book, our book, one whole book. They say that everything you wrote in your book points to what is in their book. But no! That was your book! They stole your book. They added on to your book, which was already written, complete. And they made up a whole new story, separate from anything you intended, but eerily tied to references in your book. Which would be easy to do since your book was already written! All they had to do was read it and write their new book to fit the references.

Wow. I can feel the pain, betrayal and even anger that would incite at such a visceral level. If I had written my memoir and then someone else tried to add onto it and call the whole thing their own, I would be furious. That's outright plagiarism. I feel that.

And yet, I still believe the whole Bible – Old Testament and New - really is God's book, written by men, but breathed to life by God himself. But I can't make my people see it that way, no matter how hard I try. And that makes me feel all tangled up inside. Torn between two worlds more diametrically opposed than I'd like to believe. I'm both fully Jewish and fully Christian. An oxymoron and an impossibility. A paradox. I have so much to celebrate this week- my ancestors' exodus from slavery in Egypt, and Jesus sacrificing himself for me. But my joy is shrouded by pain. Maybe joy is always clouded by pain, and we are always surrounded by paradoxes. Especially during a pandemic.

The following week, my mom and I don all the PPE - gowns, N95 masks, face shields and gloves. We enter the war zone of the assisted living facility where her brother, my Uncle Howie, has lived for several years.

By the time we get there, he can no longer talk, though I can tell he has things to say. I don't know if he wants to whisper a somber goodbye, an expression of pain, or one of his trademark corny jokes, but I see him still in there. I know he can hear us and knows we love him.

He has COVID and we have been granted a final visit. I hold his hand, help his caretakers move him into an adjustable hospital bed provided by hospice, and sing to him - both the Hebrew prayers and a few 60s hits to make him smile. Not everyone is so lucky to see familiar faces as they breathe their last breaths these days. Hospitals and nursing homes have closed their doors to visitors in order to prevent the spread, and not all facilities allow these end-of-life visits.

Hearing Uncle Howie struggle to breathe and not being able to do anything about it is excruciating. He's on oxygen and morphine to calm his breathing, but still his respirations come in quick, irregular, and obviously painful rasps. We clean his face and mouth, remove his dentures, help him sip drops of water from the little sponges that I asked the nursing staff to bring in for him. The hospice nurse tells us it won't be long.

My mom gets the call before dawn the next morning. He's gone. My sweet Uncle Howie lived a long and wonderful life, 50 plus years more than he was expected to live after surviving a bad car accident at 25 that put him in a coma for months and left him permanently brain damaged. After Grandma died in 1984, Mom moved Howie here to live in Arizona. He had his own private apartment in a large group home. We'd spend hours there on the weekends, mostly just hanging out while my mom made sure he was in good shape physically and emotionally. She was so amazing. His primary caretaker with so much weight on her shoulders.

My mom may not be a nurse, but she showed me what it is to be one, how to take care of a person selflessly, doing the messy jobs, sacrificing time and energy for another person. She taught me how to be a good sister and a good human. And having Howie in our life, all that time we spent at a residence for disabled people, we learned to love, respect, and talk to people who were different. It gave us a compassion and an understanding that I didn't realize was unique.

It's hard not to be able to mourn and celebrate Howie's life together. Because I'm sure he would say that it was a wonderful life. Everything is more complicated when someone dies now. All those things you need to coordinate and take care of, even the funeral or celebration of life, is affected. And there is a distinct lack of the social contact that is so very comforting to the mourning. Howie is one of the first 100 people in Arizona to die of COVID, the disease still such a mystery, not yet so politically charged, only a scary virus.

We decide to honor him with a small, drive-up funeral at the Jewish cemetery. Only immediate family - my mom in her own car, my sister and her family in their car, my dad in his, and my family in ours. The rabbi, a longtime family friend, pipes into our cars via FaceTime so we can hear her words despite the 100-foot distance from the graveside to our cars. We emerge from the cars only briefly for a certain prayer that requires us to stand.

After the short, somber service, each car goes its separate way. But cousins and family friends still want to send us meals, so a few days later we spread out in the grassy common area behind my mom's condo with blankets and tables and try to keep the kids at least six feet away from their cousins as we enjoy a meal together for the first time in weeks.

The week after Howie's death, I start working as a unit coordinator in Labor & Delivery. Most of my 12-hour shifts are spent doing repetitive administrative tasks that I've never been good at, like creating patient files, answering phones and stocking supplies.

But it's worth it to get to hear those newborn cries, smell the tiny Pampers Swaddlers diapers. I love the thrill of donning an N95 mask and face shield to head down to the ER for the occasional OB Trauma, bravely carrying the OB toolkit just in case they have to perform an emergency C-section. And the day I get to sit in on four different births – two vaginal deliveries and two C-sections – is eye-opening and life-changing. Every time I assist with a birth, I cry my own silent tears of joy as I watch that tiny head emerge and help encourage an exhausted but joyful mom to give one more push. This is definitely my kind of nursing.

One day I help with a different kind of birth. The baby's heart has stopped beating and everyone knows he will be stillborn. It's heartbreaking when that tiny baby emerges from his mom's womb and flops lifelessly onto the mattress. And though it's the first time I'm in the room for the birth of a deceased baby, we deal with IUFD – Intrauterine Fetal Demise - with surprising regularity. As nursing assistants, it's our job to bathe and dress the babies who have died in utero, while the nurses attend to mom. We take photos of the lifeless bodies dressed in tiny colorful outfits. We carefully stamp prints of their feet and hands onto a memorial certificate and create heart-shaped ceramic molds for the parents to keep. To be honest, I have mixed feelings about the whole thing. While it's an honor and privilege to offer that closure and some mementos of an all-too-short life to those families, I'm not sure how much of that I would want if I was the mom. But every family is different, and the hospital allows them as much time as they need with their treasured babies, something that I know was not available in years past.

One morning in early June, the pandemic in full force, my first assignment of the day is to head up to the ICU to pick up a lifeless one-day-old baby from his mother's bedside and bring him down to the morgue. I've been to the morgue a few times, and I've also been to one of the ICU units, but this is my first time in the COVID ICU Unit, a circular pod of six or eight rooms around a central nurse's station. Each room has a glass sliding door and can be monitored from outside so the nurses don't have to go in and out so much.

I don the yellow protective gown and gloves and switch out my surgical mask for an N95 and face shield, and I enter the battleground. I greet the mom, who speaks only Spanish. The nurse explains to her that I've come to take her baby. The tiny baby boy, no bigger than my forearm in width and length, is wrapped in a handmade blanket and lays on the bedside table in a white coffin-shaped box, with a pretty texture and a ribbon to wrap him up like the little gift that he is.

But the mom wants to keep the blanket as a memento instead of burying it with her baby. So, it's my job to carefully lift the baby from the box, unwrap him, and then place him back in the box. She's watching me closely, and I try to keep my hands from trembling, hoping my movements don't break any part of his perfectly formed miniature body. I take a breath and reach down gingerly. Even through my gloves, I can feel how cold the dead baby is, 24 hours after emerging lifeless from the warmth of his mother's body.

After mom says her goodbyes, I pick up the little white box containing the baby boy who only knew life as a warm and cozy place inside his mother's body. I look into that woman's eyes and assure her in my broken Spanish that I will take care of her baby. I smile at her from beneath my mask, willing her to feel my love, to know that I see her. I wish I could give her a big, tight hug.

I've just come up from the morgue when I'm tasked with sitting as a patient companion to another woman. She hadn't known she was pregnant and doesn't want her baby. She wails about the mistakes she's made and how she can't imagine how she'll move forward, now that she's pregnant with another man's baby and has no way to support them. She's too far along to get an abortion, as she'd hoped.

When I accompany her to the ultrasound, she turns her head away from the screen and refuses to see her baby's heart beating healthily. But I see it. I sit there holding her hand, praying silently for her and her unborn child, trying to infuse my love and God's love into her. I tell her that I've made mistakes too. Big ones. And that even if people can't forgive what she's done, life can go on and be better than ever. This baby could change her life in ways she can't even imagine. I tell her that she can still be, do and have anything she wants, regardless of where she came from. Maybe she didn't have a mom like mine, who told her that so often she couldn't help but believe it.

I have to be careful not to force my own beliefs onto her. That's not my business as a nurse. My job is to support her where she is, to empathize with her and to help her maintain her dignity. But I always want to give people hope, too. And here's what I know: Life can be short. Or it can be long. And any life is filled with difficulties and hardships, some more than others. But life is also filled with beautiful, meaningful moments. And God can make miracles from our messes. A miracle isn't always a grand sweeping thing. Sometimes it's just the little moments, the perfect timing, the synchronicity and abundance of everyday life.

CHAPTER 26

Final Breaths and Other Small Things

Saturday, November 21, 2020

My phone rings.

"This is Renee from Hospice of the Valley. I'm calling about your grandmother," she says. "I just came to check on her. As you may know, they gave her a COVID test Thursday, and though we don't have the results back yet, she's showing all the signs, and I wouldn't be surprised if it comes back positive. Her O^2 sats are 85, respirations 45, temp 103, heart rate 40, blood pressure 94 over 62. So, we'd like to start comfort care but just need consent."

My own heart starts beating faster and I step into full alertness as I digest the info. She's breathing more than twice as fast as normal, yet her oxygen saturation is much lower than it should be. As a nursing student and nursing assistant eight months into this pandemic, I know she's reaching the end of her life, even before the nurse says those words. At 98 years old, she's lived a long, healthy life. Dementia has taken over her brain, little by little these past several years, and it isn't much of a life now. So, I feel relief more than devastation, and a strong sense of duty. I have taken care of dying strangers at many different hospitals and facilities these last several months, holding their hands as they struggled to breathe, gently cleaning their faces, swabbing their mouths, changing their briefs. Sometimes I was the closest thing to family as they took their final breaths. As I've reflected on these deaths, I've thought a lot about how I'd like to be remembered when my time comes. I've only barely begun to make a dent in the great things I'd like to accomplish with my life, and sometimes I feel as if I haven't made much of a difference in the world.

But there's an African proverb: *Many small people, who in many small places, do many small things, can alter the face of the world.* This reminds me to just be present where I am right now. To do what I can, even if it feels small. To feel all the emotions and not try to numb them. To love even the unlovable and to do the hard things. To find and create acceptance, joy, delight, and peace in the little things. To take a breath when I'm tired or overwhelmed. To notice the beauty around me and then take another breath. It's a reminder that the smallest things are sometimes the greatest things.

I hang up the phone and Mike looks at me expectantly.

"Nana," I say simply. "It's finally time."

The girls are scattered about the house, each doing their thing. We all pile into the car and head up to the group home where Nana lives, just around the corner from my sister's house. I bring the PPE I have in my nurse pack, but we decide not to go in. Instead, we visit from her bedroom window, where we can see her lying in bed with her eyes closed, breathing peacefully, clean and well-groomed by her wonderful caretakers, even though they, too, are sick with COVID. They had only recently opened the home to visitors, after being sealed up safely for months. The guest of another resident had unintentionally brought the virus in with her, and it had spread quickly among the staff and residents, who live together like a family more than residents in a nursing home.

At home that evening, I'm scrolling through Facebook, and I'm stunned to read a friend's post about how politicians expect us to be careful when they're out having lunches and conferences. How the death rate is so small. How this is nothing more than the flu, and she won't be controlled by the government. My heart races and I feel heartbroken that this is what she chooses to *focus* on. That each side sees the other as an enemy, that there are even two sides in this. Of course, I understand where she's coming from. But doesn't she see that we're all just figuring this out as we go along? Scientists, medical professionals, and politicians scrambling to figure out how best to control this. No one truly knows what is right here, who to believe even.

And the death rate looms large in my world, regardless of percentages. I'm about to lose a second precious family member to this virus. Someone gave each of them COVID, not meaning to kill them. Maybe they thought it was just the flu, maybe they didn't have any symptoms at all.

I can't understand why everyone can't see this, why it has become a political battle, instead of a worldwide rally against a common enemy.

Not long ago, my teenage daughters were bickering, and I said to them, but also to myself, "If we could spend half the time we currently spend trying to make our own voice be heard, listening... If we could take the time to see and hear the people we encounter - even those who are different from us... If we could seek to understand them…We might be surprised by what we learn, and perhaps the world would be a better place."

There's always another side to the story, another perspective we were blind to before. Sometimes we all get caught up in our own view, our own version of the truth. There's this famous drawing that illustrates how we can get so hyper-focused on our own perspective that even looking at the same black and white picture, we can see something different from the next guy. I first encountered this exercise in Psych 101 and have since encountered it many times.

Piece of Work

My fascination with this illustration has nothing to do with the deep psychological meaning of what you see first, a young woman or an old woman. My interest lies in the fact that it really is possible to adjust your eyes to see the other side. It's hard to do. You have to step back, blur your eyes, look away for a moment, shift your perspective. And when you do, you see that there is more than one right way to look at the same set of black and white facts.

As you change your lens, the young woman's chiseled jawline becomes the old woman's gnarly nose. The choker on her slender neck becomes the old woman's thin grimace, her ear becomes the old woman's eye, etc. It may even be hard to go back to your old way of seeing it once you've seen the new image.

Though it seems impossible, sometimes both ways of looking at something are right, even if they seem diametrically opposed to one another. And sometimes they're both wrong. Usually, they're both a little bit of both, and the path is in the middle. The answer is finding a common ground, seeking to understand, and *loving* even when we don't feel loving.

We are all waves in the same ocean. Treating people with kindness and respect, listening more than we speak, seeking first to understand – this isn't just rainbows and unicorns. Forgiving ourselves and others when we make mistakes, treating people how *they* want to be treated, caring how we make them feel, and loving them as we love ourselves.

This is the basis of the teachings of Jesus - and every other coach or teacher I have learned from. But long before I knew about any of that, this is how I was *raised*. I learned this from my dad's family and their exodus from Egypt. I learned this from my mom, and the way she lives every day. And I believe this is the answer to all the problems we face as a world. This is important, life-changing stuff.

If I could go back and undo the hurt that I caused other people, I would. But I can't go back. I can only move forward and try to bring light and love to my world now. And having been in that place where I so desperately needed to be forgiven has built in me a tremendous capacity to love, understand, and forgive the people around me. And to move forward gracefully through my own life's battles with resilience and strength. My life is a tapestry and I'm still weaving it.

We are **all a piece of work**, a **work in progress** and a **work of art**, all at the same time. We are all pieces of The Master, The Great I am. No matter who we are. Or what we've done.

I hope you have enjoyed taking this journey with me. I've spent years trying to make sense of this story and its place in my life. And my greatest hope is that it will resonate with you in a positive way, despite all the negative moments.

If you'd like to learn more about what I'm up to now, head over to my website, www.DanielleTantone.com.